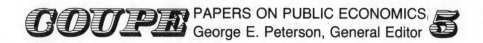

COUPE PAPERS ON PUBLIC ECONOMICS 5
George E. Peterson, General Editor

Tax and Expenditure Limitations

Edited by
Helen F. Ladd
and
T. Nicolaus Tideman

 THE URBAN INSTITUTE PRESS · WASHINGTON, D.C.

THE URBAN INSTITUTE is a nonprofit policy research and educational organization established in Washington, D.C. in 1968. Its staff investigates interrelated social and economic problems of urban communities, and government policies affecting those communities and the people who live in them. The Institute disseminates significant findings of such research through the active publications program of its Press. The Institute has two goals for work in each of its research areas: to help shape thinking about societal problems and efforts to solve them, and to improve government decisions and performance by providing better information and analytic tools.

Through work that ranges from broad conceptual studies to administrative and technical assistance, Institute researchers contribute to the stock of knowledge available to public officials and to private individuals and groups concerned with formulating and implementing more efficient and effective government policy.

Conclusions or opinions expressed are those of the authors and do not necessarily reflect the views of other staff members, officers or trustees of the Institute, or of any organizations which provide financial support to the Institute.

PARTICIPANTS IN CONFERENCE OF THE COMMITTEE ON URBAN PUBLIC ECONOMICS

Tax and Expenditure Limitations

Peter H. Aranson
Emory University

Geoffrey Brennan
Virginia Polytechnic Institute and State University

Arthur T. Denzau
Virginia Polytechnic Institute and State University

William Fischel
Dartmouth College

Jerry Goldstein
Northwestern University

Bruce Hamilton
Johns Hopkins University

Robert P. Inman
University of Pennsylvania

Helen F. Ladd
Harvard University

Julius Margolis
University of California, Riverside

Robert J. Mackay
Virginia Polytechnic Institute and State University

Richard A. Musgrave
Harvard University

William A. Niskanen
University of California, Los Angeles

William H. Oakland
Tulane University

Wallace E. Oates
University of Maryland

Peter C. Ordeshook
Carnegie-Mellon University

Janet Pack
University of Pennsylvania

A. Mitchell Polinsky
Stanford University

Robert Reischauer
Congressional Budget Office

Susan Rose-Ackerman
Yale University

Jerome Rothenberg
Massachusetts Institute of Technology

Daniel L. Rubinfeld
University of Michigan

Perry Shapiro
University of California, Santa Barbara

T. Nicolaus Tideman
Virginia Polytechnic Institute and State University

George Uhimchuk
Clemson University

William Vickrey
Columbia University

Carolyn L. Weaver
Virginia Polytechnic Institute and State University

William C. Wheaton
Massachusetts Institute of Technology

Michelle J. White
New York University

iv

CONTENTS

Tax and Expenditure Limitations

INTRODUCTION

Helen F. Ladd

The six papers in this volume were originally presented at the
October 1979 meeting of the Committee on Urban Public Economy
(COUPE), held at the University of Pennsylvania. The theme of the
conference—tax and expenditure limitations—was inspired by two
interrelated phenomena: the dramatic postwar growth of government
in the United States and the recent resurgence of interest in tax and
expenditure limitations. Richard Musgrave's paper highlights the extent and nature of this government growth: between 1948 and 1978,
public expenditures as a fraction of GNP rose from 0.18 to 0.32, or
by 78 percent, with the post-1960 increase primarily attributable to
transfer payments. Although the 1970s witnessed a slowdown, government expansion over the entire period provided a strong impetus
for research on the causes and consequences of government growth
and stimulated debate on government size. This academic discussion
gained direct policy relevance with the recent success of the tax
limitation movement.

Spurred by the passage of Proposition 13 in California in 1978,
the tax limitation movement has successfully imposed new limits on
local taxes or expenditures in almost half the states and limits on state
expenditures or revenues in nine states. The movement is now at-

[Helen Ladd is an Associate Professor in the Kennedy School of Government, Harvard
University.]

ACKNOWLEDGMENTS: I wish to thank Nicolaus Tideman, co-organizer of the conference
and co-editor of this conference volume, and Frederick Doolittle for their suggestions
and comments.

1

tempting to require by constitutional amendment a balanced budget at the federal level.[1] The movement's success has forced many economists to reevaluate their models of the collective choice mechanism and has raised new questions about public expenditures and taxes.

The six papers range from empirical studies of why voters support tax and expenditure limitations to theoretical models of the effectiveness of specific limitation devices. The first two papers use data from California and Michigan to analyze voter motivation. The next three papers take a more normative view and ask whether tax and expenditure limitations are desirable. The last examines the potential effectiveness of the initiative-referendum option as a device for controlling public sector size. Taken together, the papers, along with the comments of the discussants, highlight many important issues raised by tax and expenditure limitations. The conference discussion was lively; we hope we have succeeded in preserving some of its flavor in this volume.

Many economic models of local public-sector spending decisions focus on the pivotal position of the median voter, i.e., the middle voter when voters are arrayed by their demands for public expenditures. To the extent that public-sector outcomes reflect the wishes of the median voter, one would not expect tax and expenditure limitation proposals to receive majority support. Passage of such proposals in California, Michigan, and elsewhere, therefore, casts doubt on the simple median voter model and may provide support for the alternative view that taxpayer-voters believe that public expenditures are excessive.[2] An alternative explanation, raised primarily in the California context, focuses on the tax side. Rather than desiring overall tax or expenditure reduction, taxpayer-voters may simply want to shift taxes away from the local property tax onto state sales and income taxes.[3] The first two papers explore this question of voter motivation using two different approaches.

---

1. The enacted and proposed limitations are described in Pascal et al. (1979).

2. Voters may believe that public expenditures are too large for a variety of reasons. The pursuit of personal objectives may lead public-sector officials to expand service levels beyond those desired by the median voter; government inefficiency may make public-sector costs excessive; and public employee unions may force excessive wage and fringe benefit packages or inefficient production methods. These possibilities are discussed in Ladd (1978).

3. This view is presented in Oakland (1979) and Shapiro, Puryear, and Ross (1979).

In his paper "Popular Response to Public Spending Disequilibrium," Perry Shapiro argues that the favorable vote on California's Proposition 13 was an attempt by taxpayer-voters to reduce excessively large local public expenditures. Using a public-sector demand model incorporating income, tax price, and intergovernmental aid effects, the author simulates the expenditure changes desired by taxpayer-voters in California's school districts, municipalities, and counties between 1973 and 1978. Translating these desired changes into 1978 desired expenditure levels, he concludes that actual expenditures in 1978 substantially exceeded those desired by taxpayer-voters. This gap reflects neither a shift in preferences away from public services nor a budgetary mechanism that necessarily leads to excess spending; instead, it reflects particular conditions of the 1973–78 period, which, although not fully specified in the paper, presumably include general inflation and rapidly rising property assessments.

Shapiro also reexamines his earlier view that, instead of desiring expenditure reduction, voters wanted to shift financing responsibility away from the property tax onto state revenues. Since state revenue sources in California are more progressive than local sources, this motivation implies that higher income voters should be less likely to vote for Proposition 13 than lower income voters. Basing his analysis on those voters who did not want to reduce expenditures, Shapiro finds no correlation between income and the vote on Proposition 13, which he interprets as no support for the tax substitution hypothesis.

Paul Courant, Edward Gramlich, and Daniel Rubinfeld (CGR) use a more direct approach to examine voter motivation in their paper entitled, "Why Voters Support Tax Limitation Amendments: The Michigan Case." Shortly after the 1978 Michigan election, which included three tax and expenditure limitation proposals, the authors surveyed 2,001 Michigan residents. One of several purposes of the survey was to provide information on the political effects of public-sector employment, a topic that the authors have examined theoretically in previous work.[4] The paper in this volume reports the results of a detailed analysis of voter preferences and votes on the successful Headlee Amendment, the major provision of which is to limit the rate of growth of all state taxes and revenues (other than federal aid) to that of state personal income.

CGR find that, by themselves, variations in voter preferences for

---

4. See Courant, Gramlich, and Rubinfeld (1979).

public spending do not explain much of the variation in the probability of voting *yes* on the Headlee Amendment. In part this may reflect the relative uniformity of tastes across demographic groups. Some differences do appear, such as that employees in the private sector want less state and local spending than those in the public sector, but the differences are small. A more important reason for the low explanatory power of the simple preference model appears to be its failure to recognize interactions between voters' spending preferences and perceptions of the amendment's effects. Differing perceptions are particularly relevant in the Michigan referendum because of the complexity of the options on the ballot.

With a more complex model which fully incorporates these interactions, however, CGR find that the successful Headlee vote did not reflect a widespread feeling that government was too big. This is an important finding since many theoretical arguments for taxing and spending limits are based on the view that spending is excessive. Second, CGR find little evidence to support the view that Michigan voters were motivated by the desire to redistribute income away from public-sector employees. Instead, the analysis indicates that voters supported Headlee in order to increase their control over government, to reduce government inefficiency, or to reduce their taxes without reducing their expenditure benefits. As the authors note, a useful follow-up to their survey would be to explore how voters expected the Headlee Amendment to achieve these goals.

The next three papers focus, not on why voters support tax and expenditure limitations, but rather on whether such limitations are desirable.

Richard Musgrave's paper "Leviathan Cometh—Or Does He?" explicitly addresses the question of whether expenditures on public goods and services are "too large." On the basis of an extensive review of the literature on the size of government with particular attention to supporters of the excessive size hypothesis (referred to in the paper as the *Leviathan theorists*), Musgrave concludes that many political and bureaucratic imperfections can lead just as easily to underspending as to overspending.

Starting with Gordon Tullock's classic argument that logrolling biases majority rule toward excessive expenditure, Musgrave evaluates a range of demand-side distortions, such as the tendency for politicians to exaggerate the benefits from public services; for taxpayers to underestimate the costs because of hidden taxes, "automatic" tax increases, or deficit financing; and for government employees to incorporate income considerations into their voting behavior. On the supply side, he examines the argument that maximizing behavior of bureaucrats leads to excessive spending or that the agenda-setting power of monopoly bureaus seriously distorts output levels. Running throughout this discussion is the author's view that the narrow microeconomic and game-theoretic approach of the Leviathan theorists often leads to incorrect conclusions because it disregards the broader social-political interaction entailed in budgetary provision of goods and services.

Musgrave then briefly discusses the distribution function of budget policy, for which the optimal government role is even harder to determine. Although some models predict extensive redistribution of income through taxes and expenditures, Musgrave observes that several factors limit the amount that actually occurs. These observations lead him to support the democratic budget process as the best means of determining the proper amount of redistribution. Finally, after evaluating the reforms proposed by the Leviathan theorists, Musgrave presents his own more limited proposals, intended more to induce efficient public-sector decision making than to reduce the size of the public sector.

The author of the next paper, Geoffrey Brennan, is one of the Leviathan theorists Musgrave cites. In his paper, "Tax Limits and the Logic of Constitutional Restrictions," Brennan takes issue with the central premise of the median voter outcome model: the view that the electoral process fully constrains the actions of public officials and allows them no leeway to pursue their own objectives. He argues that neither electoral processes nor internal moral constraints provide adequate checks on the discretionary power of public officials. Electoral constraints are fully binding only when issues can be arranged along a single dimension and no one prefers both extremes to the middle; in the more common situation, Brennan argues, majority rule generates cycles with no determinate equilibrium. This indeterminacy, in turn, provides scope for political and bureaucratic discretion. Moreover, public officials tend to use this discretion to pursue their own personal objectives, internal moral constraints being insufficient to induce them to act always in the public interest. Additional non-electoral limits are therefore necessary to keep this malevolent despot or "Leviathan" under control.

The case for expenditure controls is more fully developed by Peter

Aranson and Peter Ordeshook in their paper entitled "Alternative Theories of the Growth of Government and Their Implications for Constitutional Tax and Spending Limits." While Musgrave's paper focuses on the size of government, this paper focuses on its rate of growth. In addition, Aranson and Ordeshook are concerned with the growth of government regulation as well as of taxing and spending. On the basis of a selective review of the government growth literature, the authors argue that public officials have incentives to respond to interest group demands for publicly provided services which yield private, divisible benefits, and that this fact leads to inefficient public sector growth. They show that the provision of services financed by everyone to subgroups of the population causes government growth by encouraging nonbeneficiary groups to increase their demands for public services. Aranson and Ordeshook also contend that the commonly used method of incremental public-sector decision making leads to net growth of the public sector whenever voters are unable to perceive the benefits and costs of small changes in public services.

Based on their explanations of government growth, Aranson and Ordeshook then argue that constitutional controls are the least costly way to change the incentives of public officials. Predicted benefits of controls include increased efficiency resulting from greater pressure for officials to make difficult trade-offs among programs; the end of public-sector growth attributable to increasing public employee voting strength; the reduction in demand among groups who currently are hurt by having to pay high taxes to finance benefits to other groups; and, finally, the transfer of many activities to the private sector. To counter the possibility that constitutional tax and spending limitations may lead to additional regulation as a substitute for direct spending, the authors also propose carefully constructed sunset laws.

In the final paper in this volume, "On the Initiative-Referendum Option and the Control of Monopoly Government," Arthur Denzau, Robert Mackay, and Carolyn Weaver (DMW) use mathematical monopoly game theory to examine how effectively and under what conditions the initiative-referendum process reduces public-sector budgets. DMW base their argument on a monopoly model of public-sector provision that, in the absence of additional controls, generates greater expenditures than those desired by the median voter. Building on their own earlier work and on that by Romer and Rosenthal,[5] DMW

---

5. See Romer and Rosenthal (1980) and Mackay and Weaver (1978).

envisage a government whose day-to-day activities are controlled by a dominant coalition of people with high demands for public services; their analytical task is then to compare public-sector outcomes in the case where citizen-voters have the option of initiating budget limiting referenda to the case in which they have no power.

DMW demonstrate that the initiative referendum option will be more effective in limiting the monopoly power of government when the costs of initiation are low; when such costs are large, even substantial discrepancies between actual and desired budgets may not induce voters to act. In addition, the initiative option will be more effective when referenda are permitted to constrain each component of the budget rather than when only the total budget can be constrained. In the latter case the monopoly government may force voters to accept a larger budget by altering the budgetary mix. The authors also emphasize that the threat of the initiative referendum alone is sufficient to make government more responsive to citizen-voters. In the final section of the paper, DMW incorporate the free rider problem, i.e., the fact that people can benefit from a referendum without bearing the costs of initiating it.

Out of the six papers and the discussants' comments emerge a range of views on five questions relating to tax and spending limitations. My purpose in the following paragraphs is not to provide answers to these questions but rather to indicate the nature of the debate.

1. Is the public sector too large?

Conceptually, the question is "too large in relation to what?" Economists usually use one of two norms to define the appropriate or optimal quantity of public goods. Samuelson's well known efficiency condition, i.e., that public goods should be provided up to the point where the sum of the marginal rates of substitution equals the marginal rate of transformation,[6] is appealing, but it fails to incorporate the institutional difficulties of providing services through the budgetary process. A second approach, also not fully satisfactory, because it ignores the intensity of preferences, defines a democratically appropriate expenditure level as the level desired by the median voter.

Even in this case of public goods provision, however, where economists have something relatively concrete to say about government's appropriate size, determining how actual expenditures compare to

---

6. See Samuelson (1954).

optimal expenditures is not easy. On the one hand, Leviathan theorists believe that their models of excessive expenditures accurately describe reality. The Denzau-MacKay-Weaver paper illustrates such a model. On the other hand, Musgrave argues that without further empirical testing, the assumptions leading to the conclusion that excessive spending occurs are no more compelling than others yielding the opposite result.

With respect to transfer payments, defining appropriate or optimal government size is even more complex. Again, Musgrave argues, it is difficult to make an objective case that the public sector is too large. However, support for the view that redistributive programs at the state-local level may currently be excessive in relation to the desires of the median voter comes from the information on attitudes toward the size of government that are reported by Shapiro and by Courant, Gramlich, and Rubinfeld. Survey results from both California and Michigan show that while voters on average are relatively content with expenditures for most public goods, they want to decrease spending on welfare and other redistributive functions.

The reader must decide for himself or herself whether the evidence on public sector size presented here and elsewhere is sufficiently clear to form the basis for policy recommendations to reduce the size of government. Even if one were not convinced that the public sector is excessively large, however, one might argue for tax and expenditure limitations on the grounds that the public sector is growing too fast and is out of control.

2.   Is public sector growth out of control?

Aranson and Ordeshook grapple with the concept of an optimal growth rate with no success. Significantly, their argument for tax and expenditure limitations is based on the "inefficiency" of the government growth process rather than on an excessive growth rate, the notion being that limits will force more efficient expenditure decisions. Brennan and Buchanan take a different approach and emphasize the potential for public-sector growth to be excessive in terms of the preferences of taxpayer-voters; in their view, the political process does not adequately constrain government. Under the assumption that government maximizes revenues, it overexpands unless constitutional tax limitations are imposed.

Whether expenditure growth is as inefficient or as uncontrolled as these analysts contend is almost impossible to determine. Courant,

Gramlich, and Rubinfeld provide indirect evidence on this question by showing that perceptions of inefficient government growth contributed to the success of the Headlee Amendment in Michigan. They conclude that the desire for greater governmental efficiency or increased control motivated two out of three voters responsible for the plurality. Whether this motivation represents an unrealistic search for a free lunch or an accurate assessment of the potential gains from controls remains to be determined.

By comparing actual and desired local expenditure growth in California from 1973 to 1978, Perry Shapiro sheds additional light on the hypothesis of excessive government growth. His argument that 1973 local public expenditures were in equilibrium suggests that the excessive expenditure growth he finds between 1973 and 1978 reflects characteristics peculiar to the period rather than a natural tendency for uncontrolled growth.

3. Are tax and expenditure limitations desirable?

The desirability of tax and expenditure limitations depends in part on the answers to the preceding questions. Without a general presumption of overspending or excessive growth, the case for rigid controls is weak; even when such presumption is reasonable, however, further analysis is needed. As Discussant Wallace Oates comments, the inflexibility and crudeness of tax and expenditure limitations make such measures potentially costly even when they offset real imperfections in the collective choice mechanism. Thus, the potential benefits of controls must be evaluated in light of their potential costs. Some conference participants apparently were confident that tax limit proposals would pass any such cost-benefit test; others were not so sure.

An argument can nonetheless be made for less rigid controls or fiscal reforms that strengthen the link between taxpayer-voter desires and budgetary outcomes. Even Richard Musgrave, a strong critic of the controls proposed by the Leviathan theorists, recognizes the need for reforms to strengthen fiscal discipline and to improve the collective choice mechanism.

4. Should tax and expenditure limitations be part of the constitution?

At a conceptual level, the question is whether normative tax policy issues should be discussed in a preconstitution and postconstitution framework. According to this approach, appropriate tax rules are those that citizens would agree upon in a preconstitution setting without precise knowledge of their own future income positions and knowing that the rules would be binding for an indeterminate period. This concern with once-and-for-all constitution-making underlies Brennan's paper and earlier work by Brennan and Buchanan.[7] An alternative approach, advanced by Musgrave, views constitution-making, i.e., rule-setting, as a continuing task which allows for value changes over time.

At a more pragmatic level, the question is whether specific tax and expenditure limitations should be statutory or constitutional. Musgrave contends that fiscal limitations do not belong in the Constitution since they protect no basic right or liberty, and that the Constitution is too inflexible and rigid a document to deal with the details of tax policy. To Aranson and Ordeshook, however, the only way to reduce public officials' incentives to provide private, divisible benefits is to impose constitutional restrictions over which public officials have no control. These authors counter the contention that the Constitution should not include economic policy by arguing that tax and expenditure limitations relate to rule-setting and process change rather than to policy outcomes.

5. Will tax and expenditure limitations achieve the goals of their supporters?

The Courant-Gramlich-Rubinfeld analysis indicates that the Headlee supporters in Michigan differed in their perceptions of the amendment's potential benefits. Some were motivated by the desire for a smaller public sector, others by the desire for more efficiency and voter control, and still others by the hope of lower taxes for the same services. Similarly, academic proponents of controls expect different types of gains. Brennan, for example, believes that more efficient expenditure levels will result, while Aranson and Ordeshook expect both a more efficient mix of services and a lower growth rate of expenditures.

Of the papers included in this volume, only the Denzau-Mackay-Weaver analysis examines in any detail the link between the specific form of the fiscal limitation and its objective. Focusing explicitly on various forms of the initiative-referendum option, the authors conclude

---

7. For example, see Brennan and Buchanan (1977) and (1978).

that the option can act as a significant, although imperfect, constraint on the actions of monopoly government, provided the costs to citizens of exercising the option are low. Rothenberg, in commenting on the paper, is not so optimistic. None of the papers, it should be pointed out, focuses on the related question of the unintended effects of tax limitation measures, such as increased pressure to shift financial responsibilities from one level of government to another, or differential burdens by income class.

As this discussion suggests, substantial disagreement exists among academic researchers on the issues raised by the success of the tax and expenditure limitation movement. The six papers included in this volume represent a wide range of views on these issues. We hope that their inclusion in a single volume will encourage more informed dialogue between proponents and opponents of such limitations in the future.

REFERENCES

Brennan, G., and Buchanan, J. 1977. Towards a constitution for Leviathan. *Journal of Public Economics* 8:255–73.

Brennan, G. and Buchanan, J. 1978. Tax instruments as constraints on the disposition of public revenue. *Journal of Public Economics* 9:301–18.

Courant, P., Gramlich, E., and Rubinfeld, D. December 1979. Public employee market power and the level of government spending. *American Economic Review*.

Ladd, H. March 1978. An economic evaluation of state limitations on local taxing and spending powers. *National Tax Journal* 31:1–19.

Mackay, R., and Weaver, C. 1978. Monopoly bureaus and fiscal outcomes: deductive models and implications for reform. In G. Tullock and R. Wagner, eds., *Policy analysis and deductive reasoning*. Lexington, Mass.: D.C. Heath.

Oakland, W. June 1979. Proposition 13—genesis and consequences. *National Tax Journal*. Supplement, pp. 387–407.

Pascal, A., et al. 1979. *Fiscal containment of local and state government*. Santa Monica, Calif.: Rand, R–2494–FF/RC.

Romer, T., and Rosenthal, H. 1980. Political resource allocation, controlled agenda and the status quo. *Public Choice* 33–4:27–45.

Samuelson, P. November 1954. The pure theory of public expenditures. *Review of Economics and Statistics* 36:387–89.

Shapiro, P., Puryear, D., and Ross, J. June 1979. Tax and expenditure limitation in retrospect and in prospect. *National Tax Journal*. Supplement, pp. 1–10.

POPULAR RESPONSE TO PUBLIC SPENDING DISEQUILIBRIUM: AN ANALYSIS OF THE 1978 CALIFORNIA PROPERTY TAX LIMITATION INITIATIVE

Perry Shapiro

Proposition 13, which proposed to amend the Constitution of the State of California, was passed by a majority as a referendum-initiative in the June 1978 elections. Before the election the property tax rate was approximately 2.5 percent of actual market value. The passage of Proposition 13 reduced the tax on all real property in the state to 1 percent of the 1975 market value as reflected by the 1975 property tax assessments. Because property values had increased substantially between 1975 and 1978, the passage of the proposition meant a reduction of about 57 percent in property tax revenues (about $7 billion) which initially represented a 37 percent decrease in own-source revenues of local government.[1]

[The author is Professor of Economics, University of California, Santa Barbara, and Visiting Professor of Economics, University of Michigan.]

COMMENT: The analysis represents a personal rethinking of the Proposition 13 phenomenon. It was stimulated by the recent writings of Thomas Borcherding and the perceptive comments of Helen Ladd. The process took place with the aid of long conversations with Ted Bergstrom.

1. These estimates are due to William Oakland (1979), and they slightly exaggerate the revenue effects because they fail to account for the numerous interrelationships between various revenue sources. For example, property tax payments are deductible against income for the purpose of state income tax calculation. With an average state

Proposition 13 was interpreted as the beginning of a national revolt. Indeed many other states (e.g., Nevada, Idaho, and Michigan) subsequently passed property tax limitation measures of varying severity, and in November 1979 the voters passed an amendment to the California Constitution that fixed the level of real per capita state and local government expenditures. Whether or not Proposition 13 was the beginning of a national tax revolt, it was surely the beginning of one in California.

The voters seemed to be expressing a preference for a substantial reduction in local public expenditures. But, if this is so, it is puzzling that there have been so many successful analyses of the demand for public goods employing a model which postulates voters' satisfaction with the level of public expenditures. The so-called median voter view suggests a market-like process which determines a community's supply of public goods. Within this process a community supplies public goods and services at the level the median voter would demand at the existing prices and distribution of cost shares. This process splits the dissatisfaction with government: half of the voters would want a smaller level of government expenditures and half would want a larger level. But the median level would beat any alternative in a majority rule election. In the case of Proposition 13 the status quo was rejected in favor of a substantial reduction in the level of local public expenditures. The outcome would be unexpected if local government expenditures had been at the levels favored by median voters.

Indeed, a public opinion survey conducted just prior to the election suggests that a majority of voters did not want to reduce expenditures on most local public goods. Some of the results of a survey conducted by Jack Citrin are presented in table 1. An examination of that table highlights two interesting facts. First, with the exception of two items—welfare and local public administration—a majority of the respondents did not want to reduce expenditures for public goods. Second, again with the same exception, the median respondent in each category desired expenditures to remain the same. Administrative expenses do not make a large claim on property tax revenues and welfare expenditures are financed predominately with state and federal revenues. Why then was Proposition 13 so successful?

---

income tax rate of 4.9 percent this alone would account for $343 million more income tax revenues. Furthermore, because disposable income is increased by the reduction in property taxes, sales tax revenues will be increased. Perry Shapiro and W.D. Morgan (1978)

Table 1

"[Do] You Think the Tax Money for Each [of the Following] Should Be Increased, Held the Same, or Cut Back?"

Category	Cut Back	Same	Increase	No Answer
(1) Higher education, such as university, state and local community colleges	24.5	49.7	21.7	4.0
(2) Public schools, kindergarten through 12th grades	22.2	48.9	25.0	3.9
(3) Welfare and public assistance programs	63.6	24.1	7.4	4.9
(4) Medical care programs such as medi-Cal	27.0	46.8	19.7	6.4
(5) Parks and recreation facilities	22.3	56.2	17.2	4.3
(6) Police departments and law enforcement	7.9	61.4	27.5	3.2
(7) Street and highway building and repairs	23.2	55.4	16.8	4.6
(8) Jail, prisons and other recreational facilities	9.6	42.9	38.3	9.2
(9) Environmental protection regulations	35.5	35.5	22.0	7.1
(10) Fire departments	5.9	72.5	18.4	3.2
(11) Public transportation	23.5	43.2	25.9	7.4
(12) Government backed public housing projects	42.0	31.1	17.9	9.0
(13) City and county administrative departments	67.4	24.4	1.9	6.3
(14) Courts and judges	25.7	51.5	15.7	7.1

SOURCE: University of California, Survey Research Center, *Contextual California Taxing and Spending Data Merge with California Poll 7806* (mimeo).

A possible explanation is that the voters did not wish to reduce public expenditures; they wanted only to reduce the dependence of local expenditures on the property tax base. This explanation is attractive in the light of two facts. The first is that the resident-voter's[2] property tax share had risen substantially between 1973 and 1978. In 1973 the share was approximately 45 percent and by 1978 it was approximately 53 percent.[3] The second is that the state had, over the same period, accumulated a $7 billion surplus because its revenues were growing considerably faster than its expenditures. These two facts suggested that the voters' approval of Proposition 13 was not meant to reduce the size of local government expenditures; it was meant instead to shift the financial responsibility for maintaining them from the property tax to state revenue sources.[4]

This paper examines the two alternative explanations for the success of Proposition 13. The first part of the paper deals with the possible divergence of government expenditures from their desired levels. A model is developed to calculate desired rates of expenditure change and these rates are then compared with the actual rates of change in the expenditures of school districts, municipalities, and counties. The second part of the paper deals with the possible desire of voters to transfer financial responsibility for local public expenditures from the property tax to state taxing sources. Analysis of the relationship between the potential benefits from the shift and the vote on Proposition 13 suggests that the tax shift explanation is incorrect.

Actual and Equilibrium Levels of Public Expenditures

Were local public expenditures too high in 1978? Over the period 1973–1978, educational expenditures per pupil had grown at an average annual rate of 11.3 percent. Data reported in the 1972 and 1977 *Census of Government* show that per capita municipal expenditures out of general revenues had grown at an average annual rate of 12.8 percent and that per capita county expenditures had grown

---

2. The resident-voter is a home owner or renter who is eligible to vote in local and state elections. In the analysis of the tax share, resident-voter taxes are distinct from business taxes. This distinction is somewhat artificial because a number of people who pay business taxes also vote in the state. Furthermore, in a full general equilibrium sense, the "resident-voter" may be paying a large part of the business tax.

3. William Oakland, op. cit.

4. This view is given in Perry Shapiro, David Puryear, and John Ross (1979).

at an average annual rate of 8.5 percent. If we could determine the desired rates of growth of these expenditures it would be possible to compare them with the actual rates in order to infer whether or not expenditures had grown too fast. Thomas Borcherding (1977) has done this for aggregate government expenditures in the twentieth century. To a large degree this analysis will follow Borcherding's design.

Borcherding relies on the demand studies that are based on the supposition that communities supply the amount demanded by the median voter. The median voter assumption allows community demands to be analyzed as if they were the outcome of the welfare optimization of one individual (the median voter). Under some specifications of the preference function this maximization can be shown to yield a log linear public goods expenditure equation

$$\log (E/q) = A + b_1 \log (Y/p) + b_2 \log \tau (q/p) + \Sigma C_i \log X_i \quad (1)$$

where E is nominal expenditure on public goods; q is price of public goods; p is the price of numeraire market goods; Y is income; the X_i's are factors other than price and income that affect demand and τ is the median voter's share of total public expenditures. The parameters b_1 and b_2 are the income and price elasticities of demand. If we knew the values of the equation (1) parameters, it would be possible to calculate the desired rates of growth of various public expenditures over any arbitrary time period for which expenditures were at their desired level at the beginning of the period. To see this, take the time derivative of (1):

$$
\begin{aligned}
E^* = b_1 Y^* + b_2 \tau^* - (b_1 + b_2)p^* \\
+ (1 + b_2)q^* + \Sigma C_i X_i^*
\end{aligned}
\quad (2)
$$

where the * denotes the percentage rate of change. Thus E is the rate of change in equilibrium public expenditures. However, if, at the beginning of the period over which the rate of growth is to be measured, the actual supply of public goods is smaller than the desired level, observed changes may reflect adjustments towards equilibrium as well as changes in the equilibrium value.

It is impossible to know whether or not public expenditures were at their equilibrium value at the beginning of the period to be examined (the early 1970s until 1978). However, during the first years of the decade at least three tax or expenditure limitation initiatives were defeated—two to modify the property tax and one (the Reagan initiative) in 1973 to limit the real level of per capita government expenditures. While the three defeats are not conclusive evidence of an expenditure equilibrium in 1973, such an equilibrium will be assumed in the following analysis.[5]

Education

Education is the first class of public expenditures to be analyzed. Since such a large share (47 percent) of property tax revenue is used for the support of local public (primary and secondary) education, it is reasonable to deal with it in some detail. The responsibility for financing local public education has historically been shared between local districts and the state. From personal conversations with various educators in the state, it appears that the underlying aim of the state education authorities has been to maintain equal shares for local districts and the state. The local and state shares have not always been equal: in the 1972–73 period the local share was in excess of 60 percent of spending on primary and secondary education, although in 1974–75 it fell to approximately 52 percent. While it appears that the state has sought to maintain its "fair share," by 1977–78 the proportion of local expenditures had risen to 54 percent. This was because the state school aid formula provided that the level of state aid to local school districts would fall as the assessed value in the district rose.

Whether the level of state aid affects the desired level of education expenditures is a question that needs an empirical answer. Robert Inman (1978) has reported the results of a cross-sectional study of school district expenditures for New York State. He found that the demand for educational expenditures depended upon the level of state aid. It might be reasonable to assume, in the absence of further empirical evidence, that the parameters found for New York approximate those that would have been found in California, but, since the results are derived from cross-sectional evidence, the coefficient on "state aid" cannot give us information on how changes in the aggregate level of state aid will affect the aggregate demand for educational expenditures. In order to understand the difficulty in using the cross-sectional results for these calculations of the desired change in ed-

---

5. Of course another, equally plausible, explanation is that the voters desired larger government expenditures.

ucation expenditures, consider why a person would prefer to finance local education through state rather than local revenues. After all, people must pay state as well as local taxes, and, unless people perceive that state revenues are, somehow, less costly to them than local, there is no reason to prefer one form of financing to the other. When examining variation in educational expenditures among school districts, as Inman did, it would be possible to find that state aid has an effect on educational demand because state aid is generally distributed on the basis of the assessed value of the district (the level of state aid declines with the assessed value of the district). Because of this distribution rule, ceteris paribus, a person in a relatively poorer district (as measured by assessed value) should prefer state financing and a person in a relatively richer district should prefer local financing. And because state financing redistributes revenue among jurisdictions it is reasonable that, as Inman found, the level of state aid should be statistically significant in explaining interjurisdictional variation in educational expenditures. However, additional considerations are necessary to predict the effects of state aid on aggregate state education demand over time.

The model used to analyze the aggregate effects of state educational aid starts with the assumption that statewide per capita demand for all goods—public and private—can be rationalized by the maximization, subject to a budget constraint, of a strictly quasi-concave, twice differentiable, aggregate utility function[6]

$$U\ (X,E) \tag{3}$$

where X is the per capita consumption of a private numeraire good and E is the per capita amount of the collective good (in this case educational service). The state per capita budget constraint is derived by averaging the constraints for individual school districts. The district budget constraint is complicated because its expenditures are in good part financed through grants from the state. Although some state revenue is contributed for special programs most of it is given as block grants for general educational expenditures. The level of state aid depends on the wealth of the district but does not depend on the

---

6. Sufficient condition for the existence of a utility function that rationalizes per capita demands with any group are given in Perry Shapiro (1977). Empirical tests for the satisfaction of these conditions are reported in Perry Shapiro and Steven Braithwait (1979).

amount of revenues raised locally. Under this financial arrangement total per capita educational expenditures in district i are

$$E_i = L_i + S_i \tag{4}$$

where L_i is the expenditures per person financed by local taxes and S_i is the per capita amount of state block grant aid.[7] Statewide per capita aid to education, S, is

$$S \equiv \sum_i \omega_i S_i \tag{5}$$

where ω_i is a weight equal to the fraction of the state population in i. Each district has a budget constraint

$$Y_i = \tau_{L_i} (E_i - S_i) + \tau_{S_i} T_i + X_i \tag{6}$$

where Y_i is per capita income in district i measured in the numeraire good; τ_{L_i} and τ_{S_i} are the district i resident voter's shares of local and state expenditures respectively; and T_i is the per capita state taxes for education in district i. If the variable pairs τ_{L_i} and E_i; τ_{L_i} and S_i; and τ_{S_i} and T_i are distributed independently,[8] then:

$$Y + \tau_L S - \tau_S T = X + \tau_L E \tag{7}$$

where symbols without i subscripts denote statewide averages. Since (apart from state administrative costs) S must equal T,

$$Y + (\tau_L - \tau_S) S = X + \tau_L E \tag{7'}$$

which implies that increasing the level of per capita state aid by one dollar has the same effect on education demand E as does a change of $(\tau_L - \tau_S)$ dollars in income.

7. Typically the matching grant formula is much more complicated than is given in (4). The rate of matching aid might depend upon the type of expenditure as well as the characteristic of the school district. The block grant aid is distributed on the basis of a formula such that the amount of aid decreases with the assessed property value of the district.

8. This means that the cross-sectional covariances are zero. This assumption allows us to calculate the average of a product of two random variables as the product of their individual averages. There is no way to measure these covariances but it is unlikely that they are zero.

In California τ_L (the residential property share of the property tax) was approximately 0.56 in 1976 and τ_S (estimated on the basis of the assumption that individuals paid the entire income and sales tax) was approximately 0.66. It appears that increasing state aid by one dollar would be the equivalent of reducing income by ten cents.

Using the equivalence of state aid and income it is simple to calculate the educational expenditure elasticity of state aid as

$$\frac{\partial \log E}{\partial \log S} = \frac{\partial \log E}{\partial \log Y} \left(\frac{E}{Y}\right)\left(\frac{S}{E}\right)\left(\tau_L - \tau_S\right) \tag{8}$$

The first term on the right-hand side of (8) is the income elasticity of demand for education. Although the estimates of the income elasticity vary, Inman's estimate of 0.6 is close to most others. The second and third terms on the right reduce to the state educational expenditure share of state income, which was approximately 0.015 in 1978. These values yield a state aid elasticity of educational expenditures of -0.0009.

This calculation implies that changes in the level of state aid for education will have little effect on the desired statewide level of educational expenditures. Therefore, the effects of changes in the level of state aid will be ignored in the discussion that follows.

The state is not the only source of financial aid to local school districts. There was a 41 percent increase in federal government aid to local school districts over the period from 1974–75 to 1977–78. In the case of federal aid, it is reasonable to assume that any federal assistance given is a small part of the federal budget, and it is, therefore, approximately without cost to the local district. By employing the assumption that the local share of federal education expenditures is zero, it is possible to calculate the elasticity of educational expenditures with respect to federal aid. On the basis of a calculation similar to the one used to find the state aid elasticity, the federal aid elasticity is found to be 0.05. A one percent increase in federal aid will result in a 0.05 percent increase in total education expenditures.

Estimates of income and tax share-price elasticities allow the computation of the desired percentage change in educational expenditures. The equation for desired education expenditures is

$$\log E/q = A + 0.592 \log Y/p \tag{9}$$
$$- 0.374 \log (\tau \cdot q/p) + 0.05 \log F/q$$

where A is a constant, τ is the voter's tax share, q is the price of "education," p is the price of the numeraire good (CPI), and F is the level of federal aid. The first two coefficients are the values estimated by Inman. The tax share τ is calculated by the accounting identity

$$\tau = r_L \tau_L + r_S \tau_S \tag{10}$$

where as before τ_L and τ_S are the voters' (single family residents') share of local and state taxes and r_L and r_S are the shares of educational expenditures borne by local and state revenue sources. These values are reported in table 2.

In order to use equation (9) it is convenient to translate it into a function of nominal values and absolute prices rather than real values and relative prices. In terms of nominal values

$$\log E = A + 0.592 \log Y - 0.374 \log \tau - 0.218 \log p \tag{11}$$
$$+ 0.05 \log F + 0.582 \log q$$

From this the approximate value of the desired rate of change in educational expenditures is

$$\Delta E/E = 0.592(\Delta Y/Y) - 0.374(\Delta\tau/\tau) + 0.05(\Delta F/F)$$
$$+ 0.582(\Delta q/q) - 0.218 (\Delta p/p). \tag{12}$$

Over the period 1974–78, state income increased at an average annual rate of 9.1 percent, the tax share, τ, increased at a rate of 1.8 percent per year, and the federal contributions increased at a rate of 12.1 percent per year. The prices q and p (the deflators for state and local government and for personal consumption were used) rose at an average rate of 7.9 percent and 6.5 percent respectively.

If educational expenditures were at their desired level in 1973, they were approximately 10 percent too high when Proposition 13 was approved. The desired rate of change from 1974 to 1978 was 8.5 percent per year, the actual rate was 11.3 percent per year. The average rate of growth in educational expenditures was approximately 3 percent faster than desired. Had these expenditures grown at the desired rate they would have been $1,624 per ADA in 1977–78 rather than the $1,754 which was spent. The equilibrium level of expenditures in 1978 was approximately $7.46 billion; the actual level was approximately $8.06 billion. In order to have brought expenditures on education to their equilibrium would have required a 7.4 percent

Table 2

EDUCATIONAL EXPENDITURES (PRIMARY AND SECONDARY) PER AVERAGE DAILY ATTENDANCE (ADA)

	1974-75	1975-76	1976-77	1977-78	Percent Change 1974-78	Average Annual Rate of Growth (percent)
Total/ADA	1,271.2	1,405.1	1,554.4	1,753.7	38.0	11.3/year
Local/ADA	656.2	735.6	829.7	944.3	43.9	12.9/year
State/ADA	518.7	572.0	620.3	678.4	30.8	9.4/year
Federal/ADA	85.7	86.9	93.2	120.8	41.0	12.1/year
Local/Total	51.6	52.4	53.4	53.8		
State/Total	40.8	40.7	39.9	38.7		
Federal/Total	6.7	6.2	5.3	6.9		

SOURCE: California State Controller, *Financial Transactions Concerning School Districts of California.*

NOTE: For the periods before 1974–75 it was not possible to separate expenditures on post secondary (Community College) education from expenditures on primary and secondary education.

reduction. If the demand parameters are accurate, the average citizen of the state wanted a substantial decrease in the level of primary and secondary educational expenditure.

Municipal and County Government

To compute the desired rate of growth in municipal and county expenditures (which together account for 63 percent of property tax revenues), it is assumed that the demand elasticities are the same for both levels of government. This assumption is reasonable because municipalities (incorporated cities) and counties provide many of the same services. However, there are differences in both the functions and finances of the two jurisdictional types, and these differences may invalidate the assumption of identical demand elasticities. For instance, as table 3 shows, the property tax accounts for 93 percent of county own-source revenues and 36 percent of total general revenues while it comprises 36 percent of municipal own source and 25 percent of total general revenues. Furthermore over one-half of county general revenues and less than one-third of municipal revenues are transfers from the state and federal governments. It is also interesting to notice that over the period 1971–1977, municipal expenditures grew at a much faster rate than did county expenditures. These differences may indicate that the mix of public goods provided by cities is different from that provided by counties. Even with these differences it should be possible to compute a rough estimate of the desired changes in city and county expenditures. To do so, the elasticity estimates of Bergstrom and Goodman (1973) are used.

Bergstrom and Goodman employ an estimating equation similar to that of Inman (1978), namely

$$\log \frac{M}{q} = C + \varepsilon \log \left(\frac{Y}{p}\right) + \delta \log \left(\tau \frac{q}{p}\right). \tag{13}$$

Their estimate of the parameter values for municipal expenditures (in this case M) for the State of California were $\varepsilon = 0.28$ and $\delta = 0.39$. In the case of California municipalities, the contribution by the state will have negligible effect on total spending because the voters' share of state taxes is approximately the same as the voter share of local taxes. Therefore the intergovernmental revenue elasticity is approximately zero.

The desired change in municipal expenditures is computed in a

Table 3

CALIFORNIA LOCAL GOVERNMENT TAXATION

	Municipalities			Counties		
	1971–72	*1976–77*	*Average Annual Rate of Change (percent)*	*1971–72*	*1976–77*	*Average Annual Rate of Change (percent)*
Population	15,020,511			19,252,696		
General Revenue	3,124,771	5,698,291	12.8	5,665,586	8,521,595	8.5
Intergovernmental	862,352	1,797,667	15.8	2,772,965	4,341,952	9.4
State	564,303	1,063,109	13.5	n.a.[a]	3,640,006	
Own Source	2,262,419	3,900,624	11.5	2,300,392	3,340,215	8.9
Taxes	1,544,528	2,720,183	12.0	2,177,289	3,090,939	7.3
Property	809,091	1,350,124	10.8			
Other	735,437	1,370,059	13.3			
Charges	717,891	1,180,441	10.5	592,228	839,428	7.2

SOURCE: U.S. Bureau of the Census, *Census of Government*, 1972 and 1977.

a.   Not Available.

manner similar to the one used for educational expenditures. From (13) and the estimated values of the relevant elasticities, an approximate value for t the desired rate of change is

$$\Delta M/M = 0.28(\Delta Y/Y) + 0.11(\Delta p/p)$$
$$+ 0.61(\Delta q/q) - 0.39(\Delta \tau/\tau). \quad (14)$$

The values for percentage change in Y, p and q are the same for municipalities as they are for education (the same price series were used) but the value for the tax share is different because of a differential reliance on the various revenue sources. Although both schools and cities receive substantial revenues from the property tax, approximately 65 percent of the own source revenues of cities are derived from sales taxes (35 percent) and user charges and permit fees. The allocation of the voters' share of the sales tax burden is difficult because sales tax revenues in the amount of 1 percent of taxable sales are returned to municipalities. This allocation scheme causes a problem for the imputation of burden because people pay taxes to the jurisdiction where they shop and this may not be the same as the residential jurisdiction.[9] Since it is not possible to get a direct estimate of the effect, it is assumed that the entire sales tax burden is borne by the resident-voter.

In computing the tax share it is assumed that the resident-voter pays 66 percent of state tax revenues, 45 percent (1971–72) and 54 percent (1977–78) of property taxes, and 100 percent of sales taxes and charges. Using these fractions, the resident voters' tax share was 0.71 in 1971–72 and 0.70 in 1976–77. To the order of approximation used in these examples it is reasonable to assume no change in the tax share.

Over this same period per capita income increased at a rate of 10.2 percent per year while p and q increased at 6.2 percent and 7.0 percent per year respectively. Using these rates in equation (14), the average desired rate of increase in per capita municipal expenditures is calculated to be 7.8 percent per year. During the 1971–77 period, the average rate of growth in general revenues was 12.8 percent per year; Levy and Zamolo (1978) report a rate of expenditure growth of 10.2 percent per capita over the 1973–77 period. Whichever estimate

---

9. An estimate of the inter-county discrepancies between sales tax payment and receipt is given in T. Smith and P. Shapiro (1979).

most accurately reflects the true experience, actual expenditures were growing faster than the desired rate.

There exist no separate estimates on the demand for county expenditures. The actual rate of growth in expenditures is approximately 8.5 percent a year. Since there is no appreciable change in the resident-voter tax share, if the Bergstrom-Goodman elasticities are used, the desired rate of growth would be 7.8 percent per year—the same as for municipal expenditures.

These calculations establish that local public expenditures were rising faster during the 1970s than would have been predicted by the median voter demand model. This does not prove conclusively that local expenditures were too high in 1978, but if they were not too high it is hard to understand why Proposition 13 passed so easily. As noted earlier, one possible alternative explanation is that a favorable vote was motivated by a desire to shift financial responsibility from the local to the state bax base.[10]

Shifting the Taxing Responsibility

Two facts about Proposition 13 are striking. The first is that the voters appeared to be happy with the level of expenditures on public goods; the second is that the resident-voters' share of the property tax had risen steadily over a number of years. If people really were happy with their public goods, why did they vote for Proposition 13? One answer seemed to be that the distribution of the property tax burden had changed in a way unfavorable to the resident-voter. Indeed, William Oakland (1979) reported (see table 4) that the resident-voters' share of the property tax had increased from 45.4 percent in 1973–74 to 53.6 percent in 1977–78. With the passage of Proposition 13, people did not expect the real level of public expenditures to decline: they expected the loss in property tax revenues to be made up through the state's public revenues. This interpretation of the outcome was reinforced because the passage of Proposition 13 reduced property tax revenues by about $7 billion, which was approximately the size of the state government's accumulated surplus. Therefore, in the first year, at least, government expenditures could be maintained without increasing other tax rates.

The hypothesis that resident-voters desired to shift the funding

---

10. Perry Shapiro, Puryear, and Ross, op. cit.

Table 4

SHARE OF TOTAL ASSESSED VALUE

Period	Single Family Residences	Other Residences	Non-Residences	State Assessed
1972–73	34.0	13.9	44.4	7.6
1973–74	31.6	13.8	46.9	7.7
1974–75	32.9	13.4	46.4	7.3
1975–76	35.2	13.2	44.7	6.9
1976–77	39.5	12.9	41.0	6.6
1977–78	41.0	12.6	39.6	6.4

SOURCE: William H. Oakland, "Proposition 13—Genesis and Consequences," Supplement, *National Tax Journal*, June 1979.

responsibility to state tax sources is difficult to defend. Sales and personal income tax revenues are two-thirds of the state's general revenues. These taxes are borne predominantly by individuals (although sales to businesses make up a significant portion of the sales tax base). Even though it is not possible to compute it directly, it is unlikely that the resident-voters' share of state revenues is smaller than their 0.54 share of the local property tax. However, these rough calculations of the relative advantages of state and local financing are only average values. For although a transfer of financing responsibility may not be advantageous on average it may be beneficial for some groups.

In order to establish whether or not some groups would benefit from state rather than property tax financing of public expenditures, the average tax rates (tax paid divided by income) were computed using data compiled from 1977 state income tax returns. These calculations are presented in table 5. The income tax was computed by taking the ratio of income taxes paid to reported income. Real estate and sales tax rates were computed by dividing the deduction claimed for payment of these taxes by the income of the groups claiming the deduction. This method will tend to misrepresent the rates for the low-income people particularly. A large percentage of low-income filers do not itemize deductions, and those that do are likely to use the table values for their sales tax deduction.

Table 5 suggests that, ceteris paribus, those with incomes under $12,000 would benefit substantially from a larger dependence on

Table 5

CALIFORNIA AVERAGE TAX BURDEN[a]

Average Income	Income Tax 1	Sales Tax 2	State Tax 1 + 2	Real Estate Tax
9,500	0.023	0.023	0.046	0.063
11,500	0.021	0.022	0.043	0.056
13,500	0.023	0.022	0.045	0.047
15,500	0.023	0.021	0.044	0.046
17,500	0.026	0.020	0.046	0.041
19,500	0.026	0.020	0.046	0.041
21,500	0.028	0.019	0.047	0.038
23,500	0.031	0.018	0.049	0.037
25,500	0.032	0.018	0.050	0.037
27,500	0.033	0.017	0.050	0.038
29,500	0.036	0.016	0.052	0.036
37,200	0.045	0.014	0.059	0.037
54,500	0.062	0.012	0.074	0.036
74,700	0.072	0.010	0.082	0.034

SOURCE: State of California Franchise State Board, *1977 Annual Report*.

a. The method of computation is described in the text.

state financing. Those people with incomes between $14,000 and $20,000 would benefit little or lose little from a change. And, those with incomes greater than $20,000 would be made worse off by a shift in financial responsibility. This assessment of the relative desirability of state versus local financing depends upon the belief that the success of Proposition 13 would not appreciably change the rules governing state taxation.

Even though the exact computations of the favorability of the two sources may not be accurate, the conclusion that the desirability of state financing is inversely related to income is intuitively appealing. All tax payments are positively related to income. Income taxes are obviously so related; sales and property taxes are also so related, to the extent that taxable consumption and housing values are positively related to income. For this reason, given a level of public expenditures, it is always better to be among the poorest in the taxing jurisdiction. As a simple illustrative example, suppose that individual taxes were proportional to income, i.e., individual i's tax bill (T_i) would be

$$T_i = (\tau \cdot y_i)C \qquad (15)$$

where C is the level of expenditures in the taxing jurisdiction. If total tax collections must equal expenditures

$$\sum_{i=1}^{n} (\tau \cdot y_i) \, C = C \qquad (16)$$

each individual tax price would be

$$y_i / \sum_{j=1}^{n} y_j \qquad (17)$$

Thus for any given level of expenditures C, the smaller an individual's income is relative to the income in his taxing jurisdiction, the better off he is. Since there is a tendency for high-income people to reside in districts with few poor people, people with relatively high income would be higher in the distribution of income in the state as a whole than in their residential jurisdiction. For this reason a person with high income would have a higher state than local tax price and would suffer from a shift in revenue responsibility from the local government to the state. Similarly, a low-income individual might prefer that state taxes support a larger proportion of public expenditures.

If this interpretation of the relative preferences for state versus local financing is correct, and if Proposition 13 was merely an expression of demand to shift the financial responsibility of public expenditures to the state, then support for 13 should have been inversely related to income. The problem with testing this hypothesis using voting data is that it would be difficult to distinguish between a vote for Proposition 13 motivated by a desire to reduce public expenditures from the same vote motivated by a desire to shift the financial responsibility to state taxes. To isolate the possible desire for a tax shift, I was able to rely on the data of the public opinion poll taken by Jack Citrin. For a sample of 1,317 California voter respondents, taken shortly before the election, Citrin asked how each respondent planned to vote on Proposition 13, his degree of satisfaction with a number of public goods, and various personal data such as income and party affiliation. From these data, it was possible to isolate the Proposition 13 choices of those who wanted no reduction in local public goods. It was then possible to separate the desire for reductions in expenditures from a preference for a tax shift.

A detailed examination of these data shows, first, that 78.8 percent of the voters wanted to reduce expenditure on one or more local public services. Six out of the public expenditure categories—public schools; parks and recreation; police; fire; public transportation; and local administration—were classified as local. The criterion for inclusion in this category was that the revenues were locally raised. These public goods were chosen because they were the most likely to be reduced with the passage of 13. Among the 1,202 people who gave definite opinions on all the local public expenditure categories (115 responded with "no opinion" about at least one of the seven expenditures) only 219 (18.2 percent) were satisfied with existing levels of expenditures or wanted these levels increased on all local public services. This fact alone gives some insight into the puzzle suggested earlier: why did people vote for Proposition 13 if they did not want a reduction in local public expenditures? A partial answer is that many people may have voted in the belief that only the personally undesired expenditures would be reduced. The attractiveness of Proposition 13 would of course increase with the number of desired reductions. Indeed, Citrin (1979, p. 122) reports that the probability of voting for the proposition increased monotonically with the number of expenditure reductions desired.

Of those voters who did not want a reduction in local public expenditures, 57.5 percent voted against the measure. This indicates that (at least in a probabilistic sense) people were not deceived about the nature of the proposition. Although it can be argued that 42.5 percent thought they would maintain their public services and simultaneously enjoy a tax reduction (a free lunch), a majority did not. An alternative explanation for why such people might vote for the proposition is that they believed local public services could be maintained through states taxes. We now turn to an examination of this hypothesis.

If it were true that, among the satisfied groups, those who voted in favor of Proposition 13 were voting for greater state financing, then the percentage of voters favoring Proposition 13 should decline with income. Tables 6 and 7 report the responses of the satisfied group stratified by income class. Table 6 has the responses of all satisified

Table 6

INCOME AND VOTES ON PROPOSITION 13 OF THOSE PEOPLE WHO WANTED
TO MAINTAIN OR INCREASE THE LEVEL OF EXPENDITURES ON ALL LOCAL
PUBLIC GOODS

Income	Vote on Proposition 13	
	No	Yes
Total	57.5	42.5
0–15,000	26.4[a] / 57.3[b]	19.7[a] / 42.7[b]
$15,000–$20,000	7.8[a] / 60.0[b]	5.2[a] / 40.0[b]
$20,000–	23.8[a] / 58.2[b]	17.1[a] / 41.8[b]

a. Entries above the diagonal lines are the joint (sample) probabilities of vote and income.

b. Entries below the diagonal lines are the (sample) probabilities of a particular vote conditional on the income level.

people (both homeowners and renters) and table 7 gives the response of the satisfied homeowners only. Although it should be expected that property owners might respond differently to the proposition than renters, tables 6 and 7 give little indication of this. Futhermore, on the basis of these data, we musts reject the hypothesis that people were voting for state financing. The tables provide little support for the view that voting responses varied with income. On the basis of the chi-square test for independence, it is not possible to reject the hypothesis that preference for Proposition 13 is independent of income. This finding is consistent with Citrin's (1979, p. 124) probit analysis of opinions on Proposition 13 in which he found income to be an insignificant explanatory variable.

Table 7

INCOME AND VOTES ON PROPOSITION 13 OF HOMEOWNERS WHO
WANTED TO MAINTAIN OR INCREASE THE LEVEL OF EXPENDITURES ON
ALL PUBLIC GOODS

| | Vote on Proposition 13 | |
Income	No	Yes
Total	54.7	45.3
0–$15,000	16.8[a] / 50.0[b]	16.8[a] / 50.0[a]
$15,000–$20,000	7.6[a] / 60.0[b]	5.0[a] / 40.0[b]
$20,000–	28.6[a] / 55.7[b]	22.7[a] / 44.3[b]

a. Entries above the diagonal lines are the joint (sample) probabilities of vote and income.

b. Entries below the diagonal lines are the (sample) probabilities of a particular vote conditional on the income level.

Summary

The preceding analysis only begins to explain what underlay the 1978 vote on Proposition 13. Due to the limitation of the data used and the research cited, the exact quantitative results should be treated with some skepticism. Nonetheless, the qualitative results suggest answers to questions raised by the success of the tax limitation initiative. In particular, why was the initiative so popular when for each of the locally financed public goods, over half the opinions expressed were that expenditures should remain the same or be increased? The answer given previously (Shapiro, Puryear, and Ross 1979, p. 10) was that Proposition 13 was not an initiative to reduce local public expenditures; the voters were voting merely to reduce their property taxes and supposed that the level of local public expenditures would be maintained by increased state financing. The proceeding discussion suggests that this answer is unsatisfactory. First, because state financing is not free—the resident voter must pay state taxes as well as local property taxes—and, second, because, even though all public services appeared to have majority approval, fewer than 20 percent of the people surveyed did not wish a reduction in at least one local public service.

Local public expenditures in California had risen at higher than desired rates since 1973. If the 1973 expenditure levels were equilibrium levels, then by 1978, expenditures were too high. In fact, estimates derived here suggest that school and county expenditures (the ones claiming the largest proportion of the property tax) were 7 or 8 percent too high in 1978. Since the resident-voters' share of state taxes is on average approximately the same as their property tax share, shifting financial responsibility to the state would not have equilibrated actual and desired expenditure levels. The property tax is the most visible tax. For most people, income taxes are withheld and sales taxes are paid as a small amount of each purchase, but property taxes are paid in response to a bill sent by the County Tax Collector. Hence, the property tax became an identifiable evil around which political action could coalesce. Proposition 13 appears to have succeeded because public expenditures had grown faster than desired. But it was a severe remedy: it reduced property taxes by over 50 percent to reduce expenditures that were approximately 8 percent too high.

REFERENCES

Bergstrom, T.C., and Goodman, R.R. June 1973. Private demand for public goods. *American Economic Review.*

Borcherding, T. 1977. The sources of growth of public expenditures in the United States: 1902–1970. In Thomas Borcherding, ed., *Budgets and bureaucrats: the sources of government growth.* Durham, N.C.: Duke University Press.

Citrin, J. June 1979. Do people want something for nothing?: public opinion on taxes and government spending. *National Tax Journal, Supplement.*

Inman, R.P. 1978. Testing political economy's "as if" proposition: is the median income voter really decisive? *Public Choice.*

Levy, F., and Zamolo, P. 1978. The preconditions of Proposition 13. Mimeo.

Oakland, W.H. June 1979. Proposition 13—genesis and consequences. *National Tax Journal, Supplement.*

Shapiro, P. December 1977. Aggregation and the existence of a social utility function. *Journal of Economic Theory.*

Shapiro, P., and Morgan, W.D. June 1978. The general revenue effects of the California property tax limitation amendment. *National Tax Journal.*

Shapiro, P., Puryear, D., and Ross, J. June 1979. Tax and expenditure limitation in retrospect and in prospect. *National Tax Journal, Supplement.*

Shapiro, P., and Braithwait, S. October 1979. Empirical tests for the existence of group utility functions. *Review of Economic Studies.*

Smith, T., and Shapiro, P. April 1979. Spatial equity of the California sales tax. *Economic Geography.*

WHY VOTERS SUPPORT TAX LIMITATION AMENDMENTS: THE MICHIGAN CASE

Paul N. Courant
Edward M. Gramlich
Daniel L. Rubinfeld

I. Introduction

In November, 1978, voters in Michigan were faced with three constitutional tax limitation proposals on the ballot. In light of the widely perceived "taxpayer revolt" stemming from the then recent passage of Proposition 13 in California, the Michigan proposals provided an ideal natural experiment for attempting to determine why people vote for such proposals; and in particular the nature, causes, and extent of voter dissatisfaction with the budget performance of

[The authors are members of the Department of Economics and the Institute of Public Policy Studies at the University of Michigan.]

ACKNOWLEDGMENTS: This paper represents a somewhat expanded version of a paper published under the same title in the March, 1980, *National Tax Journal*. We wish to thank Daniel Holland and the *National Tax Journal* for giving us permission to publish the article here. The survey on which this paper is based was funded by the Office of Policy Development and Research at the Department of Housing and Urban Development. We are enormously grateful to David Puryear and John Ross of HUD for their patience and helpful advice. We have also benefited greatly from working with Richard Curtin of the Michigan Institute for Social Research: he played a major role in developing the questionnaire and managing the survey. Finally, we thank Sue Goldstone, Robert Kleinbaum, James Reschovsky, Deborah Swift, and Michael Wolkoff for their extremely able research assistance, and Helen Ladd, Perry Shapiro, and Nicolaus Tideman for their helpful editorial comments.

state and local governments. Does this dissatisfaction represent a conservative push toward smaller, or limited, levels of government spending, or does it reflect the feeling that voters may be able to lower their tax bills without undergoing a reduction in public services? In more formal terms, it also provides an opportunity to answer a question that is puzzling in light of the famous median voter theorem: Why would voters add amendments to the Constitution to constrain the behavior of their elected representatives?[1]

The natural reaction of social scientists interested in understanding the motives that underlie the tax limitation movement would be to ask voters, and in this paper we report on our attempt to do that. We conducted a telephone survey of 2,001 Michigan residents sampled randomly in the three weeks immediately after the election. Questions were asked about respondents' voting in the recent election, past voting behavior, political affiliation, income, family characteristics, tax payments, and perceptions about the state of the world and the impact of the proposed amendments. This paper gives the results of our first analysis of these data.[2]

The analysis begins in section 2 with normative discussion of the use of tax limitation as a public policy tool, examining the specific Michigan proposals from this standpoint. In section 3 we analyze voter tastes for both state and local spending, disaggregated by various demographic and economic characteristics. In section 4 we develop two simple models of voting behavior. The first relates voter tastes to the vote while, in the second, the survey responses concerning spending tastes are used to predict the tax limitation vote. Both models have surprisingly limited success. Then in section 5 we construct a more elaborate model of voting behavior, focusing on the importance of interactions between voter tastes and voter perceptions concerning the likely outcome of each of the amendments. We conclude by highlighting some of the implications of this analysis.

II. Tax Limitation as Public Policy

Statewide tax and expenditure limitations generally take one of two forms. They may be constitutional or legislative limitations on the fiscal authority of *local* jurisdictions, or they may be constitutional

---

1. The median voter theorem and literature on it have been amply described by Deacon (1977).

2. Some of the theoretical underpinnings of this paper and the survey are given in Courant, Gramlich, and Rubinfeld (1979a).

limitations on the fiscal authority of the *state* legislatures. The distinguishing characteristic is whether the limitation is an attempt to limit the behavior of localities, one's own as well as others, or the behavior of the overall state government.

California's Proposition 13, which rolled back local property tax assessments and placed a ceiling on the tax rates, was clearly the first type of limitation, binding the fiscal behavior of all local governments in the state. The Michigan amendments were more complex than the California one, but they still can be broadly characterized. The Headlee Amendment, which passed with 52 percent of the overall vote, was essentially a limitation on the behavior of the state government. It limited state revenues from own sources to a constant share of state personal income, while prohibiting the state from mandating expenditures to local governments without paying for them. There was also a constraint placed on local fiscal behavior—property tax levies on existing property could not grow at a rate in excess of the inflation rate as measured by the Consumer Price Index without tax rates being cut automatically. However, these automatic cuts in rates could be prevented by an explicit local referendum on the matter.

The Tisch Amendment, which was defeated with 36 percent of the vote, would have been essentially a local limitation—requiring a large cut in the assessed value of property. In the presence of other restrictions already in the Michigan Constitution, this limitation would have forced property tax revenue cuts in some, though not all, local communities. It also would have placed a slight constraint on the fiscal behavior of the state government by limiting the state income tax rate, but other revenue sources would not have been restricted. Hence the Headlee Amendment was a limit on state taxing behavior with a modest constraint on the behavior of some localities, while the Tisch Amendment drastically limited the fiscal behavior of many localities, did not limit others, and placed a slight constraint on state taxing behavior. The third limitation amendment on the Michigan ballot in 1978, one that we asked about in our survey but are not analyzing here, called for an educational voucher plan to finance local education but left almost all details of this complex plan unspecified. It received only 25 percent of the vote.

Several authors have recently considered the effects of state imposed expenditure limitations.[3] The papers are concerned mainly with

3. See Ladd (1978); Brennan and Buchanan (1979); Goldstein and Pauly (1979); Denzau, Mackay, and Weaver (1979); White (1979b); and Courant and Rubinfeld (1979).

the first type of limitation—statewide restrictions on local behavior—but could be made applicable to an efficiency evaluation of the second type—limitation by the state government on its own behavior. In either case, the passage of tax limitation proposals in Michigan and other states raises the basic question: What "disease" do voters see infecting the behavior of their state and local governments which leads them to opt for such powerful and inflexible "cures" as constitutional limits on revenues and/or expenditures? The literature identifies three motives:

(1). Government can be too large because—given prices, incomes, and technology—the absolute level of government services provided is greater than that which would be chosen by the median voter. This is the case dealt with in Niskanen's bureaucratic maximizer models, the agenda-setting models of Romer and Rosenthal, and the monopoly models of Denzau, Mackay, and Weaver.[4] Public managers and/or bureaucrats are responsible for the excessive government size.

(2). A second way in which government can be considered too large arises when public employees earn wages that exceed competitive levels. In this case public budgets are high because rents are earned by public employees. Here the mechanism responsible for inefficiency is the familiar desire of unions to maximize their own income, a case considered in detail in our earlier work and also by Tullock.[5]

(3). A third way in which government might be too large is that it may be inefficient in the sense that bureaucracy functions inside its production frontier. For example, Fiorina and Noll (1978) have developed a model in which government is predicted to use suboptimal factor ratios given market prices.[6] In spirit, this case is different from both cases (1) and (2) above, although it shares elements of both—like (1), there is too much absolute input of real resources; like (2), the average cost of output is too high.[7]

To attempt to establish which of these notions is on the public mind, we have tried to elicit respondents' tastes for government spending and perceptions about the likely impact of the tax limitation

---

4. See Niskanen (1978); Romer and Rosenthal (1978) and Denzau, Mackay, and Weaver (1979).

5. See Courant, Gramlich, and Rubinfeld (1979); and Tullock (1974).

6. See Fiorina and Noll (1978).

7. These hypotheses are slightly different, though obviously related to the "tax shift" vs. "tax cut" hypotheses that were investigated in California by Citrin (1979) and Attiyeh and Engle (1979).

amendments with a series of survey questions. We report first the results associated with the questions on tastes for public spending, for specific types and in general, examining both how the taste distribution compares with actual spending levels and how tastes are correlated with tax limitation votes. We also see whether the tax limitation vote can be better explained by a set of predictors which include individual and family attributes as well as the price of local public services. Finally, we examine the relationship between the tax limitation vote and voter perceptions, focusing on the interaction between those perceptions and the tastes for public spending. We find that this last model helps substantially to explain why voters do and do not support tax limitation.

III. Preferences for Public Expenditure

The most striking empirical result from the survey concerning tastes for public expenditure is that by and large citizens of Michigan are satisfied with current levels of output at both the state and local levels. Indeed, with the exceptions of spending on welfare programs, there is a decided sentiment for expansion (and a stated willingness to pay for expansion) in all of the program areas for which responses were elicited. This is clear from examination of table 1, which gives information on the public spending preferences of all 2,001 survey respondents, following a question sequence that has long been used by the Institute for Social Research.[8]

The first three columns of table 1 give the program area and the number of persons who favored reductions and constancy in the level of expenditure in the areas, respectively. The column headed "More 1" gives the number of people who favored increased spending but answered no to the question, "If your taxes need to be raised to pay for the additional expenditures for [program], would you still favor an increase in spending in this area?" The column headed "More 2" gives the number of people who answered yes to that question.[9] Fi-

---

8. These questions were first analyzed by Mueller (1963); and later by Curtin and Cowan (1973). Citrin (1979) has also analyzed a similar series of questions in connection with the tax limitation votes, reaching conclusions similar to ours.

9. We mechanically adopted the ISR sequence because it was time-tested, without thinking about a weakness that later became apparent. In opting for more, less, or the same levels of public spending, respondents were not explicitly told that less spending implied less taxes. The relatively small number of respondents in the "More 1" column indicates that perhaps this problem is not terribly serious, and in any event we do correct for it in our questions that follow.

Table 1

PREFERENCES FOR SPENDING BY PROGRAM AREA
(*All 2,001 Respondents*)

Program Area	Less	Same	More 1	More 2	No Response	Mean Strong Preference[a]
Police/Fire	68	1,163	97	615	58	.282
Welfare Spending	1,262	499	44	127	69	−.587
School Spending	296	882	108	635	80	.176
College Spending	196	977	126	545	157	.189
Road Maintenance	120	824	295	698	64	.298
Parks & Recreation	209	1,117	145	485	45	.141

a. Assigning values of 1 to "More 2," 0 to "Same" and "More 1," and −1 to "Less" in the numerator, and dividing by total number of responses.

nally, "Mean Strong Preference" is derived by assigning a value of minus one to those who wanted reduced spending, zero to those who wanted the same or "More 1," and one to those who wanted "More 2," and then dividing by the total number of answers to the question.

Thus in every program but welfare, the number of people willing to pay for increases in expenditures exceeded the number expressing a desire for reduction.[10] To the extent that there is a taxpayer revolt in Michigan, it seems to be a revolt against welfare spending, ironically a type of spending that in Michigan (as in most other states) is financed about equally by the federal and state-local governments.

The preceding interpretation is strengthened when we consider stated preferences regarding state and local spending as a whole. For each of the two levels of government, respondents were informed of the major functional responsibilities of the respective levels and were then asked if they would favor an across-the-board increase, decrease, or no change in both spending and taxes, if all spending and tax categories were to be changed proportionately. Furthermore, if they favored an across the board increase or decrease in spending and taxes, they were asked to give their desired percentage amount. The results from these questions are summarized in table 2.

The first six rows give the distribution of desired spending changes, classified into cuts and increases of less and more than 10 percentage points. The seventh row gives the implied value for mean strong preferences, computed as before, and the last two rows give the mean and standard deviation of the desired percentage changes. Perhaps the most important result of the table is that the mean percentage change desired is very close to zero, only −3.53 percent at the state level and −0.22 percent at the local level. These mean changes are small relative to the within-group standard deviations, in the last row. Indeed, if a median respondent analysis were applied to this table, the desired changes would be zero. Since more than half the respondents opt for no change at both levels of government, the median respondent is apparently happy with the status quo at both the state and local levels, implying that the state is in median voter equilibrium.

There is an interesting similarity between these results and those of table 1, and one interesting difference. The similarity is that re-

---

10. The negative attitude toward welfare is confirmed by the fact that 53.9 percent of the sample stated in response to another question that they felt that *many* of those currently on welfare should not be receiving payments and 38.8 percent said that *some* should not be receiving payments.

Table 2

PREFERENCES FOR OVERALL STATE AND LOCAL SPENDING
AND TAX CHANGES
(All 2,001 Respondents)[a]

	State	*Local*
Desired Cut		
More than 10 percent	226	125
Less than 10 percent	402	174
No Change	1,027	1,190
Desired Increase		
Less than 10 percent	167	368
More than 10 percent	20	51
No Response	159	93
Mean Strong Preference[b]	−.239	.063
Mean Percentage Change	−3.53	−0.22
Standard Deviation	8.83	8.41

a. We categorized the specific quantitative responses to simplify the presentation.
b. Computed as in table 1 for comparability.

spondents were informed in the question that the state government is responsible for the nonfederal portion of welfare spending. Thus the relatively poor showing of the state government relative to localities could be due to the marked desire for reduced welfare spending found in table 1. The interesting difference is that preferences for overall spending are lower for both levels of government than are preferences for the sum of their parts. While some subtle change in the wording may have caused this difference, it is consistent with the modern theory of representative democracy and the economic analysis of log-rolling behavior presented by Downs, Buchanan and Tullock, and others.[11] With the exception of welfare, a strong majority of the population is in favor of current or increased levels of spending in each program area. But support for the total is weaker because everyone perceives the possibility of cuts in program areas favored by others. To the extent that logrolling is effective, that is exactly what one would expect to observe.

11. See Downs (1957); and Buchanan and Tullock (1962).

It is perhaps unwise to take these results too seriously because of the large number of voters opting for the same amount of public spending—over half the sample at both the state and local level. One might argue that some of the voters preferring the status quo were really either uninformed or unable to comprehend the question. To see how sensitive our results were to this possibility, we recalculated means and medians with the voters opting for the same amount of spending omitted, obtaining mean and median percentage changes of −7.8 and −8.3 at the state level and −0.5 and 4.5 at the local level. Even this strong correction—surely an overreaction because *some* of those opting for no change must have truly felt that way—did not give very large desired reductions in state spending and had very modest impacts at the local level. The clear conclusion, in line with what Curtin and Cowan (1973) and Citrin (1979) have found, is that at least as respondents answer explicit questions, there appears to be a desire for only a modest cutback in state spending and essentially no change in local spending. We might also predict that a statewide tax limitation amendment like the Headlee Amendment would have a better chance of passage than a local limitation amendment like that of Tisch, but that gets ahead of our story.

We can then look behind these preferences to see how they vary by demographic and economic characteristics. This is done by using the percentage change responses of table 2 as dependent variables in cross-section regressions, with the various characteristics as independent variables. Since we are mainly concerned at this point with the preferences of voters (those of nonvoters are unlikely to be of great importance in explaining tax limitation voting behavior), we alter the sample to include those respondents who actually voted on the Headlee or Tisch Amendments (1,028 and 1,039 respectively). Since we have no value for the dependent variable when voters did not respond to this question, we also must omit nonrespondent voters.

The results for 870 Headlee voter-respondents and 916 Tisch voter-respondents are shown in table 3. Holding constant the influence of all other variables, the table gives the mean desired spending change for each independent variable class, compared with the overall mean desired changes for the voter respondents (slightly below the numbers given in table 2).These comparisons, incidentally, are given for state spending in the case of the Headlee Amendment (because that's what it could limit) and local spending for the Tisch Amendment (because that's what it could limit).

Table 3

REGRESSIONS EXPLAINING PUBLIC SPENDING AND TAX DESIRES

	870 Headlee Voter Respondents Dependent Variable: Desired Percentage Change in State Spending and Taxes Mean = −4.13 St. Dev. = 8.66 $\bar{R}^2$ = .07		916 Tisch Voter Respondents Dependent Variable: Desired Percentage Change in Local Spending and Taxes Mean = −0.86 St. Dev. = 8.00 $\bar{R}^2$ = .06	
Independent Variables	*Adjusted Mean*[a]	*Cases*	*Adjusted Mean*[a]	*Cases*
Children				
None (of age < 18)	−4.98	474	−1.79	498
In private school	−2.55	63	0.19	70
In public school	−3.21	333	0.25	348
	Beta[b] = 0.11		Beta[b] = 0.13	
Marginal Tax Price[c]				
Price < 1.5	−3.85	135	−0.56	129
1.5 < price < 3.0	−4.00	216	−0.75	232
3.0 ≤ price < 4.5	−4.47	172	−2.16	178
price ≥ 4.5	−5.49	187	−1.24	210
Renters	−2.59	160	0.60	167
	Beta = 0.11		Beta = 0.11	

Sex				
Male	−4.91	426	−1.62	431
Female	−3.38	444	−0.19	485
	Beta = 0.09		Beta = 0.09	
Education				
< 12 years	−3.97	120	−0.14	121
12 years	−4.35	307	−0.75	338
13–15 years	−4.46	234	−1.15	241
16 + years	−3.43	204	−1.11	212
No response	−7.25	5	−1.63	4
	Beta = 0.05		Beta = 0.04	
Income				
$0–10,000	−4.18	164	−1.34	177
$10,000–15,000	−2.13	120	−0.51	124
$15,000–20,000	−5.12	143	−1.20	152
$20,000 +	−3.93	308	−0.24	316
No response	−5.24	135	−1.58	147
	Beta = 0.11		Beta = 0.07	
Religion				
Protestant	−4.10	524	−0.85	540
Catholic	−4.27	266	−1.04	293
Other	−3.86	80	−0.32	83
	Beta = 0.01		Beta = 0.02	

Table 3, continued
REGRESSIONS EXPLAINING PUBLIC SPENDING AND TAX DESIRES

870 Headlee Voter Respondents
Dependent Variable: Desired Percentage Change in State Spending and Taxes

Mean = −4.13
St. Dev. = 8.66
$18\overline{R}^2$ = .07

916 Tisch Voter Respondents
Dependent Variable: Desired Percentage Change in Local Spending and Taxes

Mean = −0.86
St. Dev. = 8.00
$\overline{R}^2$ = .06

Independent Variables	Adjusted Mean[a]	Cases	Adjusted Mean[a]	Cases
Race				
White	−4.30	790	−1.03	835
Black	−2.06	66	1.89	68
Other	−5.48	11	−4.90	10
No response	1.10	3	−2.52	3
	Beta = 0.08		Beta = 0.11	
Employment				
Unemployed	−4.30	133	−1.25	153
Local government	−2.89	43	0.31	43
School district	−2.82	72	0.05	74
State university	−3.77	13	2.00	13

State government	−3.73	23	1.32	26
Federal government	−6.99	18	−4.99	20
Private	−4.63	453	−1.14	464
Retired	−2.93	113	−0.45	120
No response	−3.02	2	2.63	3
	Beta = 0.10		Beta = 0.12	
Gloom				
Next 5 years better	−3.60	359	0.25	371
Don't know	−3.43	269	−0.93	288
Next 5 years worse	−5.84	219	−2.55	233
No response	−4.29	23	−0.96	24
	Beta = 0.12		Beta = 0.14	
Political Party				
Republican	−5.16	305	−0.97	316
Democrat	−2.78	379	−0.58	403
Independent	−5.32	178	−1.41	187
No response	−2.21	8	1.11	10
	Beta = 0.14		Beta = 0.05	

a.   The adjusted mean controls for all the other variables included in the model. It is calculated as the overall mean of the dependent variable plus the deviation from that mean associated with the coefficient for each individual subgroup.

b.   The beta statistic provides a measure of the overall importance of individual predictors in explaining variation in the dependent variable. It is calculated as a weighted average of the squares of the individual regression coefficients associated with the subgroups of the given predictor variable. (For details, see F. Andrews, J. Morgan, W. Sonquist, and L. Klem, *Multiple Classification Analysis*, 2nd edition [Ann Arbor, Mich.: Institute of Survey Research, University of Michigan, 1973]).

c.   The marginal tax price is calculated as the ratio of the individual's assessed house value (in $) to community taxable property base per capita (in $).

Perhaps the most striking result of table 3 is the relatively limited variation in the magnitudes of the adjusted means (this is also true for the unadjusted means). Other things equal, federal government employees living in the state want the least state expenditures, while blacks want the smallest cuts. However, even blacks would like slightly less spending than is now undertaken—and the difference between the two groups is only about 5 percentage points. Likewise for local expenditures: federal government employees are among the most negative and blacks the most positive. In this case, however, blacks do support increases in local spending, as do a few other subcategories of the population.

Despite the relative uniformity of tastes, there are some important differences among groups which are quite interesting and which might conform with a priori expectations. First, note that in the case of state spending, tax price bears an inverse relationship to desired spending. The low absolute value of the coefficient for renters supports this interpretation, since renters probably perceive the lowest tax price for public services. The same general result holds for local spending, except that the magnitude of the coefficient of the third tax price variable is slightly out of order. Thus, relative property tax payments clearly matter to voters, and both spending equations are consistent with what one would expect from a normal spending demand function, though with rather small price elasticities.

The results for the demographic variables indicate, as expected, that individuals in families are more likely to favor public spending, as are females. It is surprising, however, to find a very weak relationship between education and desired spending. The common view that higher education leads to a taste for relatively more government spending is weakly supported for state spending, but not for local spending. Income, although highly significant, had no clear impact on tastes for public spending. These income results appear to imply a very low income elasticity of demand for public spending, but a careful test (in progress) awaits the inclusion of the level of expenditures that is being altered.

To test the relationship between macroeconomic events such as inflation and unemployment and voter public spending preference, we defined what we might call a "gloom" variable. This variable distinguished those who thought they would be better off in the next five years from those who felt the reverse. As expected, the pessimists wanted lower public spending (but just a small amount), while the optimists were more neutral. Also we included political affiliation, and found, as expected, that Republicans want spending cutbacks at the state level and, as not expected, that Democrats do also. But persons affiliated with neither party favored less spending than party members. At the local level, political affiliation was unimportant in explaining desired spending changes.

Of greatest interest to us, in light of our concern with the political effects of private versus public sector employment, is the role of the employment status variable. Here we find that private sector voters want less state and local public spending than those in the public sector, especially if one counts federal employees as being in the private sector, from the point of view of the political economy of the state of Michigan. But the fact that the marginal effect of employment status on tastes for government spending is of the right sign does not change the fact that differences are small.

IV. Explaining Votes with Preferences

Until now we have reported and tried to explain state and local public spending demands. The next question is whether these spending demands themselves can predict the vote on the Headlee and Tisch Amendments. We are, in effect, using our survey question to develop an explanation of the vote that is more precise than the one usually given, where individual attributes such as those listed in table 3 are taken as proxies for spending preferences. To answer this question, we use preferences as independent variables in regressions explaining the vote.[12] Following the procedures adopted above, we use state spending desires as the independent variable explaining the vote of the Headlee Amendment, and local spending desires as the independent variable explaining the vote on the Tisch Amendment. As before, we restrict the sample to those who voted on the respective amendments.

The results are given in table 4. For each pair (Headlee-State,

---

12. The regression takes the form $V = \alpha + \beta M + \gamma L + \delta D + \theta N + \varepsilon$ where

V = 1 if the individual voted yes, 0 otherwise;

M = 1 if the individual wanted more spending, 0 otherwise;

L = 1 if the individual wanted less spending, 0 otherwise;

D = 1 if the individual didn't know, 0 otherwise;

N = 1 if the individual didn't respond, 0 otherwise.

Table 4

SPENDING TASTES AS A PREDICTOR OF VOTES

Dependent Variable	Headlee and State Spending			Tisch and Local Spending		
	Mean Share	Cases	t-Ratio	Mean Share	Cases	t-Ratio
Vote on amendment	.562	1,028	—	.262	1039	—
Independent Variables						
Desire more spending and taxes	.356	90	2.8	.155	193	2.2
Desire same spending and taxes	.514	510	—	.233	632	—
Desire less spending and taxes	.675	403	4.8	.449	196	6.2
Don't know	.600	15	0.2	.444	9	1.5
No response	.300	10	1.3	.444	9	0.7
Fit Statistic						
Adjusted coefficient of determination	.039			.046		
Votes correctly predicted	.591			.738		
Correct predictions with a random assignment[a]	.508			.614		
Improvement over random assignment	.083			.124		

a. Derived by assuming that the percentage of yes and no voters assigned is the same as the percentage of yes and no voters in the sample, as explained in the text.

Tisch-Local), three sets of numbers are given: The share of voters in that class voting for passage, the number of voters in the class, and the t-ratios associated with the coefficients of a regression (not shown) explaining the zero (no vote), one (yes vote) probability of voting for the amendment with just these binary variables.[13] The t-ratio tests

13. We have presented the t-ratios because they provide a useful summary of the relationship between the coefficient and its standard error; even though we

whether there is a significant difference between those in a given category and those wanting no change in spending and taxes.

The first thing to notice about the table is the difference between actual and reported voting results. The Headlee Amendment actually passed with 52 percent of the statewide vote, but 56.2 percent of our sample report voting for it. The Tisch Amendment actually received 36 percent of the statewide vote, but only 26.2 percent of our sample report voting for it. Part of these discrepancies may be due to sampling bias, but we suspect that, even though surveyed immediately after the election, voters are somewhat selective in their recollections about the vote and may not want to admit voting for the losing side.

Concerning the independent variables, the results correspond to prior expectations. Only 36 percent of those desiring more state spending and taxes voted for Headlee, while 67 percent of those desiring less state spending and taxes voted for the amendment. For Tisch the same percentages were 16 and 45 respectively. The fact that 51 percent of those desiring the same spending and tax levels supported Headlee may be surprising if Headlee is interpreted as altering the status quo, but these voters could have interpreted Headlee as preventing government spending (as a proportion of income) from growing further, and thus *preserving* the status quo.

While these results may or may not be plausible, they are not very powerful. The coefficients of determination adjusted for degrees of freedom are only .039 and .046 respectively, quite low even considering the fact that the conventionally measured fit statistic is very likely to be substantially less than one in a regression with a 0–1 dependent variable.[14] A more relevant fit statistic can be derived by measuring the percentage of votes correctly predicted by the regression as if one were using discriminant analysis.[15] The Headlee regression correctly predicts 59.1 percent of the votes and the Tisch regression 73.8 percent of the votes.[16] These numbers by themselves are

recognized that with a 0–1 dependent variable in a linear probability model, the error term is not normally distributed and the *t*-statistics are only valid asymptotically.

14. See Pindyck and Rubinfeld (1976), chapter 8 for details.

15. See Anderson (1958), chapter 6. The computational equivalence between the 0–1 linear probability model and the discriminant analysis model is given in Ladd (1966).

16. In computing these percentages we considered a vote correctly predicted whenever its fitted value was greater than .5. Other cutoff values could in general give higher percentages of votes correctly predicted. If, for example, the yes and no

not very meaningful because even a straight random assignment of voters would correctly predict close to half the votes for Headlee and even a higher percentage for Tisch (because the mean probability is farther from .5). Hence a better fit statistic can be derived by comparing the proportion of votes correctly predicted with the proportion predicted by random assignment. If, for example, .56 percent of the sample actually voted for Headlee, under a random assignment of voters $(.56)^2$ percent would be predicted to vote for Headlee and would have voted for it (in the sample); while $(.44)^2$ percent would be predicted not to have voted for Headlee and would not have voted for it (in the sample). The random assignment proportion in the Headlee case then becomes $(.56)^2 + (.44)^2 = .508$. A similar calculation indicates that a random assignment model would predict correctly with probability $(.26)^2 + (.74)^2 = .614$ for the Tisch Amendment. In some sense, then, the Headlee regression has raised the correct prediction proportion by only .083 and the Tisch regression has raised it by only .124.[17] The result is that while spending preferences and the vote on tax limitation are correlated as expected, there is a good deal of variation in the vote left to be explained.

One reason for the poor predictive power of this model may be measurement error problems associated with the survey question. This suggests the possibility of developing a different model of voting based only on voter "attributes" such as age, education, race, and sex to explain voting behavior. This attributes model, applied to the Headlee vote and estimated as a linear probability model, appears in table 5.

The state of Michigan finances its public service by a proportional income tax and a nearly proportional sales tax, so there is a very high correlation between income and tax price, and only one set of income variables is shown in the table: a categorical dummy if the family's income/needs ratio is less than 2.5 and another if the ratio is greater than 5.5. Both groups show slightly higher than average probabilities

distributions have equal variances and numbers of cases, the optimal cutoff value is just midway between the mean of the predicted vote values for the yes and no voters. We have computed these optimal cutoff values for all regressions, in general finding them close to .5. Moreover, fairly sizable changes in the cutoff value in the neighborhood of .5 make very little difference in the percentage of votes correctly predicted.

17. Even this measure could be improved upon because it assumes that a correct assignment when the predicted probability is .51 is as good as one when the predicted probability is .96, and that a prediction is incorrect when the predicted probability is "only" .49. A better measure would weight outcomes more the farther a correct or incorrect prediction is from .5.

Table 5

PREDICTING THE VOTE WITH ATTRIBUTES, 1028 HEADLEE VOTERS

Constant = .600
$\bar{R}^2$ = .046
Correct prediction rate = .628
Improvement over random assignment = .120

Variable	Coeff.	t-Ratio	N
Income/needs < 2.5[a]	.096	2.5	333
Income/needs > 5.5[a]	.056	1.3	244
One child in pub. school	−.103	−2.0	124
Two children in pub. school	−.105	−1.8	109
Three + children in pub. school	−.072	−1.2	91
Preschool children	.005	0.1	62
Private school children	.025	0.4	81
Transfer recipient	−.028	−0.3	26
Race (Black = 1)	−.162	−2.7	78
Other nonwhite	.041	0.3	12
No party affiliation	.090	0.5	11
Republican	.092	2.6	379
Other (non Democrat)	.072	1.6	161
Sex (Female = 1)	−.065	−2.1	546
Age 50–64	.026	0.6	283
Age 65 +	.015	0.2	124
Both local govt. employees	−.220	−2.8	41
Both school district employees	−.212	−2.9	48
Both state govt. employees	−.250	−2.6	27
One school district employee	−.188	−2.2	35
One state or local employee	−.067	−0.7	25
Unemployed	−.060	−1.1	162
Renter	−.071	−1.5	171

a. The income-needs variable is the ratio of family income to the estimated poverty level needs of the family as determined by the Institute of Social Research, *Panel Study of Income Dynamics: Procedures and Tape Codes, 1978 Interview Year* (Ann Arbor, Michigan, 1979).

of voting for the amendment, indicating that middle income voters are the liberals in Michigan. When families have children in the public schools, they have lower than expected probabilities of voting for the amendment, as might be predicted. Blacks have low probabilities of voting for the amendment, and Republicans and those not

affiliated with any party have high probabilities. Regarding employment, workers in the public sector show low probabilities, as would
be anticipated.

While many of the coefficient signs look reasonable, the model
again doesn't fit very well. The corrected R^2 was equal to .046, and
the prediction rate was .628, which is .121 better than would be
achieved by random assignment. The fact that the attributes model
does somewhat better than the pure spending tastes model suggests
that a good voting model must be expanded to account for more than
simply the tastes of voters for total state and local spending.

V. Perceptions About Tax Limitation

Given that spending preferences alone do not provide a very powerful explanation of tax limitation voting, we now try to do better by
having spending preferences interact with perceptions about the likely
impact of the limitation amendments. This is done by using answers
to a series of perception questions about the likely impact of the
limitation amendments. The questions followed the format: Do you
think the passage of the Headlee (Tisch) proposal will lead to:

   a)   a reduction in the overall level of taxes in Michigan

   b)   a reduction in property taxes

   c)   an increase in income taxes

   d)   a reduction in the number of state and local government
         employees

   e)   a reduction in the funds available to the local public school
         system

   f)   a reduction in the future wage increases of government
         employees.

The perception questions were followed by an open-ended question
asking respondents what they thought would be the most important
impact of the amendment. Supplying the choices listed here might
have increased the likelihood that one of our answers would be selected as having the most important impact, but other responses were
possible and were quite frequently given.

Spending preferences and perceptions about the likely impact of
the amendments should have an interacting effect on votes. If, for
example, a voter perceived that the Headlee Amendment would lower
public spending and desired less spending, the voter should support

the amendment. If the voter had the same perception but desired more spending, the voter should vote against the amendment. We have constructed regression models explaining the vote on both amendments along these lines. The dependent variable was coded as "one" if the voter voted for the amendment and as zero if he voted against it, just as in table 4. The independent variables were a series of perception-taste interactions, patterned on the above example. Whenever relevant, the variables were further split according to whether voters were in the public or private sector and hence would have a different view of such outcomes as lower government wages or employment. For these purposes all nonworking respondents were considered as private (they would still pay property and sales taxes) as were all those working in the federal government (in keeping with our spending taste results above). All those working and nonworking respondents with either the respondent or spouse working in the state or local public sector (about 11 percent of the sample) were considered public.

The results for the Headlee vote are shown in table 6. (The Tisch results appear in our *National Tax Journal* paper.) Each row of the table describes one interaction variable. The second column describes the employment group to which the variable applies (all, public, or private employees). Column three gives the perception, of those to whom the variable applies, of the most likely impact of the amendment. The entries in column four are perceived impacts of the amendment that may or may not be deemed most likely. In column five are preferences for public spending and taxes (more, same, or less) and perceptions of such matters as public employee work effort and earnings. The number of cases to which the variable applies is shown in column six, the regression coefficient in column seven and its *t*-ratio in column eight. Whenever an interaction term applied to less than ten cases it was omitted from the regression.[18] Separate constants were estimated for public and private employees through another dummy.

The first thing to be noticed is that the fit is much improved over that in table 4, when just spending tastes were used without regard to perceptions about the amendment. The adjusted coefficient of de-

18. This choice was made mainly for pragmatic reasons to keep down the number of variables, but there is also a methodological rationale: in earlier trials we found that variables with less than 10 cases were extremely unlikely to have statistically significant coefficients (even if the magnitude of the coefficients was large).

Table 6

Regression Model Explaining Headlee Vote

1,028 Headlee Voters
Adjusted R^2 = .204
Proportion of voters correctly predicted = .736
Improvement over random assignment = .228
Constant, private employees = .525
Constant, public employees = .425

Variable No.	Group	*Perceptions* Most Important Impact of Headlee	Headlee Will	Preferences	Cases	Coefficient	t-Ratio
1.	All	Reduce spending	—	More state spending	18	.012	0.1
2.	All	Reduce spending	—	Same state spending	74	.142	2.2
3.	All	Reduce spending	—	Less state spending	66	.302	4.4
4.	Priv.	Reduce taxes	—	Same state spending	80	.139	2.2
5.	Priv.	Reduce taxes	—	Less state spending	78	.212	3.1
6.	Pub.	Reduce taxes	—	Same state spending	27	.288	2.8
7.	Pub.	Reduce taxes	—	Less state spending	13	.333	2.1
8.	All	Increase taxes	—	More state spending	14	−.285	−1.7
9.	All	Increase taxes	—	Same state spending	25	−.157	−1.5
10.	All	Increase taxes	—	Less state spending	32	−.225	−2.2
11.	All	Hurt schools	—	More school spending	11	−.094	−0.6
12.	All	Increase govt. efficiency	—	Govt. wastes much	21	.358	3.4

13.	All	Increase govt. efficiency	—	Govt. wastes some	22	.201	2.0
14.	All	Increase voter control	—	Trust govt. usually	41	.391	5.0
15.	All	Increase voter control	—	Trust govt. little	36	.441	5.3
16.	All	No change		—	120	-.037	-0.6
17.	All	Don't know		—	200	-.049	-1.0
18.	Priv.	—	Reduce wage increases	Govt. workers earn more	171	.029	0.7
19.	Priv.	—	Reduce wage increases	Govt. workers earn same	136	.072	1.5
20.	Priv.	—	Reduce wage increases	Govt. workers earn less	27	-.114	-1.2
21.	Pub.	—	Reduce wage increases	Govt. workers earn more	43	-.108	-1.3
22.	Pub.	—	Reduce wage increases	Govt. workers earn same	31	-.167	-1.8
23.	Pub.	—	Reduce wage increases	Govt. workers earn less	27	-.106	-1.1
24.	Priv.	—	Reduce taxes	More state spending	12	.303	2.0
25.	Priv.	—	Reduce taxes	Same state spending	86	.095	1.6
26.	Priv.	—	Reduce taxes	Less state spending	107	.155	2.7
27.	Pub.	—	Reduce taxes	Same state spending	15	.013	0.1
28.	Pub.	—	Reduce taxes	Less state spending	15	-.011	-0.1
29.	Priv.	—	Reduce property taxes	More local spending	38	.126	1.6
30.	Priv.	—	Reduce property taxes	Same local spending	145	.090	1.9
31.	Priv.	—	Reduce property taxes	Less local spending	57	.178	2.5
32.	Pub.	—	Reduce property taxes	More local spending	15	.174	1.4
33.	Pub.	—	Reduce property taxes	Same local spending	28	.094	1.0
34.	Priv.	—	Increase income taxes	More state spending	43	-.048	-0.6
35.	Priv.	—	Increase income taxes	Same state spending	243	-.045	-1.1
44.	Priv.	—	Reduce school funds	More school spending	81	-.118	-2.1
45.	Priv.	—	Reduce school funds	Same school spending	148	-.141	-3.3
46.	Priv.	—	Reduce school funds	Less school spending	54	-.110	-1.6
47.	Pub.	—	Reduce school funds	More school spending	56	-.259	-3.4
48.	Pub.	—	Reduce school funds	Same school spending	49	-.240	-3.1

termination is now .204, more than five times greater than before. Now 73.6 percent of the votes are correctly predicted, an improvement of .228 over the random assignment naive model. This improvement is almost three times as great as in table 4.

Each regression coefficient can be translated into the proportion of yes votes in the particular category by adding either .525 or .452, the regression constants for private and public employees respectively. Most of the regression coefficients are statistically significant and are more or less internally consistent, although in some cases puzzles are raised. For example, among the voter-respondents who perceived that the most important impact of the Headlee Amendment would be to reduce government spending (variables 1 through 3), those wanting more state spending and taxes were evenly split on the amendment while those wanting less state spending and taxes voted heavily for the amendment. Among those who felt that the most important impact of the Headlee Amendment would be tax reduction, support was very strong for the amendment (coefficients of variables 4 through 7), even when voters favored the same level of state spending and taxes (as in variables 4 and 6). The obvious rationalization of this behavior is that these voters felt that taxes could be cut without a reduction in spending, either because of supposed efficiency gains or because of the free lunch illusion. We might go even further and imagine a motive based on the uncertainty about the impact of the amendment: voters feel fairly certain their taxes will be cut, but much less certain that public services affecting them will also be cut. Whatever the case, this behavior is mirrored by the 71 cynical cases (variables 8 through 10) who felt that the most important impact of the amendment would be to *increase* taxes—these voters were strongly inclined to vote against the amendment even if they wanted more state spending and taxes (variable 8). These types of findings are also reflected in the coefficients of variables representing those who felt that the amendment would increase or decrease taxes, even if that were not its most important effect (variables 24 through 39).

Far and away the strongest support for the amendment came from those who felt that it would increase either governmental efficiency (variables 12 and 13) or voter control of government (variables 14 and 15). There are 120 voters in these categories, and 90 percent of them voted for the amendment.

Regarding the wages of public employees, very few voters felt the amendment would have as its *most important* impact the limitation of future government wage increases, but many public and private voters felt the amendment would have that impact. Among public sector voters (variables 21 to 23), votes went against Headlee regardless of whether these workers felt now that public wages were above those for comparable private sector jobs (variable 21). Among private sector voters, those who felt that public wages were higher than private were fairly neutral on the amendment (variable 18), but those who felt that public wages were lower than private wages were against it. Certainly among private sector voters there appears to be little resentment directed against the high wages of government employees, and little occasion to vote for tax limitation on that account. Whether this result would obtain in other states in uncertain: perhaps the union solidarity tradition is very strong in Michigan.

The public employment findings also demonstrate the nonpunitive feelings of private sector voters. Among those who felt the amendment would reduce government employment, voters were neutral towards or against the amendment even if they felt that public employees worked less hard than private employees (variable 41). But this time public employees show some mysterious devotion to the common interest: When public employees felt the amendment would lower employment, and that government workers did not work as hard as private workers, they voted for the amendment (variable 43). Presumably they felt the other guy would get laid off.

Finally, among all voters who felt the amendment would hurt schools (variable 11 and variables 44 through 48), voting on the amendment was consistently negative.

We can summarize these results by giving a more quantitative interpretation of the extent to which passage of tax limitation amendments reflects the three motives listed earlier: less public spending, lower public sector wages, or government efficiency gains.

In our sample of Headlee voters (as shown in table 7) 578 voted for the amendment and 450 against, giving an overall plurality of 128 votes. This plurality was small or negative among those who wanted lower wages, no change, did not respond, or were in small cell sizes: among all these groups the net plurality was −36 votes. Hence the passage of the amendment can be attributed to the plurality of 128 + 36 = 164 votes among the other groups. Among those groups, voters who wanted a smaller public sector, in a sense to be defined,

Table 7

ANALYSIS OF THE PASSAGE OF THE HEADLEE AMENDMENT
(1,028 Headlee Voters)

Based on answers to most important impact question
and regression of Table 6.

Motive:	Variables in Table 5	Cases	For	Against	Plurality
Want smaller public sector	3,5,7,9,10,11	225	134	91	43
Want lower public wages	none	11	5	6	−1
May want free lunch	1,2,4,6,8	213	127	86	41
Want greater efficiency/control	12,13,14,15	120	100	20	80
Want no change	16	102	44	58	−14
Don't know	17	200	84	116	−32
Small cell sizes	none	157	84	73	11
TOTAL		1,028	578	450	128

accounted for a 43 vote plurality, those who were either looking for efficiency gains or a free lunch a 41 vote plurality, and those who were clearly looking for efficiency or control gains an 80 vote plurality.

The details involved in the calculation are important, since some strong assumptions are implicit. All groups used were determined on the basis of voter perceptions of the Headlee Amendment's most important impact. The net plurality among those who favored less public spending was the net plurality among those who desired lower spending on taxes (variables 3, 5, and 7 in table 5) and who *perceived* that the amendment would accomplish that, plus the net (negative) plurality among those with a desire for lower taxes (variables 9 and 10) but with a perception that the amendment would raise them, plus the net (negative) plurality among those who perceived that the amendment would lower spending on schools and who desired the contrary (variable 11). The net plurality among all of these groups is the plurality gained by Headlee among voters who, on balance, appeared to be calling for a smaller, or limited, public sector.

The net plurality among those who wanted lower public sector wages is the small number of voters who perceived that reduction is the most important impact of the amendment (a number not even large enough to appear as a variable in table 5). The net plurality among those whose preference could be considered inconsistent is the sum of those who voted for the amendment because it would lower taxes or spending even though they did not favor reductions (variables 1, 2, 4, and 6), plus the plurality among those who perceived that the amendment would increase taxes and so voted against it, even though they wanted the public spending (variable 8). These voters either had in mind that the amendment would generate efficiency gains, or they followed the certainty rationale described above, or they were searching for the free lunch of tax cuts without spending cuts. The net plurality among those who envisioned efficiency or responsiveness gains is also taken from table 5 (variables 12 through 15). For each group, table 7 shows the number of voters, votes for, votes against, and the plurality.

To sum up our results, 3 out of 4 voters responsible for the plurality of the Headlee Amendment were motivated by a desire for either efficiency gains or a free lunch. Only one out of 4 appears to favor a smaller-sized public sector where both spending and taxes are reduced.

It is undoubtedly unwise to try to read too much into these survey results. Voters may be unwilling or unable to articulate why they voted for an amendment, or whether they favor a larger or smaller public sector. They also may have in mind a complex package of effects, for any one amendment or for the Tisch and Headlee amendments in combination, that we are unable to test with our questions. And, as with any survey, results are always suspect to economists because voters do not have to act on the basis of their answers.

But allowing for these limitations, some suggestive results emerge from this attempt to survey voters. One is that there does not appear to be a very widespread feeling that government is too big. More people feel that way than the converse, but the differences are not substantial and in any case not strongly related to respondents' votes on the tax limitation amendment. Fundamentally, the tax limitation movement does not appear to be an attempt to correct spending imbalances between the public and private sectors.

A second result is that there does not appear to be in the tax limitation movement, at least in its Michigan incarnation, a strong desire to punish public employees. Relatively few private sector voters feel that the amendment will limit government wage increases, and even if they do feel that way, they are not strongly inclined to vote for the amendment. Relatively few private sector voters feel the amendment will lower public employment either, and when voters feel that way, they actually are more inclined to vote against the amendment. Fundamentally, the tax limitation movement does not appear to be seen as an attempt to alter the income distribution between public and private employees.

It is easier to say what this tax limitation movement is not than what it is. The strongest source of support for tax limitation comes from those who think limitations will improve voter control of government and/or government efficiency. Had we anticipated such a finding initially, we would have added questions to probe why and how voters felt this would happen, but for now that matter remains for others to investigate. Another strong source of support comes from those who think the amendment will reduce taxes, even though they have reported not desiring cuts in spending and taxes at that level of government. Thus these voters appear to perceive that their own taxes will be cut without expenditures being cut, either because of supposed efficiency gains, greater uncertainty about the spending side of the budget, or the unending search for a free lunch.

APPENDIX

I. Following are the descriptions of the tax limitation amendments, Headlee and Tisch, as they appeared on the voters' ballots:

PROPOSAL E
(Headlee)
PROPOSAL FOR TAX LIMITATION.

The proposed amendment would:

1. Limit all state taxes and revenues, excepting federal aid to its current proportion of total state personal income and to provide for exception for a declared emergency.
2. Prohibit local government from adding new or increasing existing taxes without voter approval.
3. Prohibit the state from adopting new or expanding present local programs without full state funding.
4. Prohibit the state from reducing existing level of aid to local governments, taken as a group.
5. Require voter approval of certain bonded indebtedness.

Should this amendment be adopted?

PROPOSAL J
(Tisch)
PROPOSAL TO REDUCE PROPERTY TAX ASSESSMENTS; TO ESTABLISH A MAXIMUM OF 5.6% ON THE RATE OF THE STATE INCOME TAX; TO PROHIBIT LEGISLATURE FROM REQUIRING NEW OR EXPANDED LOCAL PROGRAMS WITHOUT STATE FUNDING; AND TO ALLOW SCHOOL INCOME TAX WITH VOTER APPROVAL.

The proposed amendment would:

1. Reduce real and personal property tax assessments to 25% of true cash value of property.
2. Limit state equalization increase to 2.5% for any year.
3. Establish a maximum of 5.6% on the rate of the state income tax.
4. Allow legislature to authorize school districts to levy up to 1% income tax with local school district voter approval.
5. Prohibit legislature from requiring new or expanded local programs unless fully funded by state.

Should this amendment be adopted?

II.   Following is a list of the survey questions, as they were read to the respondents, which we used in our Headlee and Tisch "interactions" models. Below each question are the marginals for the responses of our entire sample of 2,001.

TASTES

(state spending)
—Considering just the state government in Michigan which spends mainly on education, highways, and welfare—would you favor an across-the-board increase in both state spending and taxes, a decrease in both spending and taxes, or would you favor no change?

increase	no change	decrease	don't know
10%	51%	35%	3%

(local spending)
—Considering just your local governments which spend mainly on schools, police, fire, parks, and sanitation services—would you favor an across-the-board increase in both local spending and taxes, a decrease in both local spending and taxes, or would you favor no change?

increase	no change	decrease	don't know
22%	60%	16%	2%

(state government waste)
—Do you think that people in the state government waste a lot of the money we pay in taxes, waste some of it, or don't waste very much of it?

a lot	some	not much	don't know
49%	43%	5%	3%

(state government trust)
—How much of the time do you think you can trust the state government in Lansing to do what is right—just about always, most of the time, or only some of the time?

always	most of the time	some of the time	never	don't know
5%	45%	46%	2%	2%

(government employees' earnings)

—Compared with other workers with similar skills and abilities, do you think that state government employees in general earn more, earn less, or earn about the same amount as other workers with similar skills?

more	about the same	less	don't know
45%	37%	10%	8%

(government employees' efforts)

—Compared with workers employed by private industry, do you think government employees work harder, not as hard, or work about as hard?

harder	about as hard	not as hard	don't know
4%	38%	55%	3%

(school spending)

—Do you think the local public school system should be spending more, spending less, or about the same as they do now?

less	same	more	don't know
15%	44%	38%	3%

IMPACTS OF HEADLEE

—Do you think the passage of the Headlee proposal will lead to:

——a reduction in the overall level of taxes in Michigan?

yes	no	don't know
24%	58%	19%

——a reduction in property taxes?

yes	no	don't know
30%	54%	16%

——an increase in income taxes?

yes	no	don't know
58%	25%	17%

——a reduction in the number of state and local government employees?

yes	no	don't know
39%	43%	18%

———a reduction in the funds available to the local public school system?

yes	no	don't know
39%	44%	17%

———a reduction in the future wage increases of government employees?

yes	no	don't know
42%	42%	16%

IMPACTS OF TISCH

—Do you think the passage of the Tisch proposal would have led to:

———a reduction in the overall level of taxes in Michigan?

yes	no	don't know
41%	45%	14%

———a reduction in property taxes?

yes	no	don't know
55%	32%	13%

———an increase in income taxes?

yes	no	don't know
66%	20%	14%

———a reduction in the number of state and local government employees?

yes	no	don't know
46%	40%	14%

———a reduction in the funds available to the local public school system?

yes	no	don't know
55%	29%	16%

———a reduction in the future wage increases of government employees?

yes	no	don't know
46%	40%	14%

MOST IMPORTANT IMPACT OF HEADLEE

—Overall, what do you think will be the most important change caused by the passage of Proposition E, the Headlee Amendment?

reduce (or limit) govt. spending	reduce (or limit) overall taxes, property taxes, or income taxes	increase overall taxes, property taxes, or income taxes
11%	17%	5%

increase govt. efficiency	increase voter control	hurt schools	don't know	no change
3%	5%	2%	32%	8%

MOST IMPORTANT IMPACT OF TISCH

—Overall, what do you think would have been the most important change caused by the passage of Proposition J, the Tisch Proposal?

reduce (or limit) govt. spending	reduce (or limit) overall taxes, property taxes, or income taxes	increase overall taxes, property taxes, or income taxes
12%	21%	7%

increase govt. efficiency	increase voter control	hurt schools	don't know	no change
2%	2%	4%	26%	6%

III. A question which we felt might bear further investigation is the relationship between the respondents' attributes and their perceptions of the effects of the Headlee Amendment. Following are two two-way tables. The first shows the relationship between the attribute education and perceptions of Headlee; the second shows the relationship between job status (public or private) and perceptions of Headlee. The percentages presented within these tables are *conditional* probabilities; i.e., of those respondents with a given attribute, *x*-percent perceive that Headlee will have a certain effect.

EDUCATION

(Headlee Voters, N = 1014)	(1) less than high school	(2) high school graduate	(3) some college	(4) college graduate
PERCEPTION: Respondent thinks passage of Headlee will . . .				
(1) reduce overall level of taxes	32.2%[a]	27.7%	20.3%	15.1%
(2) reduce property taxes	39.6%	30.8%	26.7%	20.9%
(3) increase income taxes	62.4%	62.8%	61.7%	54.8%
(4) reduce the number of state & local government employees	41.6%	38.3%	39.8%	37.7%
(5) reduce funds available to local public school system	41.6%	36.7%	39.8%	41.8%
(6) reduce future wage increases of govt. employees	40.3%	44.4%	44.4%	49.0%

a. For example, 32.2% of those with less than high school education (versus 27.7% of high school graduates) perceive that Headlee will lower taxes

JOB STATUS

(Headlee voters, N = 1028)	(1) private employee	(2) public employee
PERCEPTION: Respondent thinks passage of Headlee will . . .		
(1) reduce overall level of taxes	25.1%[a]	15.1%
(2) reduce property taxes	30.0%	22.7%
(3) increase income taxes	60.3%	61.6%

(4) reduce the number of government employees	40.0%	35.5%
(5) reduce public school funds	36.4%	54.7%
(6) reduce future wage increases of government employees	44.4%	48.3%

a. For example, 25.1% of private employees (versus 15.1% of public employees) peceive that Headlee will lower taxes.

REFERENCES

Anderson, T. W. 1958. *An introduction to multivariable statistical analysis.* New York, N.Y.: Wiley.

Attiyeh, R., and Engle, R. June 1979. Testing some propositions about Proposition 13. *National Tax Journal.*

Brennan, J., and Buchanan, J. June 1979. The logic of tax limits: alternative constitutional constraints of the power to tax. *National Tax Journal.*

Buchanan, J., and Tullock, G. 1962. *Calculus of consent.* Ann Arbor, Mich.: University of Michigan Press.

Citrin, J. June 1979. Do people want something for nothing: public opinion on taxes and government spending. *National Tax Journal.*

Courant, P., Gramlich, E., and Rubinfeld, D. June 1979a. Tax limitation and the demand for public services in Michigan. *National Tax Journal.*

_____. December 1979b. Public employee market power and the level of government spending. *American Economic Review.*

Courant, P., and Rubinfeld, D. 1979. On the welfare effects of tax limitations. *IPPS Discussion Paper* no. 142. Institute of Public Policy Studies, The University of Michigan.

Curtin, R., and Cowan, C. 1973. Public attitudes towards fiscal programs. In B. Strumpel et al., eds., *Surveys of consumers*, 1972–73. Ann Arbor, Mich.: Institute of Survey Research, The University of Michigan.

Deacon, R. December 1977. Private choice and collective outcomes: evidence from public sector demand studies. *National Tax Journal.*

Denzau, A., Mackay, R., and Weaver, C. June 1979. Spending limitations, agenda control, and voters' expectations. *National Tax Journal.*

Downs, A. 1957. *An economic theory of democracy.* New York, N.Y.: Harper and Row.

Fiorina, M., and Noll, R. April 1978. Voters, bureaucrats, and legislators: a rational choice perspective on the growth of bureaucracy. *Journal of Public Economy.*

Goldstein, G. S., and Pauly, M. V. 1979. The effect of revenue and tax limitation on property values. *National Tax Journal.*

Ladd, G. October 1966. Linear probability functions and discriminant functions. *Econometrica*.

Ladd, H. March 1978. An economic evaluation of state limitations on local taxing and spending power. *National Tax Journal*.

Mueller, E. May 1963. Public attitudes toward fiscal problems. *Quarterly Journal of Economics*.

Niskanen, W. May 1968. The peculiar economics of bureaucracy. *American Economic Review*.

Pindyck, R., and Rubinfeld, D. 1976. *Econometric models and economic forecasts*. New York, N.Y.: McGraw-Hill.

Romer, T., and Rosenthal, H. Winter 1978. Political resource allocation, controlled agendas, and the status quo. *Public Choice*.

Tullock, G. Fall 1974. Dynamic hypothesis on bureaucracy. *Public Choice*.

White, M. J. June 1979. Government response to spending limitations. *National Tax Journal*.

Discussion of Perry Shapiro, "Popular Response to Public Spending Disequilibrium: An Analysis of the 1978 California Property Tax Limitation Initiative"; and Paul N. Courant, Edward M. Gramlich, and Daniel L. Rubinfeld, "Why Voters Support Tax Limitation Amendments: The Michigan Case"

William H. Oakland, Discussant

It has become fashionable in fiscal circles to regard 1978 as the year of the taxpayer's revolt. Citizen-based initiatives to reduce the size or growth of government expenditures were placed on the ballot in numerous states. While such measures met with a mixed degree of success, they have nevertheless prompted economists to inquire into the root causes of taxpayer dissatisfaction with the state of fiscal affairs. The essays by Shapiro and by Courant, Gramlich, and Rubinfeld (C–G–R) are in this spirit.

Shapiro's essay argues that the "tax shift" hypothesis which he and others (including myself) have used to explain the emergence of Proposition 13 is incorrect. Briefly stated, the tax shift hypothesis asserts that Proposition 13 was an attempt by voters to shift a significant share of the responsibility for financing local public services to the state government. This transfer was motivated by rapid increases in the unpopular property tax, attributable to sharply rising real estate prices, and the presence of a substantial accumulated budgetary surplus at the state level.

Shapiro bases his case for rejecting the tax shift hypothesis upon the observation that, among those favoring no cuts in local service, there was no correlation between income and vote for or against Proposition 13. According to Shapiro a transfer from local to state finance should benefit those with lower than average incomes because their share of state taxes is less than their share of local taxes, and vice versa for higher income groups; hence, income should have been correlated with voting behavior if a "tax shift" was the motivating factor underlying Proposition 13.

As an alternative, Shapiro argues that voters were motivated by excessive local government expenditure. He points out that, among voters surveyed, a small minority did not favor cuts in at least one local spending program. A voter may have believed that the cuts required by the referendum would have occurred in those areas he felt to be excessive. Equally important, Shapiro provides evidence that local expenditures may have grown excessively in the recent past. Using a median voter model, he argues that educational expenditure was 10 percent too high by 1977–78, and municipal and county expenditures "were growing faster than the desired rate."

My own view is that Shapiro's arguments are unconvincing. For reasons set out below, the case for excessive expenditure is unpersuasive and the test of the "tax shifting" hypothesis is inconclusive. I will treat these in turn.

To establish his overexpenditure result, Shapiro employs income elasticity estimates derived from cross-sectional studies. For education he uses .59, and for other expenditure a paltry .28. Such estimates are simply incompatible with the growth of government expenditure in Western societies over the past one hundred years. While the desired growth of government might well have leveled off in recent years, an elasticity of near unity (allowing for rising real costs) would be needed to maintain a constant share of income. In California, growth of personal income has averaged more than 10 percent in recent years, which does not seem incompatible with the expenditure growth reported by Shapiro.

Even if one accepts the cross-sectional elasticities, the .28 used for general local government seems far too low. Indeed, in the Bergstrom–Goodman piece from which the estimate for California was taken, the average elasticity for all states was .65. If one substitutes this figure, the growth of municipal and county expenditures is in line with the "desired" rate. This leaves us with the author's estimate of $800 million in "excess" education expenditure. Considering that Proposition 13 would have reduced local government by $7 billion, voters were using a sledgehammer to kill a fly.

The other strand in the author's over-expenditure argument is that a large majority of taxpayers favored cuts in at least one local government spending program. In this sense, government expenditure is argued to be excessive. This line of reasoning overlooks those voters who, while favoring cuts in some programs, also favor increases in others. It is not clear whether such voters perceive government to be too large overall. Indeed, it is puzzling why nearly 47 percent of those favoring no cuts whatever, voted to support the amendment. This apparent contradiction points to the pitfalls of using survey data to determine preferences on the size of the government budget.

Turning to Shapiro's alleged counterfactual argument about the "tax shift" hypothesis, I find it is too simplistic. First, it is tacitly based upon the assumption that people are spatially stratified perfectly according to income. In fact, the majority of Californians reside within the boundaries of local governments whose citizens are heterogeneous with respect to income. It is not clear that the "higher income" households of such jurisdictions would not prefer state to local financing. For, in this way, the burden of carrying the costs of public services of the poor can be shared with their affluent counterparts in the suburbs. Hence, there can be no presumption that votes will be correlated with income. Indeed, a much more conclusive test would be voting patterns among city and suburban residents.

In sum, it is premature to label the "tax shifting" hypothesis as incorrect. While such a hypothesis implies a high degree of rationality among taxpayer voters, it is the only story which seems to hang together with the facts.

The difficulty in using survey data to uncover taxpayer motives with respect to tax limitation issues is nicely brought out by the C–G–R paper. Not only do the authors test for overexpenditure directly but they also check for consistency between voters' stated preferences and their actual voting behavior. The results of the latter exercise are rather startling. While most Michigan voters expressed the opinion that existing public expenditure was satisfactory or below desired levels, many of the same individuals voted in favor of tax limitation.

These results, in themselves, can be rationalized on the grounds that the Headlee Amendment does not severely constrain the growth of state expenditure; hence, those satisfied with existing spending levels may have interpreted the amendment as a precaution against future public sector excesses. However, when C–G–R examine voter perceptions as to the predicted effect of the amendment, the inconsistency remains. This leads the authors to conclude that many voters believe that they can obtain public services without having to pay taxes—what the authors refer to as a "free lunch."

While acceptance of the "free-lunch" hypothesis is tempting, a full resolution of the question must await further study. This is because voters were not voting on a single issue in the Michigan case. Indeed there were three separate limitation questions on the ballot. It is not implausible that voters favoring one form of limitation may have voted against the other two. Alternatively, a voter who did not favor any type of limitation whatever, but who felt that some sort of limitation would be adopted, might strategically vote for the lesser of the evils—in this case the Headlee Amendment. Resolution of this conjecture awaits analysis of elections where a single initiative is placed on the ballot.

LEVIATHAN COMETH—OR DOES HE?

Richard A. Musgrave

The events of the past decade have brought two striking changes in intellectual climate. One is a remarkable rise of intellectual conservatism, ranging from those who consider themselves liberals—but hard-nosed liberals—to the minimal-state position of the libertarians. With its advocacy of free markets and capitalist institutions, this new breed challenges what Schumpeter had described as the inherently left based, anticapitalist role of the intellectual in society.[1] This change is paralleled by a disenchantment with public controls on the far left, leading to a shift in emphasis from centralized direction to decentralized if communal control. Both these developments, but especially the former, have left their mark on how the role of the public sector is viewed, be it in the press or the more learned journals of the public finance fraternity. Indeed, our fraternity has been a leading force in the process of change. Where the traditional theme since Pigou and then Keynes had been to show how governmental action must correct for market failure, the new thrust is to stress government failure and to view the public sector as an impediment to the market. Central to the new doctrine is the proposition that government has become too large and that constitutional constraints

[The author is H.H. Burbank Professor of Political Economy at Harvard University.]

ACKNOWLEDGMENTS: Thanks for helpful comments are due to Helen Ladd and Nicolaus Tideman. I am especially indebted to Robert MacKay who generously provided me with a detailed review of an earlier draft. His assistance was most helpful but should not be taken to implicate him in the contents of this paper.

1. Schumpeter (1942), chap. 13, part 2.

are needed, lest Leviathan (hence my subsequent reference to Leviathan theorists) will swallow the private sector and with it the remainder of our liberties.[2]

What is the basis for this proposition? Is the overexpansion hypothesis supported by the facts, and how valid is its analytical foundation? In addressing this question, I limit myself to budgetary activities of government, omitting other aspects such as monetary policy, regulation and the courts. This is a somewhat arbitrary division, especially since one arm of government may frequently be substituted for another, but it will have to do for purposes of this essay.

"Market Failure" and "Government Failure"

By way of introduction, a word is needed about the implications of the terms "market failure" and "government failure." Market failure may be interpreted to mean (1) that the market, as it actually functions, does not live up to the competitive norm and therefore does not deliver the Pareto-optimal outcome in the provision of private goods which a competitive market would produce. Such market failure is more or less avoidable and calls for appropriate controls over market structure, such as assurance of free entry. Or, (2) failure may arise because even a perfectly competitive market cannot, left to its own devices, secure efficient resource allocation. This may be the case due to decreasing costs, to the presence of externalities, and to the provision of social goods. Finally, (3) the market cannot provide for what are considered appropriate corrections in the distribution of income.[3] The latter failures, especially those of type (2), have been the concern of

---

2. The practice of borrowing the title of Thomas Hobbes' famous treatise may be credited, I believe, to James Buchanan (1975, p. 147), and since then has been used widely by members of his school. In line with Webster's definition as that "sea monster, often symbolizing evil," the term is well suited to conjure up the dangers which are said to follow from fiscal expansion and the resulting emergence of an all-powerful state. But it would be wrong to claim Hobbes's support for the position taken by Leviathan theorists. The message of Hobbes' *Leviathan*, after all, was that a strong and indeed absolute state ("that mortal God") is needed to permit man to emerge from his natural state in which life "is solitary, poor, nasty, brutish and short," so that he may enjoy the laws of nature, calling for "justice, equity, modesty and mercy." Though awesome in his power, the sovereign as seen by Hobbes was far from evil. This being the case, one wonders why Hobbes chose so ambiguous a title! See Hobbes (1651, pp. 107, 142).

3. Other types of "market failure," bearing on maintenance of macrostability and the resulting function of stabilization policy, are omitted from this discussion.

traditional public finance theory and call for remedy by nonmarket mechanisms rather than for repair of avoidable market imperfections.

Can we define a concept of government failure in the provision of social goods parallel to type (1) market failure in providing for private goods? Yes and no. Government may indeed perform below par, because decision makers may disregard consumer (voter) preferences, taxes may be unduly burdensome, and public services may be delivered in a wasteful fashion. But absence of government failure is not defined as readily as it is for the market provision of private goods. In the latter case, we have the Pareto efficient outcome achieved in perfectly competitive markets. In the former case we have the efficient solution provided by Samuelson's omniscient referee who can place the use of resources on the utility frontier. But such a referee does not exist. With the system of the market inoperative, a political process using a voting mechanism is needed to secure preference revelation. This is an additional obstacle to efficient provision, not encountered in the case of private goods where consumers, in response to the auctioning mechanism of the market, must reveal their preferences. Depending on the institutional arrangements (e.g., voting rules and the role played by the executive and legislative branches of government) the outcome may differ by a smaller or larger margin from the efficient result, but it will hardly reach a Pareto efficient solution. Some voters will remain dissatisfied and the efficiency cost of taxation will persist. Notwithstanding interesting recent work in the analysis of voting processes,[4] policy performance will not be perfect. It follows that public sector failure should be defined as failure to reach the best feasible (if second best) solution, rather than as falling short of truly optimal outcome.

Defining government failure is even more difficult if we consider the distribution function. Assuming that the desired state of distribution or social welfare function has been determined, absence of failure might be defined as efficient implementation of the required pattern of distribution. Since redistribution by lump-sum taxes (that most counterfactual and useless fiction of the economist's imagination) has no operational meaning, the condition of efficient implementation must be interpreted once more in terms of "as efficiently as possible."

---

4. See Johansen (1978) who argues that the difficulties of the free rider problem are largely overcome under representative government, and Tideman and Tullock (1976) for a discussion of voting processes which render it in the voter's interest not to cheat.

Once extended beyond voluntary giving, redistribution involves efficiency costs which must be considered; and as shown by the literature on optimal taxation, such allowance may be made with the standard tools of economic analysis. But determining the "proper" target of redistribution policy is a different matter. Some will view entitlements to income or property as rooted in natural law (e.g., Locke and Nozick, who hold that one has the right to the fruits of one's own labor), others begin with the premise that entitlement is only to fairness (e.g., Rawls's choice under the veil of ignorance), and still others (Bentham and the utilitarians) postulate that society should maximize utility, average or total, whatever the resulting distribution.[5] Given the multiplicity of possible rules, it is obvious that government failure in conducting distributional activity cannot be defined without specifying this underlying rule and the social welfare function which derives therefrom. Since the choice of distributive rule (or, one step back, the choice of rules by which to choose this rule) is controversial, we have no ready basis for determining what a "perfect" government would do, and hence we cannot say in an objective sense whether budgetary redistribution is too large or too small.

Moreover, the issue of efficiency costs of redistribution has to be seen in relation to prevailing economic institutions. While effects on labor–leisure choice are present under all forms of economic organization (short of slave-labor), effects on saving, investment, and risk taking are of much greater importance in a decentralized market economy with private ownership than under public ownership and planning. In considering "the correct size" of the budget it is thus appropriate to allow for its effects on the viability of particular economic institutions and the implications of alternatives. Moreover, these effects include not only economic efficiency but other aspects of the social setting, such as individual freedom. This nexus greatly expands the range of considerations which are relevant in dealing with the proper size of the budget, a complication which is inconvenient but no excuse for ignoring it.

How Big Has the Budget Become?

I now turn to some figures on the growth of the public sector, defined here in budgetary terms. Obviously, this growth cannot be

---

5. Locke (1690); Nozick (1974); Rawls (1971).

measured meaningfully in absolute dollars but must be related to the expanding size of the economy. The changing ratio of expenditures to GNP, though a crude measure only, will serve the purpose of this brief survey. As shown in table 1, the salient features of more recent developments may be summarized as follows:

1. To begin with, the overall ratio of total expenditures (all levels and types) to GNP rose by 5.6 percentage points during the fifties, 4.9 points during the sixties, and 1.6 points during the seventies. Taking a span from 1940 to 1978, the expenditure-to-GNP ratio rose from .18 to .32, or by 78 percent. The rise was substantial but it has proceeded at a distinctly declining rate, and during the seventies it slowed down to only a trickle.[6]

2. From 1940 to 1960, the growth in the expenditure-to-GNP ratio was accounted for very largely by national defense. Thereafter, defense declined relative to GNP with the entire expansion in the civilian ratio.

3. From 1940 to 1960 the ratio of federal expenditures (grants included) to GNP rose by 83 percent, while the state-local ratio remained almost constant. Since then, the latter has risen slightly relative to the federal share, expressing the declining weight of defense and reversing an earlier tendency towards increased centralization of civilian functions. If grants are included at the recipient's level, the increase in the state-local share is substantially larger. Viewed this way the ratio of federal expenditures to GNP falls from 17.3 percent in 1960 to 16.8 percent in 1978, while the state-local ratio rises from 14.6 to 15.7 percent.

4. Government purchases of goods and services as percent of GNP rose sharply during the fifties and moderately in the sixties but have declined since then. Almost the entire increase in the overall ratio during the sixties and seventies was thus accounted for by transfers.

---

6. Taking the longer view, the ratio of total expenditures to GNP is estimated at 7.3 percent for 1902 and at 10.4 percent for 1927. The increase in the ratio was accounted for almost entirely by civilian expenditures. The size of the public sector has increased substantially over the longer run and, though the rationale of "Wagner's Law" (See Wagner, in Musgrave and Peacock, 1958) may be debatable, his early projection was essentially correct. Borcherding's scathing critique of "Wagner's Law" (Borcherding, 1978) seems to be based on a misreading of Wagner's position as reflecting nothing but an income elasticity of demand for social goods in excess of unity. As careful reading of Wagner will show, his prognosis was much more comprehensive, allowing for technological, social, political, and institutional changes of industrial society and their impact upon budgetary policy.

82TAX AND EXPENDITURE LIMITATIONS

Table 1

BUDGET TRENDS

	1940	1950	1960	1970	1978
I. Public Expenditures as Percent of GNP, Current Prices					
1. Total Expenditures	18.4	21.3	26.9	31.8	32.4
2. National Defense	2.2	4.9	8.8	7.5	4.7
3. Civilian	16.2	16.4	18.1	24.3	27.7
4. Total Expenditures	18.4	21.3	26.9	31.8	32.4
5. Federal	10.0	14.2	18.3	20.8	20.5
6. State and Local	8.4	7.1	8.6	11.0	9.9
7. Total Expenditures	18.4	21.3	26.9	31.8	32.4
8. Purchases	14.2	13.4	19.8	22.3	20.6
9. Transfers	4.2	7.9	7.1	9.5	11.8
10. Total Purchases	14.2	13.4	19.8	62.3	20.6
11. National Defense	2.2	4.9	8.8	7.5	4.7
12. Civilian	12.0	8.5	11.0	14.8	15.9
II. Public Expenditures as Percent of GNP, 1972 Prices					
13. Total Purchases	19.0	18.3	23.5	23.2	19.9
14. National Defense	2.8	6.5	10.3	7.9	4.7
15. Civilian	16.0	11.8	13.1	15.4	15.3
III. Public Employment as Percent of Total					
16. All Levels	13.1	13.3	15.6	17.6	18.0
17. Federal	3.1	4.2	4.3	3.8	3.2
18. State and Local	10.0	9.1	11.3	13.8	14.8

Source: *Economic Report of the President*, January 1979, pp. 183, 187, 267.
Line 2: Includes National Defense purchases only.
Line 3: Line 1 minus Line 2.
Line 6: Federal grants included at federal level.
Line 9: Includes interest.
Line 13: Ratio of government purchases at 1972 prices to GNP at 1972 prices.
Line 14: National Defense expenditures are deflated by index for federal purchases.
Line 15: Line 13 minus Line 14.
Line 16: Government employment as a percent of total wage and salary workers in nonagricultural establishments. *Economic Report of the President*, January 1979, p. 222.

5. If both purchases and GNP are expressed in 1972 dollars (adjusting thereby for the more rapid increase in the cost of public services) we find the ratio of purchases to GNP to have risen less rapidly. The move now is from 14 percent in 1940 to 20 percent in 1960 and 22 percent in 1970. Since then, the adjusted ratio declined to 20 percent in 1978. Considering civilian purchases only, the ratios were 16, 12, 13, 15, and 15 respectively. Both the adjusted purchase ratios now stand at about their pre-World War II level.

Summarizing, the overall expenditure ratio rose substantially from 1940 to 1970, but only slightly since then. Both civilian and defense outlays shared in the growth, with civilian expansion largely in the transfer sector. Government purchases of goods and services since 1960 have expanded in line with GNP, not more; and if considered in real terms, the total purchase ratio has fallen and is now substantially below its 1960 level. In all, it appears that the growth of Leviathan, especially in the recent past, is in the eyes of the beholder. Much depends on which aspect is considered.

Problems of Measurement

There are some obvious and some not so obvious difficulties in measuring public sector growth in these terms. The more obvious difficulties involve the questionable aggregation of purchases and transfers and the choice of GNP versus national income as the denominator. These need not be considered here, but two other—and more intriguing—aspects might be noted.

Treatment of Social Goods

If the growth of GNP is interpreted as an index of welfare (a rough one, to be sure), the change should be viewed in per capita terms. This is evident for a world of private goods only. If population doubles with output constant, GNP is unchanged while per capita GNP or income, and hence (by rough approximation) welfare, is cut by one half. But the situation is less evident in a world of social goods. If social goods are truly nonrival in consumption (as they are taken to be in textbooks), per capita welfare should be invariant to population growth. Holding the output of social goods constant while population rises, per capita welfare should remain unchanged so that total welfare (defined as per capita times numbers) rises. But this is not allowed

for in the customary view of GNP under which per capita income falls
as population increases, with the entire GNP treated as if in private
goods. Does it follow that in a period of rising population (1) the
growth of per capita GNP understates welfare growth, and (2) the
changing ratio of government purchases to GNP understates the rising
share of social goods entering into per capita output?

At closer consideration, this line of reasoning is questionable. The
individual consumer should be expected to value his consumption of
social goods at his tax price, not at the cost of social goods to the
community as a whole. We may thus write $\text{GNP} = Q_P P_P + Q_s P_s^c$,
where Q_P and Q_s are the quantity of private and social goods, P_P is
the unit price of private goods and P_s^c, is the unit price of social goods
to the community. Since $P_s^c = P_s^t N$ where P_s^t is the average tax price
of the social good and N is the number of consumers, we also have
$\text{GNP} = Q_p P_p + Q_s P_s^t N$. Similarly, per capita income equals not
$\dfrac{Q_f P_p}{N} + Q_s P_s^c$ but $\dfrac{Q_p P_p}{N} + Q_s P_s^t = \dfrac{Q_p P_p}{N} + \dfrac{Q_s P_s^t N}{N} = \dfrac{\text{GNP}}{N}$ which is
the usual definition. Note, however, that this assumes social goods
to be provided in line with consumer evaluation as reflected in the
tax price.

Should One Deflate?

Whether GNP growth is viewed as measuring output performance
or as an index of welfare growth, it is necessary to correct for inflation.
This would have no effect on the ratio of government purchases to
GNP if relative prices did not change, but since public purchases
have risen faster, the ratio of nominal expenditures to nominal GNP,
shown in lines 1–12 of the table, rises more sharply than do the
constant price ratios of lines 13–15. Assuming the supply of public
services to have been determined in line with consumer preferences,
this suggests an income elasticity well above unity, sufficient to overcome the adverse substitution effect of rising public goods prices. But
it remains to consider which view is correct.[7]

A simple illustration may help to pose the problem. Suppose that
in year one the economy produces five units of goods purchased
privately and three units of goods purchased or produced by govern-

---

7. Peacock and Wiseman (1967) consider nominal ratios only, but real ratios have
been used in the recent writings of Beck (1976) and Durbin (1977).

ment. Both cost $1.00, GNP equals $8.00, and the public expenditure share is .38. Next year, the output mix is unchanged but prices of goods purchased by government have doubled while those of private goods are unchanged. GNP in year two rises to $11.00 and the nominal public share now equals .55, a 45 percent increase above the initial level. But after deflating government expenditures by 50 percent to account for the doubling of prices and deflating GNP by 27 percent to account for the 37 percent rise in the GNP index, the adjusted ratio remains at .38. Has there been public-sector expansion? Clearly, there has been no change in the *physical units* of resource inputs or product outputs, or in the set of physical resources claimed by the public sector. To express this, the adjusted ratios should be used in measuring public sector growth. But it is also evident that the rise in the nominal ratio has caused the required tax rate (assuming a balanced budget) to increase from 38 to 55 percent, causing a larger share of income to be channeled through the budget and a larger share of output (as measured in *value terms*) to be provided by it. This may well be the crucial point. Assuming that the relative prices of social and private goods reflect consumer valuations, it is the change in the nominal and not the real ratio that matters.

Turning to a more realistic illustration, consider the period from 1960 to 1970 during which current expenditures on elementary and secondary education rose by 177 percent. This was the combined result of (1) a 26 percent increase in school age population and enrollment, causing a shift in demand from other uses towards education, relative to given levels of income and costs, (2) a 70 percent rise in per capita personal income, causing the demand for education to rise for a given school age population and costs, and (3) a 117 percent rise in per student cost, as compared to a rise of 31 percent in the general cost of living, causing a shift in demand away from education for given levels of income and school population. The net result thus reflects a change in the school age population as well as a change in responses to income and price elasticities. Undoubtedly, the increase in education inputs would have been larger if relative costs had not risen, so the increase in the relative cost of education is a significant factor in the outcome. But this does not displace the fact that the observed increase in inputs *was* purchased at the higher prices and hence should be valued accordingly when it comes to determine the public sector share. By the same token, a secular increase in the relative cost of public services due to lagging productivity gains, as postulated by Baumol and others,[8] will be reflected in a more rapid rise in the nominal than in the deflated share. But given the assumption that public services are worth their cost, it is the change in the nominal share that should be considered in measuring public sector expansion.

Baumol's proposition has significant bearing not only on the *relative* behavior of the real and nominal ratios but is relevant also for their absolute movement. Noting that an increase in the relative cost of public services calls for an increase in the nominal share even if the real share remains constant, Peacock and Wiseman (1979) conclude that an actual increase in the nominal share may be expected to result.[9] Indeed, Baumol's theory of "unbalanced growth" is viewed as the "modern counterpart to Wagner's Law." I have some reservations about this. For one thing, an increase in the relative price of public services will increase outlays enough to raise the nominal share only if the price elasticity of demand is above unity. Moreover, Baumol's observation applies to outlays on public services only and not to transfers, and within public services it applies to government produced services rather than to the purchase of private output (pencils for civil servants or military hardware). Yet, these are the parts of the budget which have expanded most rapidly. For these reasons, I would not consider Baumol's point, interesting although it is in a narrow range, a major source of public sector expansion. Moreover, our earlier distinction between P_s^c and P_s^t also has a historical role. As population increases and (for spatially limited social goods) as density rises, we may expect P_s^t to fall relative to P_s^c, so that P_s^t/P_p need not rise with P_s^c/P_p and may even fall. To be sure, publicly provided goods are not typically pure social goods, and this weakens the weight of the latter consideration.

The various problems noted here do not exhaust the list of difficulties encountered in designing a meaningful measure of public sector growth. Other points that might be explored include (1) how to interpret the growth of public services which complement, rather than rival, private consumption, (2) how to deal with the growth of intermediate public services entering into private production, (3) whether or not to adjust for changing needs due to demographic factors, e.g., share of school age children or retirees in the total

---

8. See Baumol (1967).

9. See also the reference to Borcherding in note 46 below.

population, (4) how to deal with changing needs for public services due to adverse changes in "environmental" factors, such as density and the resulting need for antipollution measures, and (5) how to deal with changing defense budgets in response to changing international conditions. Designing a meaningful measure of change in the public sector share is a complex task which remains to be resolved.

Is the Level of Public Services Excessive?

Even if a meaningful measure of "share" is agreed on, a finding that the budget is too large (or too small) must be supported by explicit criteria for what size is "proper." Without this, we only have the protagonist's own value judgment. To examine such criteria, I make use of my familiar distinction between two objectives of budget policy, i.e. (1) the provision for public goods and services and (2) the adjustment in the distribution of income.[10] Of course, the two become intertwined in practice, since proportional taxes may be used to finance "pro-poor" or "pro-rich" services, just as progressive or regressive taxes may be used to finance proportional services. However, it is helpful to begin with this distinction.

As noted before, provision for public services may be said to be at its optimal level if a change in the output mix (public and private) cannot improve A's position without hurting B's. Given the previously noted difficulties of implementation, the level of provision is proper if this outcome is approximated as well as possible.[11] Leviathan theorists, therefore, must demonstrate that there is a systematic bias which pushes the budget over its proper or efficient level. There now exists a large body of literature devoted to making this case, and it is growing steadily. Efforts at exploring the fiscal system "as it really works" are all to the good and I will welcome the development of a truly positive theory of fiscal behavior. But I do not see it in the making. The theory of fiscal crisis which emerges from the Marxist literature has the merit of viewing the problem in terms of social structure and the interactions of groups, but it suffers from a too simplistic and one-dimensional (capital versus labor) view of social conflict, as well as a total neglect of social cooperation.[12] The theory

---

10. See R.A. Musgrave (1958), chap. 1.

11. Reference to "provision," throughout means that the goods and services are provided free of direct charge and paid for through the budget. Whether they are produced by government or purchased in the market does not matter in this context.

12. See R.A. Musgrave (1980).

of government failure which emerges from the Leviathan literature is
not one of social structure but one that derives its conclusions (in the
tradition of micro and game theory) from behavioral assumptions for
the major actors, e.g. voters, officials, and politicians, all of whom
operate in set institutions. While claiming to offer a positive approach,
this literature reflects the consequences (derived neatly and on occasion, gleefully) from a preconceived model of behavior, designed
so that it cannot but result in the demonstration of government failure.
As we shall see, many of the arguments employed to show budget
excess may, by a change of underlying assumptions, also be used to
predict deficient service levels. It thus remains for careful empirical
work to test alternative hypotheses in order to establish the degree
and direction of actual bias. While such testing may be difficult, it
is essential if the models are to have scientific merit.[13] My purpose
here is not to fill this gap but merely to examine the plausibility and
implications of certain propositions drawn from the Leviathan model.
In the process, reference will be made to important parts of this
expanding literature, but my coverage must necessarily fall far short
of completeness.[14]

Voting Bias

The centerpiece of the argument is that majority rule involves an
inherent bias towards excessive budget size. The initial presentation,
given, I believe, in Gordon Tullock's seminal 1959 paper, examines
two situations.[15] In the absence of vote-trading or logrolling, a majority
vote on the size of the budget (assuming well-behaved, single-peaked
preferences) reflects the preference of the median voter. This outcome
may be excessive or deficient, depending upon the relative intensity

13. Gordon Tullock (1974) in concluding his presentation of an overexpansion
model based on government employee voting concludes happily that "The hypothesis
here presented may be difficult to test but this does not mean that it must be wrong."
True enough, but if so, it also means that the hypothesis is of little scientific interest.

14. The spirit of this body of literature is well captured in Borcherding, ed.
(1977a) and Niskanen (1971). See also the review by Amacher, Tollison, and Willett
(1975). As is the case with any body of lively literature, there may be many variants
of the doctrine, ranging from its most extreme form (see for instance, Brennan and
Buchanan, 1977) to more relaxed versions as in Borcherding's imaginative analysis
of government growth (Borcherding, 1977a).

15. Tullock (1959). Thereafter the argument appears and reappears in many
places, e.g., Buchanan and Tullock (1962), chap. 7; Buchanan (1975), p. 155; and
Riker, W. (1978).

of preferences of those who would like more or less, i.e., as compared
to the budget size which would result if side payments were permitted
and no "transaction costs" (I use quotes since I consider this to be
an ambiguous term of many meanings) intervened in the *tâtonement*
process. The agreed-upon budget share will not be optimal, but no
presumption on the direction of error can be established. But a presumption for excess arises, so Tullock argues, when logrolling (in the
sense of vote-trading only, but not side payments) is permitted.

Tullock addresses the case of public services (maintenance of access roads to a throughway) which are useful to some members of the
community (farmers living on the particular road) but not to others.
At the same time, all maintenance costs are distributed by a fixed
tax formula (e.g., a head tax) among all farmers, and all repairs are
decided upon by majority vote. Consider the case of five farmers, or
groups of farmers, A to E, living on five access roads respectively.
Farmers A, B, C will form a coalition to vote for maintenance of their
roads up to a point where the cost to each (measured by *his* per capita
share in the maintenance cost) equals the benefits which he derives
from the repair of his own road. Since the two/fifths of the cost borne
by D and E are not allowed for, maintenance of roads A, B, and C
is overexpanded. Similar and overlapping coalitions are formed among
other groups, say D, E and A, providing for repair of their respective
access roads, and so forth. In each case the cost share borne by
outsiders is neglected and overexpansion occurs. Each farmer, so
Tullock argues, maximizes his interest but the budget is overexpanded
and the overall result is inefficient.[16]

The argument leaves me troubled in several respects. Even if one
accepts the underlying modeling of the problem, Tullock's result need
not emerge. If farmers A, B, and C can coalesce to have their road
adopted, so can D, E, F, and G join to defeat it. The project may
be rejected even at a reduced scale for which A, B, and C would
have been willing to pay the full cost. The reason is that the opponents
must contribute even though to them the road is worthless. The outcome may thus be the rejection of projects which should have been
adopted (as measured by the test of a hypothetical case of perfect side
payments) as well as the adoption of projects which should have been

---

16. I here disregard the possibility, noted by Tullock, that all voters may behave
as "Kantians" and agree on the level of maintenance (for all roads) which is desired
by the median voter.

rejected. To break the symmetry of the argument and to establish an overexpansion bias, it must be shown that the cost of organizing a coalition is less relative to the gains for proponents than for opponents of the project. And this is by no means a foregone conclusion.

Next, I feel uneasy with the way in which the problem is formulated. Is it not strange to demonstrate the oversupply of public goods with a model which deals with public provision of what essentially are private goods? Take the extreme case where access to Road A is of use to Farmer A only, access road B to farmer B only, and so forth. In this situation, what rationale is there at all to provide for road maintenance through the political process? Provision should be left to the market, where quantities can be varied with the preferences of particular consumers. Or suppose that there are a large number of farmers on each road. In this case, what reason is there for submitting the residents of all roads to a central fisc rather than dividing it into "local fiscs" in which each group of residents can deal with their own problems? The cause of failure thus arises from uniform budgetary provision of private goods, or from too centralized a provision of local social goods, but the fault is not inherent in the voting process as applied to the provision of social goods within the appropriate benefit area. If, on the other extreme, we assume that all roads are equally useful to all farmers, maintenance will be as desired by the median voter, and the outcome, as noted before, may err on either side of the proper level.

Finally, and most important, there is the assumption that cost shares are totally independent of benefit shares. Thereby, Wicksell's key requirement of simultaneous determination is rejected and the stage for public sector failure is set.[17] Nor is there reason for so damning an assumption on empirical grounds. While specific expenditure decisions are made typically without immediate consideration of how the resulting tax cost is to be assigned, in the long run there surely emerges some relationship between how voters feel about their tax bill and about the benefits which they receive from public services. Farmer A, who values road maintenance more highly, will be willing to cooperate with B who values them less and to assume a larger share in total cost; politicians will consider the tax as well as the expenditure wishes of their voters, and so forth. The extent to which the political process is responsive to both sets of voter wishes

---

17. Wicksell (1896) and Musgrave and Peacock (1958).

will depend on legislative and executive institutions. As noted below, public officials who have control over what is to be voted on may limit the choice among tax-expenditure bundles so as to keep voters from choosing a preferred solution.[18] But this power is surely limited. Governments fall, administrations change, and voter satisfaction (or displeasure) with their tax-expenditure packages remains a major determinant of the political process. While only a 51 percent majority is needed for passage, most major tax and expenditure programs command a larger support. Moreover, reforms may be undertaken, as shown below, to strengthen the process.

Bureaucrats

I now turn to the role of the "bureaucracy," that bête noire of the Leviathan syndrome. This role is obviously a key factor in the operation of the public sector and it is appropriate therefore to illustrate it in modeling government behavior. The question is how?

Here, as in other contexts of social controversy, the choice of terminology is far from harmless. By referring to public officials as "bureaucrats" and agency heads as "bureau heads," the Leviathan literature appeals to current U.S. usage in which "bureaucracy"—as distinct from, say, "civil service"—has come to be a perjorative term. But it need not be interpreted in that fashion. The classical formulation was given in Max Weber's treatment, where the role of bureaucracy is seen as conducting organizational behavior (within government or out) in a rational fashion and performing assigned tasks in a strictly hierarchical order.[19] The virtue of bureaucracy thus interpreted is efficient conduct in the performance of assigned tasks. The danger of bureaucracy is an excessive routinization of life and loss of spontaneous or charismatic leadership and innovation. The Leviathan theorists, in disregard of this twofold connotation, go back to von Mises' dismal view of the bureaucrat as the tyrannical and uncontrolled agent of an all-powerful (Prussian if not Nazi) state.[20] In Niskanen's basic contribution, the official or "bureau head," far from being the public's servant, becomes the monopolistic supplier of public services.[21] Acting in analogy to the profit-maximizing firm in the private sector, he

---

18. See MacKay and Weaver (1978) and p. 95 below.
19. See Gerth and Mills (1970), p. 21
20. See von Mises (1944).
21. See Niskanen (1971 and 1975).

will do so because his personal interests, be they income or prestige, are linked thereto. For this purpose he will provide services at a level where total benefits equal total cost, this being the highest scale of output which the "sponsor" may be expected to accept. This scale exceeds the level at which marginal benefits and costs become equal, thus resulting in oversupply. While qualified and extended in various ways by Niskanen and subsequent writers, such is the essential model of bureaucratic behavior and the premise upon which the discussion proceeds.

Beginning with this characterization of the "bureau head," it seems to me mistaken to model his or her behavior in so close an analogy to that of the profit-maximizing business executive. To insist that profit maximization is the only mode of behavior (the "only game in town" as I have heard it put) extends the market calculus beyond its proper sphere. I have no quarrel, of course, with viewing bureau heads as maximizers, if this is taken merely to reflect purposeful (means-and-end oriented) action. Rather, my point is that maximization may involve targets other than personal economic gain and power, e.g., duty, respect of one's colleagues, realization of what one considers to be a "good society," and the satisfaction of having contributed thereto.[22] These motivations may go hand in hand with concern for personal gains (be they in income, power, prestige, or security) but they may conflict as well. Libertarians who fail to see this should consult Adam Smith on the complexities of human nature.[23] Human motivation is too many-sided and complex to be captured by the caricature of bureau-grabbing officials which permeates the Leviathan literature.

This critique stands even though Niskanen and others recognize that "bureau heads" may be nice people who believe in their bureau's function (this being why they are there), and thus their personal

---

22. Becker (1976, p. 5) includes such objectives in the preference function upon which the "economic approach" is based but requires stable preferences and choice through market processes as further characteristics. Since bureaucratic action to implement the public interest is not (or largely not) operative through market processes, an alternative (call it noneconomic) mode of behavior is required. There *is* a need for more than one game in town.

23. Not, of course, the *Wealth of Nations*, but the *Theory of Moral Sentiments* (1759), which shows human motivation as highly multidimensional, with "prudence" but one (and lesser) virtue. I am indebted also to Howard Margolis, whose interesting thoughts on a multidimensional model of motivation are in line with my own thoughts on the matter.

fortune and their view of the public interest happily coincide in calling for bureau expansion. In my view, this coincidence frequently does not apply. Responsible public policy requires awareness on the part of department heads (a term which I prefer) of competing needs within an overall budget constraint, and not simply exclusive concern with the function of a single department. My point is not that all "bureau heads" act exclusively in the public interest but that such motivation plays too significant a part in the typical case to be erased from the model.

The crucial importance of this issue becomes apparent when we compare the roles of bureau and business heads in society. Whereas the profit-maximizing behavior of the businessman may claim social sanction through the (more or less perfect) operation of the invisible hand, bureau-maximizing behavior carries no such sanction. By its very nature the conduct of the bureau head—if performed in the social interest—must be based on an intent to pursue such interest. To deny the possibility of such conduct is to deny the very role of government as a beneficial force, and a governmental model based on such denial cannot but demonstrate the preconceived conclusion of performance failure.

Moreover, Niskanen's model, in my view, makes insufficient allowance for the constraints which the checks and balances of the executive system place on the individual bureau head. This system provides not only a check on efficiency in performance (cost effectiveness analysis) but also calls for comparative evaluation of alternative projects within a budget constraint (marginal cost-benefit analysis). Operating in such a system, agency heads in search of promotion may well find it to their personal advantage to be efficient in service delivery and to recognize the need for comparative evaluation of alternative projects.[24] To be sure, this mechanism, even at its best, lacks the penalty of bankruptcy which *may* be (note Chrysler) the penalty of inefficiency in the private sector, and civil service rules may reduce the penalties for inefficient performance. Nevertheless, there are budget and examination procedures which play an important role in the executive structure, a role which, though not perfect, must be accounted for in a balanced view of governmental behavior. The

---

24. As noted by Julius Margolis (1975) careers are frequently made by bureau hopping. Restraint in the conduct of one bureau may lead to a larger position in another.

budget requisitions of particular departments serve as inputs into a budget making process. The department head, while pressing his particular function, operates in the context of an adversary process (see the budget preparation of OMB) and does not decide single-handedly on how much he should spend. Surely, this budgetary process—involving balancing between functions in the context of a budget constraint—must be given an important role in an unbiased model of governmental operations. In recent decades, the federal budget process has come to be essentially concentrated in what is now called the Office of Management and Budget. Department heads appear before Congress in defense of their programs as incorporated into the executive budget, and not as advocates of their own decisions. The executive function on budgeting is crucial and I fail to understand why it is largely if not entirely disregarded in much of the Leviathan literature.

Nor can I buy the role of the sponsor or review committee as willing to accept the monopolists' service level (where total benefit equals total cost) without objection. If the sponsor is viewed as an imbecile, no such rationalization is needed because anything will go. If he is granted the capacity of rational decision making, why should this rule be appealing to him? Given a sponsor who is concerned only with his particular type of service, he may well wish to go further, since the opportunity cost of reducing other services will be a matter of indifference to him. Given a sponsor who is aware of the need for budgeting and willing to allow for such opportunity costs, the rule of equating total benefits with cost will be rejected as inefficient and marginal criteria will be applied. There may be some merit to Niskanen's hypothesis that review committees are composed of high demanders, but this is not necessarily so. Doves have been known to serve on committees dealing with appropriations to the armed services, legislators hostile to taxation choose to serve on tax committees, and so forth.

Finally, as in the executive branch, allowance must be made for the fact that the legislative budget process involves some degree of apportionment between functions (although not as effectively as it should). If committee A is staffed by high demanders, the same will be true for committee B with which A must compete in the context of an overall budget constraint. Moreover, legislators stand to gain by appeal for expenditure and tax reduction as well by the offer of increased service levels. All this makes for a complex process, the outcome of which (whether for over- or underexpansion) is by no means evident.[25]

Agenda Setting

The Niskanen model of bureaucratic behavior, under which the bureau head is in the position of monopoly supplier, has been extended in the more recent literature to examine the consequences of situations where government is able to determine the agenda of issues on which voters are permitted to vote.[26] Various forms of monopoly practice in agenda setting are considered. These may range from all-or-nothing offers of single services at fixed prices, to setting discriminatory tax prices to various groups of taxpayers, and to commodity bundling in the group of services that are offered. In posing the problem, it is assumed that the agenda will be set so as to maximize the service level and that the voting public has little if any control over the proposals on which it is permitted to vote. Once more the role of review committees is allowed for, but as in the Niskanen model, they are mostly taken to be dominated by high demanders. Once more, the model cannot but yield oversupply.

While the earlier presentations involved agenda setting by a single bureau,[27] later work has come to allow for interaction among multiple

---

25. Niskanen (1971, chapter 14) in addition to the initial bilateral monopoly case noted above, also offers a more complex model in which action by the review committee becomes subject to acceptance by the legislature. This keeps the review committee (acting in cahoots with the monopoly bureau) from simply reflecting the preferences of the high demanders which it represents, since it cannot ask more than the median voter (in the entire population), and hence the legislature will accept. Thus the level cannot exceed that at which the gain to median voters becomes zero or (if reached earlier) that at which the gain to the high demanders is maximized. In both cases, optimal supply is exceeded. High demanders gain, low demanders lose, and the middle is indifferent.

As Niskanen notes (1971, p. 139) the model still excludes the role of the executive, bargaining between the executive and the legislature, as well as bargaining within the legislature, over different issues. Each service is determined by itself, so the essential function of budgeting remains excluded, as is the formation of platforms and coalitions. These factors are of major importance in the real setting, as distinct from the simplified single-issue, median-voter model which underlies Niskanen's analysis. Moreover, tax and expenditure decisions remain separated, in itself a defect sufficient to assure budget failure.

26. For an excellent review of this literature, see Robert J. Mackay and Carolyn L. Weaver (1978).

27. See Romer and Rosenthal (1978).

bureaus, providing for different services.[28] This has made for a richer analysis, since it helps to determine the composition of the total budget. Nevertheless, the composition thus determined remains different from that arrived at by a budgeting process which allocates funds among different services within a given budget constraint, or in a competitive model of costless agenda setting. Interesting and ingenious though these models are, my critique remains essentially similar to that of Niskanen's earlier version. Once more, I question the extreme behavioral assumption underlying budget-maximizing agenda setting, note the neglect of budget-making constraints among bureaus within the executive branch, and doubt that monopoly control over agenda setting does in fact rest with the executive in general and (even less likely) with particular bureaus.

To be sure, the political process falls short of the perfectly competitive model, but Leviathan theorists, to my mind, undervalue the democratic mechanism by denying all responsiveness of officials and legislators to the agenda-setting wishes of the voters. Surely, elected officials will not be at the mercy of bureaucrats whose action means a loss of votes; surely, legislators must be aware that voters want a say on what is brought to a vote; and surely, voters may reject proposals which in their view result in excessive budgets. Deviations may occur for a while, but sooner or later the public gets what it wants and governments stand to win or lose with fiscal issues. I am not persuaded that monopoly bureaus are a potentially far more serious threat than are private monopolies[29] or, for that matter, that power over agenda setting is *the* critical defect in the fiscal process.

Public Employee Voting

As a further cause of overexpansion, Leviathan theorists point to the voting behavior of government employees.[30] The hypothesis is that public employees will be more inclined to support large budgets than are private employees. Thus, as public employment increases, so does the voting power of public employees, generating a snowball effect. As shown in a recent study, this hypothesis may be questioned or at least qualified, even on theoretical grounds.[31] After all, public

---

28. See Mackay and Weaver (1978).

29. See Mackay and Weaver (1978), pp. 142, 161.

30. For an early statement of this proposition, see von Mises (1944). See also Tullock (1974), Bush and Denzau (1977), and Borcherding, Bush, and Spann (1977).

31. See Courant, Gramlich, and Rubinfeld (1979).

employee demands are limited, at least at the local level, by out-migration of private employees, public wage rates for a given budget size must fall as the number of employees increases, and the size of the budget is constrained by voter control. Nevertheless, some such bias may be expected to exist. The question is how important a factor this has been in leading to budgetary expansion.

As shown in table 1, lines 16 to 18, public employment now accounts for about 18 percent of the total, with 3 percent at the federal and 15 percent at the state and local level. With employed voters accounting for about two-thirds of eligible voters, public employees may be taken to make up 12 percent of the total.[32] This, however, is a lower limit, since retirees from public employment and members of public-employee families need also be accounted for, pushing the public-employee voting sector to an upper limit of 18 percent. Their effective voting impact further depends on (1) their relative voting participation and (2) the cohesiveness of their vote. Voting partici-pation varies greatly among eligible voters and, although I am not aware of current statistics on voting participation by public as against private employees, one may expect a higher participation among the former.[33] With voting participation of, say, 50 percent for voters as a whole, suppose that participation among public employees is 80 percent (the percentage generally applicable to union members), leav-ing that of other groups at 44 percent. Public employee votes would then account for 28 percent of the total. If voting in a bloc and in favor of budget expansion, this is a sizable group, which may have a substantial impact on election outcomes, especially at the municipal level. But the assumption of perfect bloc voting overstates this weight. Employees with seniority may view potential hiring differently from new employees, and family members may not share the public sector bias. Strangely, little empirical work has been done on this interesting and eminently researchable hypothesis.[34]

To demonstrate public employee voting as a cause of public sector expansion in past years, it is not enough however to show that there exists such bias. It must also be shown that this is an expanding

---

32. See *Statistical Abstract of the United States*, 1978, p. 520 (data for 1974).

33. Bush and Denzau (1977) refer to a study by Rosco Martin reporting local public employee participation in local elections in Austin, held in 1933, at 87.6 percent, as against an overall participation of 58.1 percent.

34. The papers referred to in note 28 only hypothesize on the basis of Martin's 1933 ratio. Also see Greenstein (1970) for voting participation of union members.

force. Attention should be given therefore to what has happened to
the share of public employment over time. As shown in table 1, the
rising ratio of expenditures to GNP has in no way been matched by
an increase in the ratio of public to total employment. Whereas the
ratio of total expenditure to GNP rose by nearly 80 percent from 1940
to 1978, the employment ratio rose by 46 percent only. The share
of federal expenditures paid as compensation to federal employees
fell sharply. Since almost the entire increase in public employment
occurred at the state–local level, it can offer no explanation for the
rising federal expenditure ratio but runs well ahead of the rising
state–local ratio.

Tax Illusion

The preceding argument has been that taxpayers are forced to pay
for a larger public sector than they want to have. Next it is argued
that overexpansion occurs because of fiscal illusion.[35] Taypayers are
taken to underestimate the full cost of public services and thus opt
for too large a budget.

Taxpayers, so it is argued, fail to perceive their full burden because
taxes are hidden in higher prices and lower incomes, or because the
tax system is too complex to be understood.[36] I recognize this potential
defect and have steadily favored visible taxes as a precondition of
efficient decision making. I do not feel comfortable with the proposition frequently advanced on the liberal side that hidden taxes are
desirable to offset a bias towards deficient budgets which results from
imbalance in campaign contributions and other forces. Visibility is
one of the main advantages of direct as against indirect taxes. Although
withholding has reduced this advantage of income taxes, emphasis

---

35. For an earlier discussion of fiscal illusion see Schmölders (1960) and Downs
(1960).

36. Goetz (1974) expands the hypothesis but without empirical evidence, while
Wagner (1976) makes an attempt at empirical verification. In search of a positive
relationship between the complexity of the tax structure and public sector size,
Wagner relates city expenditures to (among other variables) a measure of tax concentration (i.e. lack of dispersion among revenue sources) and finds a significant
negative relationship. The result is difficult to interpret, however, since the reader
is not given the characteristics of revenue composition which go with the various
degrees of concentration. For instance, if lack of concentration means heavy reliance
on the property tax, as it probably does, the result may simply indicate taxpayer
dislike of the property tax as against alternative revenue sources such as sales or
income taxes. A more searching analysis of the problem is called for.

on direct taxation in our federal tax system ranks it highly in this respect. But once more there are two sides to the hypothesis. Tax illusion may also work the other way. Apart from visibility, many other factors such as frequency and lumpiness of payment also affect the degree of tax perception. Just as consumers are more aware of the prices of items which absorb a large part of their household budget than they are of items which are purchased in small units, so taxpayers feel more burdened by taxes which come in lumpy installments as is frequently the case with the property tax. Moreover, the responsiveness to taxes depends on their perceived rather than actual incidence, and while the incidence of some taxes may not be perceived at all, that of others (e.g., the employer contribution to social security) may be perceived more than once. Moreover, people may well perceive declines in disposable income due to taxes as more burdensome than similar losses due to declines in earnings. It hurts more "to lose what you have," than not "to get what you don't have."

However this may be, fiscal illusion is not limited to the tax side only. It is no less plausible to maintain that the benefits of public expenditures are undervalued. The acquisition of private goods which are purchased personally and carried home is evident, and their benefits as valued by the purchase price are highly visible. Publicly provided and jointly consumed goods are not thus personalized. Their benefits are more remote and taken for granted, much like sunshine, and hence may not be given an adequate evaluation.[37]

These potential sources of underestimation of benefits are conveniently disregarded in the Leviathan literature.[38] Instead, the expenditure side is dealt with as a critique of political advertising. Where Galbraith argued that private-sector advertising leads to undervaluation of public services and deficient budgets,[39] the Leviathan position holds that political advertising leads to overexpansion.[40] While private advertising is taken to inform consumers, political advertising is said to support the state monopolist and to lead to overexpansion.[41] I find this position questionable. Surely political advertising is directed at urging tax reduction and budget cutting as

---

37. Downs (1960) argued precisely this point. Budget size will tend to be deficient because expenditure benefits seem more remote whereas tax burdens are felt directly.

38. Goetz (1974) and Wagner (1976) consider the tax side only.

39. See Galbraith (1956), p. 261.

40. See the contributions by Tuerck, Wagner, and Staff in Tuerck, ed. (1978).

41. See Wagner (1978).

well as service expansion, and it would be interesting to investigate the comparative amounts spent in both directions. Moreover, it can hardly be doubted that outlays on advocacy of private services much exceed that spent on advocacy of the public sector. Once more, the Leviathan literature leaves one with an altogether one-sided impression.

Putting the tax and expenditure sides together I can see how various forms of fiscal illusion may distort the outcome but I see no a priori reason to expect a net bias towards overexpansion. Empirical analysis is needed to test one or the other proposition.

Deficit Finance

A further aspect of fiscal illusion stressed in the Leviathan literature arises in the context of deficit finance.[42] Deficit finance of public services, by not calling for taxes, gives the impression that services may be obtained at zero cost and thus encourages overexpansion. There is merit to this argument and I have long been aware of a potential conflict between (1) the need for deficit finance to maintain high employment under depressed conditions and (2) the desirability of maintaining fiscal discipline by assuring that consumers of public services are aware of the opportunity cost which is involved.[43] To be sure, the conflict may be avoided by relying on tax reduction rather than expenditure increase but, in practice, arguments for expansionary fiscal action are likely to make for program expansion.

While granting the conflict, I do not think that deficit finance has in fact been *the* or even *a* major cause of U.S. budget expansion. State and local budgets have been essentially in balance with regard to current outlays and even finance of capital expenditures is typically subject to public vote. The conflict between deficit finance and fiscal discipline is thus essentially a federal issue. The question is how much the option of deficit finance has in fact contributed to the increase in federal expenditures. Federal deficits during the sixties and seventies ranged from zero to 10 percent of expenditures with an average of 8 percent. The potential impact of these deficits on expenditure levels might be viewed in various ways:

1.   Suppose expenditure determination operated under a rule permitting

---

42. See Buchanan and Wagner (1977) for what seems to me a highly alarmist presentation of the case.

43. See Musgrave (1958), p. 38.

8 percent of total outlays to be covered by deficit, thus reducing the tax price by 8 percent. Assuming unit price elasticity of demand for public services, tax financed expenditures would be unchanged and, adding a matching rate of 8/92, total expenditures would be raised by 8.69 percent. Taking the initial 1960 expenditure/GNP ratio of 26.9 percent, this will explain an increase to 29.2 percent only. This however would be a once and for all increase and could not serve to explain a continuing rise in the expenditure to GNP ratio.

2. Suppose next that the deficit is charged against the marginal expenditure dollar, cutting its tax cost to zero. Assuming the size of deficit to be constant and fixed independent of expenditure level, the resulting expenditure increase would (in analogy to the effects of a lump sum grant) at most reach the size of deficit, i.e. 8 percent of outlays.

3. A much larger effect on expenditure levels might result if deficit dollars can be created at will and charged against the marginal expenditure dollar, in which case an infinitely large budget level would come to be financed at next-to-zero tax cost, with the expenditure to GNP ratio approaching 100 percent.

The latter pattern clearly did not apply, as the deficit to expenditure ratio showed no upward trend. Even during the second half of the seventies the ratio did not exceed 10 percent. It appears that "cost free" expenditure increases induced by way of deficit finance hardly exceeded the increase in deficit which in fact occurred. With an increase in deficit of about $40 billion from the early sixties to the late seventies, and an increase in expenditures of about $300 billion, this calculus suggests that at the most only slightly more than 10 percent thereof may be imputed to the deficit effect.

But all this is a rather tenuous interpretation. Annual fiscal behavior shows no evident relationship between expenditure increase and deficit, and it is difficult if not impossible to determine what parts of the annual expenditure changes are imputable to the availability of deficit finance. The reason of course is that changes in deficit do not only reflect discretionary changes in expenditure behavior but also built-in changes in tax revenue. Indeed, the full employment budget was close to balance throughout the period, with fluctuations in deficit reflecting very largely built-in changes in revenue from their full employment level. Rising deficits due to built-in revenue losses, in fact, might be viewed as retarding expenditure expansion, given a congressional desire to avoid excessive deficit levels. Contrary to the

Leviathan message, experience does not suggest that a massive break-down of fiscal discipline, generated by the impact of Keynesian eco-nomics, has been a major cause of expenditure increase.

Inflation

We have noted that depressed economic conditions calling for an expansionary fiscal policy may generate excess budgets. But once more, objective analysis calls for a further proposition. This is the no less plausible and more timely hypothesis that restrictive policy, called for under the inflationary conditions of the present setting, may depress the budget unduly.

Given a high rate of inflation and the popular if mistaken belief that inflation is to be blamed primarily on excessive public spending, there is strong pressure to fight inflation by curtailing the budget deficit.[44] This might be done by raising taxes but, as in the expansion case, there is likely to be major pressure for the expenditure cuts. Resulting cutbacks or the omission of expansion that would otherwise be undertaken might well exceed what would be called for as a matter of efficient budgeting if no compensatory action was needed, i.e., if resource allocation between social and private goods was in line with consumer preference at a noninflationary full employment level of income. This is simply the mirror image of overspending under pres-sure for expansion. Given our inflationary age, the bias of stabilization

---

44. I do not share the contention, so popular in an election year, that the federal deficit has been the main cause of monetary expansion and thereby of inflation. This contention (1) overlooks inflationary forces on the supply side, including the dynamics of wage-price escalation and the rising cost of crude oil; (2) errs in relating demand-side inflation to monetary expansion only; and (3) is mistaken in viewing the expansion of the federal deficit as the prime cause of money growth.

My immediate concern is with (3). Here the strategic variable in monetarist analysis is the growth in high powered money or in the monetary base. What has been the linkage between its growth and the federal deficit? During the 1960s, the deficit averaged $1.3 billion while the average annual increase in the monetary base was $2.7 billion. For the first half of the 70s, the deficit averaged $14 billion while the average increase in the base was $6 billion. For the second half of the 70s the corresponding levels were $42 and $9 billion. The lack of correspondence between deficit and growth of monetary base is evident and should not be surprising. Changes in monetary base are a function of Federal Reserve policy, mainly open market operations. This policy is adjusted to respond to changes in economic conditions, changes which involve consumers, investors, the foreign sector and (but by no means only) federal finance.

policy may well be the very opposite of that postulated by the Leviathan doctrine.

I would, however, add another and perhaps more important way in which inflation bears on fiscal discipline. This is through the effects on built-in revenue gains. Nominal increases in income under the progressive income tax generate an increase in effective tax rates at given levels of real income. Assuming the cost of public services to rise in line with the general price level, this permits expansion of public services without requiring the explicit sanction of legislative action to increase tax rates, a factor which may tend to generate a budget in excess of that resulting if such action was required. At the federal level, the tendency towards a built-in increase in the ratio of income tax revenue to personal income was largely offset by repeated legislative action for reducing rates and increasing exemptions or deductions.[45] But even this does not entirely neutralize the problem. By gaining approval for tax reduction which in fact tends merely to offset the built-in increase, legislators may avoid pressures for genuine tax reduction or for expenditure cuts that may have resulted otherwise. Moreover, the offsetting tax reductions resulted in substantially shifting the distribution of the income tax burden (from both ends towards

---

Following the same development from a somewhat different angle, it is interesting to note the weight of U.S. debt in the expansion of bank assets. In the 60s, total loans and investments of commercial banks doubled while their holdings of U.S. debt declined. During the first half of the 70s total holdings rose by 70 percent with less than one percent thereof accounted for by U.S. debt. For the second half of the 70s total holdings rose by 57 percent with 10 percent thereof in U.S. debt. Taking the 70s as a whole, only 6 percent of the increase in total holdings took this form. This picture is qualified by extending the analysis to Savings and Loan Associations, but the essential finding remains the same: the main source of expansion of bank assets, and with it of bank credit, has been the deficit of the household sector, i.e. the issuance of private debt in the form of consumer credit and mortgages, and not of U.S. obligations. By the same token, the expansion of the monetary base provided for (rightly or wrongly) by Federal Reserve policy was directed very largely at accommodating the supply of private and not of public debt.

Our focus has been on the relationship of the deficit to monetary expansion, since this is usually taken to be the key factor in blaming inflation on the federal budget. But, as was noted under (2), the monetary implications of the deficit are not all that matters. The effects on aggregate demand of an "active" deficit caused by budget expansion will be quite different from those of a "passive" deficit due to a shrinkage in the tax base, and so forth. There is more to the story than effects on money supply, but to complete the tale would transgress (if I have not already done so) the statutory limitations for the length of footnotes.

45. See Pechman and Sunley (1977).

the middle) which most likely would not have received legislative approval had there been an explicit adjustment.

The offsetting federal action was not matched with regard to state income taxes, and sales tax revenue as well showed a surprisingly high income elasticity over the inflationary decade of the 70's. Both these developments enabled the ratio of state expenditures to personal income to rise without matching legislative action to increase rates, permitting some states, such as California, to generate surpluses in state budgets. Much the same development occurred in some instances of local finance, where the property tax base rose faster than the price level. This was the case especially in California where the combination of rather current assessment practices and rapid rise in the value of residential housing resulted in a sharp increase in the ratio of property tax to homeowner's income, a development which goes far towards explaining the Proposition 13 climate and subsequent constitutional amendments.

Conclusion

Having sketched the main lines along which Leviathan theorists advance the hypotheses of overexpansion, I conclude that there are indeed many reasons why one would expect budget decisions to be imperfect, but on balance no clear bias emerges which tells me that the budget is over- rather than underexpanded. As I see it, the voting bias can go in either direction. The conclusion of bureaucratic overexpansion largely follows from the behavioral assumptions of the model and from its disregard of the checks built into the budgetary process. Public employee voting may be a factor but little effort has been made to provide empirical support for the hypothesis. Fiscal illusion works in both directions, with an uncertain net effect. The bias introduced through deficit finance poses a problem in fiscal discipline, but it has hardly been a major factor in U.S. budget growth. The need for inflationary constraint may well work in the opposite direction. The bias resulting from built-in revenue gains has been a factor at the state and local level, and so forth. In all, there is no simple a priori reason to conclude that the net effect of all these factors has been towards excessive expenditure growth.

My contention, to repeat, is not that budget levels are "just right." There may or may not have been overexpansion. Rather it is that Leviathan reasoning, although presented as positive theory, has been

largely drawn from biased and untested models.[46] Little effort is made
to view both sides of the hypotheses and important aspects are omitted,
including the role of campaign contributions and of political pressures
resulting from supplies of products purchased by government. More
generally, the approach suffers from its exclusive reliance on a micro
and game theoretical framework, disregarding thereby the broader
aspects of social-political interaction which enter into the actual world
of fiscal politics and into the shaping of fiscal institutions.[47] All this
would not matter if it were simply a question of playing theoretical
games. But having created the devil, Leviathan theorists must then
proceed to exorcise him or her; and this, as shown in my concluding
section, distorts the pattern of proposed fiscal reform.

Is the Level of Transfers Excessive?

I now turn to the distribution function of budget policy. Since this
has been given less emphasis in the Leviathan literature, I shall deal
with it more briefly.

As shown in table 1, rising transfers have been responsible for the
entire growth in the budget-to-GNP ratio over the last two decades.
While the overall ratio rose from 27 percent in 1960 to 32 percent
in 1978, that for transfers rose from 7 to 12 percent. Of this, nearly
two-thirds was accounted for by social security and welfare, mostly
the former, with the remainder reflecting interest, veterans benefits,
and other items. Estimation of the resulting degree of redistribution
is difficult, and this is not the place at which to consider the complexities involved. Much depends on how the problem is formulated,
which groups are considered, and on whether changes in annual or
lifetime incomes are to be determined.[48] However, some conclusions

---

46. An interesting exception may be found in Borcherding's study (Borcherding,
1977b). Reviewing the expenditure growth from 1902 to 1970, Borcherding finds
that about one half of the actual growth can be traced to price income and population
changes leaving the other half to be accounted for by varying "political" and presumably distorting forces. It is not possible here to review this analysis with the many
assumptions which enter. However, it would seem at the least that separate treatment
should be given to (1) defense and civilian outlays in the purchase total and (2)
purchases and transfer components in the expenditure total. Nevertheless, this is an
interesting and instructive study.

47. For a discussion of fiscal sociology, see Musgrave (1980).

48. For a discussion of the problem, see Musgrave, Case, and Leonard (1974).

may be ventured. Clearly, the major redistributional impact results from the expenditure side of the budget since the overall tax structure is more or less proportional. Moreover, the major redistributive impact on the expenditure side stems from the transfer system. While low income-oriented service programs have grown, benefits of many programs accrue more heavily to middle- and upper-income groups. In all, it appears that the impact of fiscal redistribution on overall measures of inequality such as the Gini coefficient is quite modest, but that the fiscal factor becomes much more important if the share of the bottom decile or quintile is considered.[49]

Normative Aspects

Beginning with a normative appraisal of this outcome, I distinguish between two issues. One is whether the implicit policy target "correctly" reflects the norms of fairness or justice in distribution. The second is whether the policies chosen are efficient means of implementing the target.

As noted before, the usefulness of economic analysis in setting norms for the proper distribution and, hence, redistribution policy is limited. In determining what constitutes legitimate redistribution, various approaches may be taken:

1. The argument may begin with the premise that the given state of distribution is just, so mandatory redistribution is not permissible. This leaves open only a process of voluntary redistribution, where Mrs. Rich gives to Mr. Poor because she derives satisfaction from his improvement.[50]

2. The state of equality or inequality may be viewed as a social good, where A prefers a Gini coefficient of .5 whereas B prefers one of .3. Acting alone, neither can make a significant contribution to bringing about the desired change in the coefficient from its existing level of say, 0.4. The desired state of distribution thus becomes a social good, automatic provision of which is blocked by the free rider problem. Budgetary action and mandatory execution are required to secure the adjustment.[51]

---

49. Here transfer receipts are a high multiple of earnings.
50. See Hochman and Rogers (1969).
51. See Thurow (1971). Note that the conditional nature of the entitlement to prebudget earnings is considered subject to amendment by vote only in the context of overall redistribution in which equal treatment is given to people with equal income, thus ruling out changes aimed at individual income recipients.

3.   Retaining the premise that the distribution of earnings (prior to budgetary adjustments) is just, the initial entitlement may nevertheless be considered subject to change by a voting rule (simple majority or otherwise) aimed at securing whatever state of distribution the majority desires.[52]

4.   All these approaches take the existing state of distribution as points of departure—although (1) more absolutely than (2) and (3)—and hence allow for secondary redistribution only. Alternatively, it may be postulated that the given distribution has no basis in entitlements, thus calling for budgetary redistribution as the means of implementing an optimal pattern, be it "fair" or welfare maximizing.[53]

Approach (1) may be dealt with as a market problem, subject to the efficiency analysis of economics. No budget is required. Approach (2) requires budgetary action to implement what is essentially a social goods problem. Approach (3) similarly involves a budgetary process. Approach (4) finally poses the basic array of issues involved in establishing norms for a just distribution, be it on the basis of natural law, or some form of social contract. As noted before, this is a range of options among which economics offers no clear choice.

Setting aside the perplexities of determining legitimate redistribution objectives, critical examination *can* be applied to whether policies are in fact designed so as to accomplish the desired objective. For instance, the rural electrification program which was voted half a century ago to assist small farmers may now go to support well-to-do owners of summer homes. Or, the policy objective may be valid but the policies used may be ineffective in achieving it or do so at a higher than necessary efficiency cost. Here the economists' contribution becomes essential since cost-effectiveness analysis must be applied to redistributive policies as well as to the delivery of services. Redistribution policies should be designed so as to involve the least efficiency cost, as developed in optimal taxation theory.[54] Beyond this, economic analysis may be helpful in ascertaining the distributive implications of alternative approaches to policy objectives which in themselves are not distribution oriented. An especially important illustration is given by policies to further economic growth. Much depends on how growth is achieved. While growth ultimately tends

52. Such a scheme is described though not subscribed to by Buchanan (1975).

53. See Rawls (1971) and Arrow (1973).

54. Tullock (1971) and (1974) and Browning (1974) note the additional cost of lobbying for redistribution programs.

to benefit almost all groups, it also involves initial costs and it remains relevant (especially in the shorter run) to consider how these costs are shared. Since investment decisions tend to be made by high income people, such policies tend to conflict with redistributional goals and little thought has been given to developing growth incentives in which distribution is neutral.[55]

Positive Aspects

Turning from the normative to the positive side of the problem, it is difficult to ascertain to what extent the actual budget reflects each of the four categories set forth above. Surely, the voluntary giving approach (1) accounts for only a minor part. Treasury matching of charitable contributions at the taxpayers' marginal rate (a tax expenditure which does not appear in our expenditure-to-GNP ratio) is perhaps the major item, but most such transfers occur outside the budgetary framework. Items (2) to (4) are difficult to distinguish, even on a conceptual level. Moreover, voting on redistribution may reflect not only the implementation of adjustments as legitimated by some prior social contract or constitutional agreement, but also a Hobbesonian free-for-all in the grabbing of income shares. This need not be overt, but voting may reflect responses to the actual or perceived threats to the stability of the system, with potentially more drastic events forestalled if social pressures are appeased.[56]

May one expect redistribution to be of growing importance as the Leviathan framework would suggest? The dynamics of policy change will differ with our four cases. In line with (1), giving will proceed until the marginal gain to the donors matches their loss and then terminate. Under (2) and (3), which combine initial endowments with subsequent budgetary adjustment, the equilibrating process is more complex. Choice by voting in this case cannot be modeled in simple median voter terms, since voters with a median Gini preference may not also be voters with a median income. Moreover, views regarding the desired Gini coefficient (or, say, the desirable share to be received by the lowest quartile) change over time.

However, even here it appears that the redistribution process will proceed at a declining rate. Assume for the extreme case that everyone votes for such redistribution as leaves him or her in a better position.

---

55. For an early discussion of this problem, see Musgrave (1963).
56. See O'Connor (1973).

A vote in favor of complete levelling of incomes can carry a majority only as long as the median voter's income is below the average, a condition which in fact is met. But sequential votes in favor of successive levellings from the top down will command majorities only until the levelling reaches down to the median income.[57] The lower the median income relative to the mean, the more levelling will occur.

Tracing the path of redistribution, it may well be that successive redistribution measures (working from the top down) have lowered the level of income up to which voters may expect to gain from further such policies. At this level drops towards the median income, the majority available for further redistribution shrinks and finally disappears. This suggests an outlook rather different from that presented in the Leviathan prognosis. Note, however, that a distinction must be drawn between the median voter and the median income recipient, and allowance must be made for the fact that voting participation tends to increase with income. Future political development may bring about an increased voting participation at the lower end of the scale, a process which would lower the income of the median voter relative to average income, thereby increasing the scope for redistribution by majority vote.[58]

Given these possibilities it seems surprising that in fact so little redistribution has occurred. There are various reasons for this. For one thing, lower income people may reject levelling as they expect to do better later—witness the fate of McGovern's estate tax proposal in 1972. For another, they may allow for the effects of levelling on their own earnings and the earnings of others available for transfer, be it immediately through labor supply effects or via the longer run responses through growth effects. Also, redistributive voting may be inhibited by respect for accepted ethics of entitlement to earnings.

A further deterrent to continuing redistribution results from the previously noted shift in political values from centralization to decentralization. While there is much to be said for neighborhood concern in the context of voluntary giving, it is also apparent (although not evident to small-is-beautiful romantics) that redistribution based

---

57. This pattern disregards the possibility of discontinuous redistribution, e.g. transfers from the lower and upper end of the income scale towards the middle. For a discussion along these lines, see Niskanen (1971) and (1975).

58. For a discussion of this point, see Meltzer (1979). It is also interesting to note that a similar argument already appears in de Tocqueville (1835). For a discussion of his view, see Peacock and Wiseman (1979).

on majority vote can function only on a nationwide scale. If concentrated locally, the very effort is aborted by low-income people pursuing those with high incomes, and the latter fleeing those with low incomes, i.e., the familiar urban–suburban patterns. Emphasis on decentralization therefore provides a further barrier to continuing redistribution.

Conclusion

In all, it is evident that both normative and positive modeling of budgetary redistribution is exceedingly difficult, but the analytical intractability of the problem is no reason for ruling it out of court. Some writers view consideration of distribution as slightly naughty, upsetting as it were an otherwise harmonious order, and involving jealousy or greed. This view is unacceptable on both normative and positive grounds. Distributive justice, as seen by most people, is not divinely preordained but depends on society's sense of entitlement and fairness; and adjudication of claims to shares in scarce "goods" is at the heart of the social problem and not limited (as some seem to believe) to poverty settings. Distributional disputes rightly enter into the political process of a democratic society, and it is proper, indeed preferable, that they should find their expression in budgetary rather than other policy tools. There is no universal criterion which tells us that this or that degree of redistribution is too much but there is much to be said for choosing a democratically determined budget process (as distinct from, say, street riots) as the proper arena.

Fiscal Reform

There are plenty of reasons why fiscal policies, like other forms of human endeavor, may fall short of efficient performance. Constructive reforms are needed to improve the framework of decision making. There can be no disagreement about this. Indeed, my early distinction between and separation of the "three branches" (allocation, distribution, stabilization) of fiscal action was directed precisely at this purpose.[59] Where I disagree with the Leviathan theorists is on the content of reform. The objective of institutional adjustment, as I see it, should be to induce more efficient decision making, be it towards expansion or contraction. It should not be to correct for an unproven hypothesis of overexpansion, or to implement value judgments in favor

---

59. See Musgrave (1958), chap. 1.

of small budgets. Moreover, the process of implementation should be by congressional procedure and not by constitutional limitation.

Brakes on Leviathan

Reform proposals, advanced in the Leviathan literature, include various suggestions, most of which are based on the presumed need to correct for overexpansion. Suggested reforms, designed to restrain Leviathan, include:

1. Overall limitations on the size or rate of growth of the budget;
2. A requirement of two-thirds majority;
3. Increased use of executive veto;
4. Interbureau competition in the supply of public services;
5. Competition among review committees;
6. Reducing the monopoly power of agenda setting;
7. Use of progressive rates of taxation;
8. Avoidance of broad-based taxes.

Among these, item 1 has received most attention, and economists, including Milton Friedman and William Niskanen, have been leaders in the movement. Various states have imposed tax or expenditure limitations, the limit being defined, in most cases, in relation to personal income in the jurisdiction. Similar proposals are being advanced at the federal level. In other instances, the permissible increase in expenditures is limited to the rise in the price level, so as to keep expenditures from rising in real terms. Such limits which fix the public sector share in income, to be sure, are less objectionable than would be the setting of absolute ceilings, but they still place an arbitrary shackle on the fiscal process.[60] Since upper limits tend to be transformed readily into floors, they in fact establish a constant share as a norm. Clearly, this is incompatible with an efficient budgetary system. The income elasticity of demand for public services need not be unity—changes in relative prices may affect the appropriate share, as will changing requirements due to altered demographic, international, and other conditions. All these factors suggest that the efficient expenditure ratio will not be constant but will call for adjustment to changing conditions.

If it is assumed that simple majority rule leads to overexpansion

---

60. For an analysis of the effect of various types of limitations, see Ladd (1978) and Courant and Rubinfeld (1979).

of the budget, a requirement for a larger majority is, of course, a move in the right direction. If the hypothesis is mistaken, such a move would cause inefficiency.[61] Moreover, even if there is some presumption regarding the direction of error, it remains to be determined whether two-thirds (rather than 60 or 70 percent) is the proper level. To be sure, budgeting by unanimous agreement would be ideal if there were no difficulty in securing the revelation of preferences. But since such difficulty exists, it in no way follows that increasing the required majority will improve the solution. If each voter were given a veto right, no provision for social goods would result and the efficiency loss to the economy would be enormous. In the absence of a more conclusive demonstration that a higher majority is called for, the proposition that all voters should be given equal weight, and the implicit sanction of simple majority rule, remain appealing.[62] At the same time it appears that adjustment in the required majority level (provided that it could be determined correctly) would be superior to the rigidities introduced by imposition of a ceiling.

The suggestion that increased use be made of executive veto on particular budget items falls outside the Leviathan framework as it emphasizes the role of the executive. Nevertheless, it is a useful proposal, which has had broad support for some time. Given the right to such veto, the executive would be enabled to prevent passage of marginal legislation which cannot be checked if attached to essential bills.

Proposals to increase competition among bureaus are in logical response to the hypothesis of oversupply based on bureau monopoly.[63] I find it difficult to visualize just how such competition would function. A multiplication of bureaucratic institutions (imagine, for instance, 10 HEWs) would seem to be needed and, contrary to consolidation, would add to the bureaucratic apparatus. Integration of bureau claims into an effective budgetary process, increased use of contracting with competing private firms for the delivery of public services, improved

---

61. Niskanen's attempted demonstration (Niskanen, 1971, p. 181) that a two-thirds rule would be more efficient is based on an ingenious but highly simplified model of the U.S. fiscal system. All the reservations noted in my earlier pages again apply.

62. This concern seems to be shared by Niskanen, who urges prior attention to other measures.

63. See Niskanen (1975) and Mackay and Weaver (1978).

bidding procedures, and similar measures seem to me a better approach.

Proposals to facilitate broader participation in agenda setting, similarly, follow from the hypothesis of agenda monopoly. While widening participation in agenda setting is attractive, I doubt the overriding importance of agenda monopoly as a source of difficulty. Moreover, I would not like to see such a widening lead to large-scale use of public referenda. While attractive under the rubric of "grass roots democracy," such procedures induce single-issue voting with its divisive consequences. As I see it, coalition building, which can operate only in the framework of representative government, is an essential prerequisite for a functioning democracy. Needless to say, commodity bundling to maximize bureau output does not fulfill this same function.

A progressive distribution of tax burdens may be helpful in approximating a system of Lindahl pricing, given the assumption that income elasticities for demand are in excess of price elasticities, as they may well be. However, this argument applies to general social goods only and not to programs whose benefits are addressed to particular income groups, and it certainly does not hold for transfer programs. It has also been suggested that the revenue-raising ability of government should be curtailed by excluding part of the potential base from taxation (a recommendation in stunning conflict with the widely accepted notion that broad-based taxes are desirable) and that tax bases should be chosen so as to be complementary to the public service rendered. These latter suggestions spring from so extreme a drawing of the Leviathan monster as to permit exclusion from our consideration.[64]

Alternative Reforms

As I see it, most of these reform proposals mirror the Leviathan image, thereby reflecting an unrealistic reading of the sources of government failure. In my view, reform should address the major needs, for (1) integration of tax and expenditure decisions, (2) integration of decision making so as to combine the components of the budget into a coherent overall program, and (3) separation of programs addressing the provision of public goods from others addressing objects of redistribution. I will note briefly the rationale for these re-

---

64. See Brennan and Buchanan (1977, 1978).

quirements, without however attempting to spell out the detailed institutional arrangements which would be needed to meet them.

The case for integrating tax and expenditure decision is evident. It is clearly impossible for voters to express preferences for programs unless they know the cost, and preferences will differ depending on how the cost is divided. This is the essence of the Wicksellian message (and not the much-emphasized concern with unanimity) which, notwithstanding some attention to earmarking, seems largely neglected in most of the Leviathan modeling of the problem.[65] In some instances, linkage between the two blades of the scissors is provided, more or less effectively, as in the case of property taxes which specify assignments of revenue shares to particular program areas. In others, a vague beginning is made, as in the new congressional budget process where the overall size of the budget is related (if only too loosely) to tax legislation, or in the executive budget proposals in which attention is paid to both the tax and expenditure side. These are beginnings, but clearly more need be done. The previously noted relation of budgetary balance to fiscal discipline is also relevant in this context. The requirement to balance the budget makes sense as an instrument of fiscal discipline, were it not for the conflicting needs of stabilization policy.[66] Nevertheless, it seems unfortunate that consideration of rules relating to full employment or marginal balance, which were in the center of attention a decade or two ago, have now been replaced with the cruder techniques of overall expenditure and tax limitation.

Similarly, integration of partial program decisions into an overall budgeting process is of central importance for achieving an efficient use of public resources. I find it distressing that this central requirement is given so little attention in the Leviathan literature, partly because the role of the executive is disregarded and partly because "by its nature" government is assumed to be incapable of such constructive action. The budget reforms of 1974 again provide a step in the right direction but once more the task is far from complete. How much better it would be if all of us concerned with fiscal reform were to join in pushing this aspect, rather than advocating limits which stand to impair as much as improve the scope for efficient action. Of course, there can be no detailed and comprehensive review of all

---

65. See, for instance, Buchanan (1963).

66. I here pass over the distinction between current and capital outlays, and the argument that the latter (on grounds of intergeneration equity) should be debt financed.

programs each year, but even marginal adjustments are important, supplemented by a more detailed analysis of various parts of the budget on a rotating basis. Various plans for sunset legislation offer a useful approach, as does what appears to be a current shift in budget procedure from detailed analysis of each item to a more comprehensive if less detailed balancing of the merits of alternative programs.

Separation of policies designed to provide for public services from others to achieve redistributive objectives, is, perhaps, a more controversial issue, but I continue to believe that it is of major importance.[67] I recognize, of course, that public service programs may have significant distributional objectives, so that the distribution function is not simply one of transfers. I also recognize that the efficiency cost of redistribution may, in some instances, be less if undertaken through services in kind than through transfers; and that equity considerations, in line with concepts of categorical equity, may indeed call for redistribution in kind.[68] Yet I think that these are exceptions rather than the rule and that mixing of the two objectives greatly increases the difficulty of efficient political action. In principle, public services should be financed by benefit taxes (which may or may not be progressive depending on income and price elasticities), while redistribution should be implemented through a negative income tax. In theory this calls for two tax systems which, of course, may be integrated in practical administration.

The Constitutional Issue

In concluding, I offer some comments on whether fiscal reforms should be made through legislative and executives measures, or whether they should be written into the Constitution. Emphasis upon constitution-making and the distinction between constitutional and postconstitutional action plays a major part in the Leviathan literature and should therefore be noted here.[69]

The basic question is how to draw a dividing line between what does and what does not belong in a constitution. A first purpose of constitution-making is to protect basic rights and liberties, freedoms which are inviolate and cannot be tampered with. These include such matters as freedom of worship and protection against bodily harm.

---

67. See Musgrave (1958), chap. 1.
68. See Tobin (1970) and Okun (1975).
69. See Buchanan (1971) and Frey (1979).

While there is no sharp dividing line between "basic" liberties and lesser goods, the case for a fiscal constitution can hardly be made on grounds that not having the expenditure-to-GNP ratio exceed 33.2 percent, or not having marginal tax rates rise above 50 percent are basic rights of this sort.[70] Surely, there are many other issues (e.g., abortion vs. right-to-life) which are more fundamental and would have prior claim to constitutional prescription. However, it must be admitted that the United States Constitution, as a historically arrived-at instrument, is not limited to "basic" provisions of this sort and that the literature on constitutional law is painfully short of guidance as to what should or should not be included.[71]

A second case for constitution-making is to determine the rules by which other and lesser issues are to be decided. The generally accepted rule is majority vote with two-thirds required for certain exceptions only. The specific question then is whether fiscal matters belong to the group of issues for which a more demanding majority should be required by constitutional provision. To so conclude, one might argue that entitlements to the acquisition of income are inviolate except by abridgement through two-thirds majority and that, therefore, a special constitutionally guaranteed exception from the simple majority rule is called for. As noted before, I do not find this persuasive. If, instead, it is argued that fiscal issues need special constraints because (due to technical reasons, not applicable to other issues) majority rule gives biased results, it seems to me that the remedy for such a technical fault should be provided for in the more flexible framework of executive or legislative action. Moreover, there are serious difficulties in writing a provision for constitutional limitation so as to (1) maintain sufficient flexibility when exceptions are needed, (2) prevent circumvention by techniques such as tax expenditures, placing programs outside the budget, or substitution of regulation for public services, and (3) retain sufficient clarity and simplicity to permit judicial interpretation of the constitutional content.

I do not wish to deny of course that the ongoing process of political decision making has to proceed in the framework of a constitutional rule. It would be too cumbersome and destabilizing to remain in

---

70. Nozick (1972) argues in the context of his entitlement theory that taxation in general involves violation of the basic Lockean principle of entitlement. This makes sense if that principle is accepted. Yet, it can hardly be maintained that a rate of 51 percent is in conflict with such entitlement while one of 50 percent is not.

71. This includes even so recent and basic a work as that of Tribe (1978).

permanent constitutional convention.[72] Yet, I find it difficult to conceive of constitution-making as a once-and-for-all, initial act by which basic rules are established for all future. The "initial state" from which social choices are to be made is not to be viewed as a unique historical event long behind us, but remains present and choices are subject to reexamination. The role of constitution-making as a philosophical issue should thus be seen as a continuing task. Values may change and new issues may arise which will have to be met by new provisions. This does not deny the role of tradition and the wisdom of the Founding Fathers, but neither does it close the door for reassessment. I realize that this conception of constitution-making as a continuum runs into conflict with the fact that a historically determined constitution must set the rules for its own change, leaving the idea of constitutional process (which is needed for day-to-day operation) in conflict with the idea of continuum of the "initial condition." While I cannot resolve this problem (and, unhappily, find little guidance thereto) my instinct tells me to be wary of constitutional constraints which narrow options, especially where the proposed constraints (e.g., budget limitations) may be based on a misreading of the actual defects in the prevailing system.

REFERENCES

Amacher, R., Tollison, R., and Willett, T. 1975. A budget size in a democracy: a review of the arguments. *Public Finance Quarterly* 3:99–120.

Arrow, K. 1973. Some ordinalist-utilitarian notes on Rawls' theory of justice. *The Journal of Philosophy* 70:245–64.

Baumol, W. 1967. Macroeconomics of unbalanced growth, the anatomy of urban crisis. *American Economic Review* 58:415–26.

Beck, M. 1976. The expanding public sector: some contrary evidence. *National Tax Journal* 29:15–22.

Becker, G. 1976. *The economic approach to human behavior*. Chicago, Ill.: University of Chicago Press.

Borcherding, T.E., ed. 1977a. *Budgets and bureaucrats: the sources of public sector growth*. Durham, N.C.: Duke University Press.

Borcherding, T.E. 1977b. One hundred years of public spending, 1870–1970. In *Budgets and bureaucrats*, T.E. Borcherding, ed., pp. 19–70. Durham, N.C.: Duke University Press.

Borcherding, T., Bush, W., and Spann, R. 1977. The effects on public spending of the divisibility of public outputs in consumption, bureaucratic power and the size of tax sharing groups. In *Budgets and bureaucrats: the sources of public*

---

72. For emphasis on institutional arrangements as a device to reduce transaction costs, see Mackay and Weaver (1979).

sector growth, ed. T.E. Borcherding, pp. 211–29. Durham, N.C.: Duke University Press.

Brennan, G., and Buchanan, J. 1977. Towards a constitution for Leviathan. *Journal of Public Economics* 8:255–73.

Brennan, G., and Buchanan, J. 1978. Tax instruments as constraints on the disposition of public revenue. *Journal of Public Economics*, 9:301–18.

Browning, J. 1974. On the welfare cost of transfers. *Kyklos* 27:374–77.

Buchanan, J. 1963. The economics of earmarked taxes. *Journal of Political Economy*.

Buchanan, J. 1974. *The limits of liberty*. Chicago, Ill: University of Chicago Press.

Buchanan, J. 1975. The political economy of franchise in the welfare state. In *Capitalism and freedom: problems and prophets*, ed. A. Selden, pp. 52–77. Charlottesville, Va.: University of Virginia Press.

Buchanan, J., and Tullock, G. 1962. *The calculus of consent*. Ann Arbor, Mich.: University of Michigan Press.

Buchanan, J., and Wagner, R. 1977. *Democracy in deficit*. New York, N.Y.: Academic Press.

Bush, W., and Denzau, A. 1977. The voting behavior of bureaucrats and public sector growth, In *Budgets and bureaucrats: the sources of public sector growth*, T. Borcherding, ed., pp. 45–76. Durham, N.C.: Duke University Press.

Courant, P., Gramlich, E., and Rubinfeld, D. 1979. Public employee market power and the level of government spending. *American Economic Review* 69:806–17.

Courant, P., and Rubinfeld, D. 1979. On the welfare effects of tax legislation. Manuscript.

Denzau, A., Mackay, R., and Weaver, C. 1979. Spending limitations, agenda control and voters' expectations. *National Tax Journal*, Supplement 32:189–99.

Downs, A. 1960. Why the government budget is too small in a democracy. *World Politics*. 13:541–63.

Durbin, E. 1977. Comment. *National Tax Journal* 30:97.

Galbraith, K. 1956. *The affluent society*. Boston, Mass.: Houghton Mifflin.

Gerth, H., and Mills, C. 1970. *From Max Weber: essays in sociology*. New York, N.Y.: Oxford University Press.

Goetz, C. 1974. Fiscal illusion in state and local finance. In *Budgets and bureaucrats: the sources of public sector growth*, ed. T. Borcherding. Durham, N.C.: Duke University Press.

Greenstein, F. 1970. *The American party system and the American people*. Englewood Cliffs, N.J.: Prentice Hall.

Frey, B. 1979. Economic policy by constitutional constraint. *Kyklos* 32:307–19.

Hobbes, T. 1651. *Leviathan*. The Library of Liberal Arts. 1958. Indianapolis, Ind., and New York, N.Y.: Bobbs-Merrill.

Hochman, H., and Rogers, J. 1969. Pareto optimal redistribution. *American Economic Review*, pp. 219–234.

Johansen, L. 1978. The theory of public goods: misplaced emphasis? *Journal of Public Economics* 7:147–52.

Ladd, H. 1978. An economic evaluation of state limitations on local taxing and spending powers. *National Tax Journal* 31:1–13.

Locke, J. 1690. *Two treatises of government*. Ed. P. Laslett. Cambridge, England: Cambridge University Press.

Mackay, R., and Weaver, C. 1978. Monopoly bureaus and fiscal outcomes: deductive models and implications for reform. In *Policy analysis and deductive reasoning*, ed. G. Tullock and R. Wagner. Lexington, Mass.: D.C. Heath.

Margolis, J. 1975. Comment. *Journal of Law and Economics* 51:645–59.

Meltzer, A., and Richard, S. 1979. Taxes, votes and the distribution of income. Manuscript.

Musgrave, R.A. 1958. *The theory of public finance*. New York, N.Y.: McGraw-Hill.

Musgrave, R.A. 1963. Growth with equity. *American Economic Review*, Proceedings, 53:323–33.

Musgrave, R.A. 1980. Theories of fiscal crisis. In *Essays on tax theory and policy*, ed. H. Aaron and M. Boskin. Washington, D.C.: The Brookings Institution.

Musgrave, R.A., Case, K., and Leonard, H. 1974. The distribution of fiscal burdens and benefits. *Public Finance Quarterly* 2:259–311.

Musgrave, R.A., and Peacock, A. 1958. *Classics in the theory of public finance*. London, England: MacMillan.

Niskanen, W. 1971. *Bureaucracy and representative government*. Chicago, Ill.: Aldine.

Niskanen, W. 1975. Bureaucrats and politicians. *The Journal of Law and Economics*, pp. 617–59.

Nozick, R. 1974. *Anarchy, state and utopia*. New York, N.Y.:

O'Connor, J. 1973. *The fiscal crisis of the state*. New York, N.Y.: St. Martins Press.

Okun, A. 1975. *Equality and efficiency*. Washington, D.C.: The Brookings Institution.

Peacock, A., and Wiseman, J. 1967. *The growth of public expenditures in the United Kingdom*. Princeton, N.J.: National Bureau of Economic Research.

Peacock, A., and Wiseman, J. 1979. Approaches to the analysis of public expenditure growth. *Public Finance Quarterly* 7:1–23.

Pechman, J., and Sunley, E. 1977. Inflation adjustments for the federal income tax. In *Inflation and the income tax*, ed. H. Aaron. Washington, D.C. The Brookings Institution.

Rawls, J. 1971. *A theory of justice*. Cambridge, Mass.: Harvard University Press.

Riker, W. 1978. The cause of public sector growth: resources and minority advantages. Manuscript.

Romer, T., and Rosenthal, H. 1978. Political resource allocation, controlled agenda, and the status quo. *Public Choice* 33–4:27–45.

Schmölders, G. 1960. *Das Irrationale in der öffentlichen Finanzwirtschaft: Problem der Finanz Psychologie*. Hamburg, West Germany: Rowohlt.

Schumpeter, J. 1942. *Capitalism, socialism and democracy*. New York, N.Y.: Harper.

Smith, A. 1759. *The theory of moral sentiments*. Indianapolis, Ind.: Liberty Classics, 1976.

Staff, R. 1978. Homo politicus and homo economicus: advertising and information. In Tuerck, D., ed., *The political economy of advertising*, ed. D. Tuerck. Washington, D.C.: American Enterprise Institute for Policy Research, pp. 135–58.

Tideman, N., and Tullock, G. 1976. A new and superior process for making social choices. *Journal of Political Economy* 84:1145–61.

Thurow, L. 1971. Distribution as a social good. *Quarterly Journal of Economics* 85:327–36.

Tobin, J. 1970. On limiting the domain of inequality. *Journal of Law and Economics* 13:263–79.

Tocqueville, A. de 1835. *Democracy in America*. Tr. Henry Reeve. Oxford World Classics, 1965.

Tribe, L. 1978. *American constitutional law*. Mineola, N.Y.: Foundation Press.

Tuerck, D. 1978. Introduction: the theory of political advertising. In *The political economy of advertising*, ed. D. Tuerck, pp. 1–11 and 61–68. Washington, D.C.: American Enterprise Institute for Policy Research.

Tullock, G. 1959. Problems of majority voting. *Journal of Political Economy* 67:571–80.

Tullock G. 1971. The cost of transfers. *Kyklos* 24:629–41.

Tullock, G. 1974a. Dynamic hypothesis on bureaucracy. *Public Choice*, 19:127–31.

Tullock, G. 1974b. More on the welfare cost of transfers. *Kylos* 27:378–81.

von Mises, L. 1944. *Bureaucracy*. New Haven, Conn.: Yale University Press.

Wagner, A. 1883. *Finanzwissenschaft*, part 1, third edition. Leipzig: C.F. Winter. For excerpts therefrom see Three extracts on public finance. In *Classics in the theory of public finance*, ed. R. Musgrave and A. Peacock, pp. 1–16. London, England: MacMillan, 1958. Also New York, N.Y.: St. Martins, 1967.

Wagner, R. 1976. Revenue structure, fiscal illusion and budgetary choice. *Public Choice*, pp. 45–61.

Wagner, R. 1978. Advertising and the public economy: some preliminary ruminations. In *The Political Economy of Advertising*, ed. D. Tuerck, pp. 81–100. Washington, D.C.: American Enterprise Institute for Policy Research.

Wicksell, K. 1896. A new principle of just taxation. In *Classics in the theory of public finance*, ed. R. Musgrave and A. Peacock, 1958, pp. 72–119. London, England: MacMillan.

TAX LIMITS AND THE LOGIC OF CONSTITUTIONAL RESTRICTIONS

Geoffrey Brennan

I. Introduction

The object of this paper is to mount a defense of the Leviathan model of government as an appropriate one both for understanding the taxing process and for deriving policy prescriptions about desirable changes in tax institutions. In offering this defense, I wish to sketch a view of the taxing process that is quite different from that embodied in the reigning orthodoxy and to lay the foundation for what we might call, in dust-jacket journalese, a "radical new approach to tax analysis."[1]

Let me say at the outset that I do *not* want to argue that Leviathan is upon us, or that the tax limitation movement, currently so voguish, supplies incontrovertible evidence to that effect. I shall leave that sort of argument to other people and other occasions. Indeed, my only concern with tax limitation here is that it provides a reasonable point

[The author is Professor of Economics in the Center for Study of Public Choice, Virginia Polytechnic Institute & State University.]

ACKNOWLEDGMENT: The argument developed here follows closely one that James Buchanan and I develop jointly in a forthcoming book—*The Power To Tax: Analytic Foundations of a Fiscal Constitution* (Cambridge University Press, 1980). Buchanan's contribution, shorn of any responsibility for inadequacies, is gratefully acknowledged, as is the support of the National Science Foundation.

1. This is an approach, incidentally, which James Buchanan and I pursue in our forthcoming book on the power to tax. See Brennan and Buchanan (1980).

of departure for the essentially analytic and methodological issues I wish to raise. It provides that point of departure by bringing into focus the question: should the power to tax be limited, and if so how?

We should note immediately that this is a very different question from that which is the preoccupation of current public finance ortho- doxy. In that orthodoxy, we are concerned with the question: given a particular revenue requirement, what is the "best" way to raise it? The procedure used to answer this question involves specifying nor- mative criteria by which the tax system can be evaluated, and testing alternative tax arrangements by appeal to these criteria. Is the tax system fair? Is it appropriately redistributive? Does it minimize waste—in terms both of administrative costs and of the costs of avoid- ance and evasion? (The minimization of waste thus defined includes, but is broader than, the minimization of "excess burden" as tradi- tionally conceived.)

What is clear is that such a procedure does not really provide any means of answering the earlier question concerning the desirability of limits on the government's power to tax. For this reason, it seems to me that public finance orthodoxy is ill-equipped to provide any analytic or prescriptive input into the tax limitation debate. Tax lim- itation is concerned mainly with the *magnitude* of revenue require- ments—a matter which the tax orthodoxy, armed with its "differential incidence" and "equi-revenue" form of analysis, completely sweeps away.

At one level, the tax limitation issue raises questions about the plausibility of the assumption that the *level* of revenues is completely independent of the means used to raise revenues. To the extent that this assumption is invalid, the analysis surely ought to take account of changes in the level of revenues that result from changes in the tax system, and evaluate the implications of those revenue changes for distributive and efficiency objectives. There seems no good reason for believing such tax-induced changes in expenditure levels to be of negligible significance. The redistributional and allocative effects may well, it seems to me, dominate their more familiar analogues on the tax side.

To take account of the effects of changes in the level of revenues requires no necessary alteration in the basic normative framework, though it does require the introduction of explicit treatment of the political nexus between the way taxing arrangements are organized and the levels of public spending that they finance. And it does require some judgment as to whether the political mechanism is such that levels of public spending are likely to be roughly efficient or not, since otherwise the efficiency implications of revenue changes cannot be assessed.

Once this connection is made, however—once tax institutions are placed firmly in a political setting—then the standard normative framework seems to lose much of its relevance and appeal. The domain of normative evaluation shifts from alternative tax systems to alternative political settings, of which tax arrangements may be a part: it is these alternative political settings and their fiscal dimensions rather than specific *outcomes* of those political settings that have to be evaluated. To conduct such an evaluation requires an explicitly constitutional perspective.[2] In other words, the examination of the power to tax and of the way in which the power to tax might be constrained offers an alternative perspective on taxing arrangements that is both of direct relevance to the tax limits movement and of considerable analytic interest in its own right. In what follows, I wish to sketch the basic elements of this alternative perspective, and indicate its implications for the standard tax policy advocacy as it emerges from orthodox public finance.[3]

Clearly, any analysis of the "power to tax" along such lines requires some model of government. As I shall argue—I hope persuasively— the appropriate model for such purposes is a "monopoly government" or "Leviathan" model. But even if this aspect of my argument is rejected, it will surely be admitted that it is a profound methodological weakness of standard tax analysis that crucial political assumptions remain entirely implicit.

II. The Power to Tax

The power to tax is the power to impose upon individuals and upon private institutions charges that can be met only by a transfer to government of economic resources, or financial claims to such resources—charges that carry with them effective powers of enforcement under the very definition of the taxing power. Possession of this power in no way carries with it of itself a legal obligation to use the resources

---

2. The shift to the constitutional perspective involves a shift from evaluation of acts to evaluation of rules (or "processes" in Nozick's terms).

3. In doing so, it follows pretty much the spirit of an earlier paper by James Buchanan and myself (Brennan and Buchanan [1978]).

so obtained in any specific way. Nor is the capacity to exercise the taxing power in any way contingent on any current expression of willingness to pay. The power to tax is the power to coerce, or as John Marshall put it, "the power to destroy."

We can, of course, rationalize government's possession of that power in terms of public provision of "public goods" that citizens desire but cannot provide for themselves through voluntary bilateral interactions. But we should distinguish sharply between a *rationalization* of the government's possession of the power to tax and an understanding of that power in and of itself. If we wish to understand the power to tax, it seems logical to examine it *in abstraction*, and then proceed to analyze how it might be constrained in order to achieve outcomes that the citizens who are to be subject to it might desire. This latter question is, after all, the central one here.

I think we can distinguish, in response to this central question, three distinct forms of constraint. First, there are the internal moral rules that shape or may shape the conduct of those who hold office in government. Second, there are the electoral constraints that have occupied the attention of modern public choice scholars—the processes of interparty competition and so on. Third, there is a set of nonelectoral constitutional rules—rules that operate independently of, or possibly in complementary fashion to, purely electoral constraints.

Explicit limits on the taxing power, whether they be rate limits, share limits, or of some other form, fall clearly into the latter category. To understand the pure logic of tax limitation, therefore, requires that we understand something of the role of nonelectoral constraints in the design of "optimal" constitutions; and in one sense all I wish to do in this paper is to establish the fact that there is an important object of study here, and to indicate what assumptions seem to be required to permit us to focus on the role of nonelectoral constraints and to analyze that role in a satisfactory manner.

At this point, let me make a simple observation. There would be no role *at all* for nonelectoral constraints if it were the case that electoral and internal moral constraints between them (or, a fortiori, either operating on its own) were sufficient to ensure outcomes that the citizenry desires. A basic assumption of any analysis of nonelectoral constraints must therefore be that electoral processes and morality within government are insufficient to ensure desired outcomes.

There are then two ways of proceeding in principle to establish the case for tax limitation. One is to indicate on presumptive analytic grounds why we might believe electoral and moral constraints to be insufficiently binding. The other is to observe that the set of nonelectoral constraints in almost all known "democratic" constitutions is non-empty. This fact must represent an interesting challenge to the explanatory powers of models of government in which electoral processes and/or internal morality are completely constraining. In what follows, I shall make appeal to both lines of reasoning.

III. Nonelectoral Rules

Constitutions typically lay down a whole range of restrictions on the behavior of governments that do not bear directly on electoral processes. Such things as basic "inviolable" rights, eminent domain laws, restrictions on the domain of government spending, requirements of government accountability, specification of the structure of government (e.g., the establishment or maintenance of a federal structure) and the separation of powers, all exemplify this. So too do existing rules about how the tax system should be organized—rules of uniformity and the like. The existence of all such restrictions presumes that ordinary political processes generate results that would on occasion violate these rules.

Consider some simple examples. It is, I think, instructive to ask how the "power to tax" differs from the power to "take." Clearly, both involve taking of a sort. Suppose the government wishes to obtain a particular tract of land. It can take it directly from the existing owner, Mr. A, but in doing so it would (one might hope) be seen to violate "eminent domain" requirements and be compelled by the courts to pay to Mr. A just and proper compensation. Suppose, however, that the government purchases the land from Mr. A in an open market transaction and then levies upon him a tax that raises an amount of revenue equal to the full purchase price. Mr. A is clearly no differently placed from the situation in which government takes his land directly. In what way, then, does the power to tax differ from the power to take? Presumably the answer lies in the fact that taxes are understood to exhibit properties, such as generality, that direct appropriation does not. It may be that the requirement of uniformity/generality of treatment means that tax financing implies that all those in similar circumstances (for example, with the same aggregate wealth) will have to pay identical taxes and hence that, whereas the direct appropriation alternative might survive electoral scrutiny, the tax alternative would not do so. In this case, the generality requirement is seen to increase the likelihood that electoral processes will operate within tolerable limits: fiscal constraints complement electoral constraints. But can we be certain that the effects of "taking" are ruled out by such a generality requirement? Is there not some risk that "taking" will become legitimized simply on a broader scale than in the absence of the uniformity constraint? And is it sufficient to impose generality restrictions on the tax side when corresponding limits are not placed on the spending side? In other words, is the only restriction on the power to tax that is desirable a constraint that requires generality, or do we seek for something more?

A second example may be useful here. Most governments operate under fairly elaborate accounting procedures, designed in part to ensure that politicians and bureaucrats do not simply pocket tax revenues for their own purposes. Apparently, it is recognized that neither electoral processes nor the in-dwelling ethical instincts of government officers are sufficient to ensure that all corruption will be precluded. Of course, even the most elaborate procedures cannot ensure that some politician or bureaucrat will not dip a hand into the till one way or another sometime or another: the objective is simply to keep such behavior as far as possible within reasonable bounds.

To consider a third case, examine the question of the federalization of government. Orthodox public finance offers an elegant justification of a federal structure based upon the spatial properties of the "public goods" that the market cannot provide optimally. But it does not and cannot offer any explanation of the *political* decentralization that is characteristic of genuinely federal constitutions, because it cannot explain why a purely administrative delegation of spending decisions to subnational areas cannot achieve everything that political decentralization can. If the central government, constrained by electoral competition (or conscience) works "perfectly" (whatever this may mean exactly) then the appropriate outcomes will emerge in each local area. That is, a party that offers the differentiated levels of public goods supply and appropriately differentiated tax rates (differentiated by area) will defeat the party that offers homogeneous treatment, ceteris paribus. Why do we need a federal structure, then? One possible answer[4] is that competition for residents (and their tax dollars)

---

4. This is a matter that James Buchanan and I explore in detail in chapter 9 of our forthcoming book (Brennan and Buchanan [1980]).

between governments represents a means of reducing their monopoly power—an aspect of Tiebout's mobility model that has received rather too little attention in the federalism literature.[5]

This is by no means the only conceivable justification for federalism. My point is simply that whatever justification is offered must take as its point of departure the assumption that electoral processes and internal moral constraints are inadequate to constrain the government's exercise of its coercive power, and must develop its analysis in the context of a model of government that is structured accordingly. This must be true for the analysis of all nonelectoral constraints—and for all tax rules specifically.

IV. Are Electoral Constraints Really Binding?

Apart from this general observation about the model of government appropriate for the study of nonelectoral constraints, we should ask a further question. Just how strong is the analytic and empirical base of the argument—or perhaps more accurately the hope—that electoral processes really do constrain?

There are a number of ways of approaching this question. One would be to ask whether there are means whereby electoral constraints could be made more constraining than they currently are. To the extent that there are, current political institutions must be less constraining than they might be. Another, related, approach would be to ask whether and to what extent politicians and bureaucrats do exercise discretionary power. Are governments simply puppets acting out the will of the median voter as they perceive it, or do they genuinely "govern" in some meaningful sense? Of course, to the extent that governments *are* totally constrained by electoral outcomes, the notion of offering policy advice to government (an activity incidentally that has been worth a lot of money to a lot of economists) becomes totally ludicrous;[6] the "median-voter" theory of government does not admit much scope for moral suasion. A third approach would be to examine abstract models of political process, of the type that have emerged from the so-called "theory of public choice," and indicate the analytic evidence for the belief that electoral processes do constrain.

---

5. See David Friedman (1979) and Richard McKenzie and Robert Staaf (1978) for arguments along such lines.

6. One could, of course, argue that the economists' role here is to indicate those things most likely to be congenial to the median voter, although one would also have thought that the pollsters would have put us out of business long ago if this were the case.

In what follows, I shall rely predominantly on the last approach. As it happens, I do believe that politicians and bureaucrats exercise very considerable amounts of discretionary power. I also believe that electoral processes *could* conceivably be used to constrain governments much more severely than is typically the case in Western democracies. Decisions could be taken by popular referenda much more commonly. Nor are the reasons for avoiding the referendum option entirely technical: computer and telephone voting techniques seem to provide inexpensive means of popular voting (or large sample voting) on an extensive range of issues over which politicians and bureaucrats currently exercise discretion.[7] One might argue that the reason for *not* relying more extensively on popular government is that it is simply undesirable to do so. Indeed, if my assessment of the costs of voting is accurate, then the whole theory of representative democracy must now be based on such reasoning. Accordingly, one set of arguments that might be investigated here relates to the question as to why one might avoid reliance on majoritarian political processes, even where this is taken to provide effective constraint. In this connection, one might mention Downsian "rational ignorance"[8]; the need for some expenditures (such as those on legal institutions) to be decided independently of majority will.[9] I shall not explore such arguments here, however. That general line of reasoning is concerned with the possibility that individuals might, at the constitutional level, explicitly choose nonelectoral means of constraining government in preference to relying on electoral processes, given that those electoral processes generate outcomes in line with majoritarian preferences. Here, however, it is preferable to focus on the issue of whether, and to what extent, majoritarian electoral processes will constrain where it is intended that they do so.

I think it is useful in this connection to distinguish between two possible sources of "slack" in the political process. One arises "on the supply side" by virtue of the fact that many public services are provided by a single bureaucratic supplier, effectively under monopoly conditions. The other arises "on the demand side" via the peculiarities

---

7. See James C. Miller, III, (1969) for an argument along such lines.

8. See Anthony Downs (1957).

9. Buchanan's "punishment dilemma" and "Samaritan's dilemma" are illustrative of one aspect of the problem here. See James M. Buchanan (1975), chapter 7, and "The Samaritan's Dilemma" in E.S. Phelps (1975).

of majority rule as an institutional device for "adding up" individuals' preferences. Although these sources of slack can in principle exist independently[10] the distinction is a little artificial, because a monopoly bureau can exploit the peculiarities of "nonconstraining" voting rules to secure larger monopoly rents. In what follows, however, I shall ignore any independent power that might be exercised by the bureaucracy in its role as the supplier of policies and policy proposals. The question of monopoly bureaus is handled in some detail by my colleagues Arthur Denzau, Robert Mackay, and Carolyn Weaver, in another paper in this volume, and I happily leave it to them. I shall focus solely on majoritarian political-electoral processes, with an eye to the question: to what extent do those processes constrain?

A brief explanatory word is in order at this point. The question at issue here in asking whether processes "constrain" is whether those processes drive surplus to zero. Presumably, electoral processes may constrain *at the margin*, just as market processes may constrain monopoly at the margin. The question we are here interested in is whether those electoral processes are sufficiently constraining to drive out virtually all slack—as the market does in perfect competition—or whether they are not.

Space here hardly permits any serious discussion of public choice theory, but we can briefly catalogue some of the main results.[11] First, we all know that, unless the "issue space" is unidimensional, majority rule generates cycles: there is no unique equilibrium. In fact, it has been shown that there exists a cyclical sequence that can incorporate all points in utility space. It follows from this result that if we were to stop a majoritarian cycle after some sequence of arbitrary length, the resultant "equilibrium" could be anywhere. (This does not, of course, imply that all points are equi-probable.) We also know that, if the issue space is unidimensional and individuals' preferences are single-peaked, there is a determinate equilibrium at the median voter's preferred location (under certain assumptions we need not specify here). The question as to whether majority rule constrains,

<hr/>

10. "Supply side" slack can arise, for example, if supply of some public good is inherently monopolistic but the political decision rule is unanimity. "Demand side" slack can arise if all public services are supplied via competitive contract, but majority rule prevails.

11. An interesting and broad-ranging discussion of many of these issues is contained in Dennis Mueller's recent book on public choice (Mueller 1979).

therefore, seems to depend on whether institutional rules can be developed that establish a unidimensional issue space. One possible means of doing this might involve the following tripartite procedure:

(1) Earmark every revenue source to some expenditure, with revenue sources determined so that marginal cost-sharing is well-defined;[12]

(2) Define for each expenditure that quantity-share for each individual (with pure public goods, equal shares are ensured; for private goods, the sharing must be specified);

(3) Vote on each tax-expenditure decision separately.

Now it may be that some such procedure implicitly underlies orthodox tax thinking, because in this setting, the tax system is determined ex ante and, once set, establishes a context in which desired *levels* of spending can be determined. There would, specifically, be no need for any tax-spending limits in this setting. Nor could tax decisions be determined by in-period political process: one would need constitutionally appointed institutions for determining the tax system (royal commissions and the like) and perhaps constitutionally appointed rules (such as "efficiency," "equity," and "simplicity") for application to the tax determination process. But the whole rationale here depends on the other conditions obtaining. Since they don't, we must assume that in actual majoritarian politics "cycles" are the norm; and we must examine normative tax theory in a different analytic setting.

Our response to this fact may be twofold. We might argue that the implication is a politics of chaos—a *necessarily* random walk over policy space. Alternatively, we might argue that the absence of determinacy establishes scope for the exercise of political and bureaucratic discretion, scope for the creation of political surplus which politicians can "spend" in any way that their tastes suggest or moral principles allow. Note that in *either* case, some constitutionally determined limits seem desirable—and *at both ends*! That is, a spending maximum and a spending minimum would be required. Whether we are led to excessive spending by bureaucratic enthusiasm or by an occasional random fluctuation hardly seems to matter: we would like to bound the outcomes.

Now, I don't myself believe that political process *forces* random political outcomes. (Politicians may seem to behave randomly at times

---

12. A progressive or regressive income tax does not in general exhibit this property.

but I don't think this is something forced on them by majority rule). I am, therefore, led to the conclusion that politicians and bureaucrats exercise genuine discretion over some range.

Perhaps it may be useful at this point to introduce a simple little model to offer what some might construe as some logical foundation to this conclusion. Consider the simplest version of the simplest and probably best-known model of majoritarian politics, attributable to Downs.[13] In this model, there are two homogeneous parties, I and II. Suppose that one party, say I, has to announce its policy before the other, party II, and the announced platforms are binding. Downs shows that party II will always defeat party I. Suppose we consider a simple three voter world, with no utility interdependence, and party I announces a payoff to the three voters a, b, and c of $100 each. This platform can then be depicted as the payoff vector (100, 100, 100) where the first term indicates the payoff to a, the second term the payoff to b, and the third term the payoff to c. Party II can then announce a policy involving the payoff vector (101, 101, m) where m is less than 98 (or any permutation of these payoffs) and win the election. This possibility leads Downs to the conclusion that interparty competition does not in general lead to Pareto optimality, except perhaps by accident: a party can always ensure victory by announcing its policies last and organizing appropriate transfers from some minority to the corresponding majority.

One important feature of this model, however, is an implicit inconsistency in the behavior of politicians. Politicians are postulated to maximize their expected returns, which depend on their election— and hence are modeled as maximizing the probability of being elected. It is therefore somewhat bizarre that they are not postulated to maximize the advantages of election when they are successful. Since party II *knows* that it can win the election if it has the right to announce its policy platform after party I, then II will respond to party I's platform involving payoff vector (100, 100, 100) with a platform which *both* assures II of being elected, *and* maximizes the "surplus" which it has at its disposal. In this case, party II's "best" policy is one involving the payoff vector (101, 101, 0) (or any permutation of these payoffs), with the party itself appropriating the excess of total product over that product which is required to be left in the hands of voters in order to secure election. The implications of this simple model are

---

13. Downs (1957) ch. 10.

then twofold: first, the rational party will exploit the maximal minority to the maximal extent feasible; second, it will expend in payments to the majority the minimal sum necessary to secure election. As a result, a significant proportion of total resources is available for discretionary use by the successful party. In the non-single-peaked case, therefore, with sequential announcement of policy platforms, important dimensions of "monopoly government" emerge out of simple majority rule.

Of course, to the extent that there are constraints of the type earlier mentioned on the inequality of tax-shares, and on the inequality in benefit shares under various sorts of government programs (transfers, particularly), the extent of feasible redistribution from the minority will be rather limited. It will emerge in the form not so much of cash transfers as of special interest expenditures, regulations, and so forth. But redistribution from minority to majority will occur and "political surplus" will result, in all cases except where genuine "single-peakedness" is assured.

V. The Benevolent-Despot Model

Suppose we accept the notion that those who occupy office in government do exercise discretion. As I have tried to point out in the preceding section, the analytical grounds for believing the contrary are pretty thin. And in any case, the idea ought to be congenial to mainstream public finance specialists and indeed to policy economists more generally, because the whole normative theory of government policy seems to be predicated on just this assumption.

The next question we should pose is whether and to what extent we can expect those individuals who exercise discretionary judgment in government to behave "morally"—to be constrained by the internal dictates of conscience. In other words, how descriptive is the "benevolent despot" model of politics?

Now, unlike what I detect as the prevailing attitude in the profession, I happen to believe that morality is important, both intrinsically (a fact which hardly bears here) *and* empirically (a fact that does). That is, most people do behave morally, according to their lights, at least some of the time; and most people are apt to be influenced to some extent by coherent moral reasoning. And I have, in some of my research, indicated this belief.

But if I believe in the empirical relevance of moral considerations,

I also believe in the reality of "sin"—or, if you object to that much-misused word, in the capacity of people to ignore the dictates of conscience. Nor would I want to deny that most people have considerable capacity for fiendishly inventive self-deception in rearranging their moral frameworks so as to justify what they would like to do anyway. Furthermore, I see little historical evidence for the view that individuals' ethical intuitions are identical. Rather, the record seems to me to be full of tales of people doing quite wicked things for the best possible reasons (like burning one another at the stake in the interests of one another's immortal souls, and so forth). Moral perceptions, like tastes, differ. The Spanish inquisition may have been a totally moral enterprise according to Phillip II's lights, but one can't imagine that it was a desired outcome from the point of view of the Spanish Jews or the Flemish Protestants.

Of course, we don't need to go to such extremes to indicate the ambiguity of "moral" behavior. A reasonable model of job selection suggests that individuals will tend to inhabit jobs they consider "worthwhile." Those individuals who have visions of changing the world via governmental means will tend to favor jobs in the bureaucracy. And each will gravitate towards the bureau that most relates to his vision: health bureaucrats can be predicted to believe that health is more worthwhile than other things; military personnel will tend to believe in the virtues of a strong defense operation; and so on. In a world where people behave morally, simple self-selection will have the effect of allocating decision-making power to relatively high-demand individuals. There will be a natural tendency for government officials to seek expansion of their own sphere of activities whether individuals behave out of self-interest *or* morality. More generally, because perceptions differ as to what precisely morality requires, there can be no necessary presumption that widespread moral behavior on the part of all individuals will generate outcomes that satisfy standard Paretian criteria (including the purely "moral" elements in individuals' utility functions).

For these reasons, I do not believe that the introduction of some elements of moral behavior into the politico–economic model rescues us from anxiety about the desirability of political outcomes under quasidictatorial regimes. But there is another issue at stake here— one of method. Even if as an empirical matter we believed that bureaucrats and politicians might, by virtue of moral considerations, be induced to behave in the citizens' interests much of the time, this is still not a satisfactory *assumption* for a model of politics in the context under consideration here. For the purposes both of comparative institutional analysis, and more particularly of constitutional design, a deliberately cynical model of government is obligatory. To suggest why, let us consider a couple of simple analogies.

Let us, first, go back to homo œconomicus, the selfish savage who devotes himself single-mindedly to maximizing the present value of his measurable wealth. As a psychologically descriptive hypothesis of the way that individuals do in fact behave, this model of man may be unacceptable. Any theory that depends for its predictions on the hypothesis that all persons behave in such fashion at all times and in all circumstances must, of course, be rejected out of hand from ordinary introspection. It is difficult to deny, however, that this simplistic model of pure economic man has been shown to have powerful explanatory potential.

More importantly, however, even if the model of pure economic man should be severely limited in its positive explanatory usage, it may prove to be, and has proven to be, very helpful in the comparative analyses of alternative social orders and arrangements. As Sir Dennis Robertson observed, we need not at all deny the existence of "love" to believe that we ought to point up institutional ways and means of economizing on it. Or, if we prefer to return to Adam Smith's illustration, we may acknowledge that our butcher and our baker are occasionally, and perhaps frequently, benevolently inclined, but surely we should all feel more secure if the institutional structure is so organized as to make their self-interest coincident with our own rather than the opposite.

In this way, what may appear to be a highly cynical or skeptical model of politics may be justified in much the same way that classical and neoclassical economic theory justifies its economic-man hypothesis, particularly in the context of comparative institutional evaluation. A nonbenevolent model of government may be acknowledged to be useful, not necessarily because it predicts how governments always, or even frequently, work, but because it is only from such a base that we can organize our institutions so that government will operate to generate "nonbenevolent" results less often.

Take another example that is perhaps closer to the problem of constitutional design. Suppose a house is being built for you and you wish to draw up a contract with your builder. You do this not because you really think your builder isn't trustworthy. If you really thought that he was out to exploit you, you presumably wouldn't employ him. But the mutual trust that is the common cement in such commercial transactions hardly represents a basis for drawing up the legal contract. There would be no point in having a contract at all if you couldn't conceive that your builder might in some manner welsh on the deal. In setting the terms of the contract, you would rationally assume, for the purposes of that exercise, that the builder would act so as to exploit every opportunity for cheating you because it is the possibility of such exploitation that you seek to forestall.

The analogy with the social contract is clear. The constitutional documents that might be predicted to emerge from agreement among citizens in some original position behind a veil of ignorance must be predicated on the assumption that moral constraints will be inadequate because it is precisely that contingency with which they are designed to cope. I can really do no better here than quote John Stuart Mill in his *Considerations on Representative Government*:

> The very principle of constitutional government requires it to be assumed that political power will be abused to promote the particular purposes of the holder; not because it always is so, but because such is the natural tendency of things, to guard against which is the especial use of free institutions.

A model of government in which political power is "abused to promote the particular purposes of the holder" is what James Buchanan and I chose to call "Leviathan" government in our earlier work, more or less following the usage of Thomas Hobbes and others. The particular formulation we chose was a model of surplus-maximizing government, which, on the assumption that surplus is a constant proportion of aggregate spending,[14] becomes a simple revenue-maximizing model. I hold no particular brief for this particular formulation beyond its simplicity and familiarity—familiarity because it is precisely identical to the standard monopoly theory of the firm. This is a possible virtue, it seems to me, because we can very easily lift many results from standard literature and because the conventional maximizing methodology can be directly applied.

More subtle formulations, particularly those in which the interrelationships between individual political agents are incorporated, in which electoral constraints perform some, though not a totally constraining, role, and which include more complex maximands than

---

14. This is a fortiori the case if surplus is an increasing function of spending.

aggregate tax revenue, ought surely be developed. The characteristic that all such models must exhibit, however, is that such political power as lies with government officials is systematically exploited to the holder's ends. Without such a model, no understanding of the "fiscal constitution" is possible.

VI. The Tax Implications

Perhaps by way of conclusion, it might be interesting to indicate some of the implications of this model for tax policy, and how they differ from those that emerge from the more familiar public finance orthodoxy. In the conventional analysis, there is a virtually unquestioned belief in the desirability of greater broadness of the tax base. Under equi-revenue assumptions, the broader the tax base, ceteris paribus, the smaller will be the excess burden induced per dollar of revenue raised. There is, moreover, a strong presumption that the tax burden will be spread more evenly and hence "fairly" over the voting population the broader the tax base. Standard tax advocacy has long seen increased broadness of base as a major objective of tax reform.

With perspectives informed by the Leviathan model of government, however, we recognize that assigning a particular tax base to government is analytically equivalent to assigning government a monopoly franchise in the "sale" of that "tax base." Even if, for whatever reason, this monopoly franchise is not exploited to its maximum potential, there is a very clear logical implication that aggregate government revenue will increase when the government's collection of monopoly franchises is expanded (i.e., when the tax base is broadened). It is also clear that, beyond some point, such increases in aggregate government revenue will be regarded by the citizenry as undesirable: levels of public spending (and "political surplus") will be pushed too high. Once this is recognized, we see that implicit revenue limits embedded in any particular tax system are systematically undermined by the pressure for increased broadness of base, characteristic of conventional tax advocacy. Moreover, I think this is a point that the much-benighted "man in the street" recognizes. Much of the difficulty associated with broad sweeping changes in the tax system (inclusion of imputed rent on owner-occupied dwellings in the income tax base, expanding the coverage of the sales tax, introduction of a broadly-based value-added tax, and so on) arises because people simply cannot be led to accept the equi-revenue methodology. This may, of course, be due to a genuine confusion; but I suspect that it may have its roots in a well-based disbelief of the equi-revenue assumption.

It seems to me that we ought to be able to discuss the political and empirical relevance of the equi-revenue methodology *independently of* the question of the appropriate size of government. Whether current tax orthodoxy is a well-disguised push for increased government activity or whether increased government is simply an unintended by-product of orthodox tax reform is beyond the point. That this *is* the result of broadening the tax base under conceivable and reasonably plausible models of government is surely something of which we ought to take account.

VII. Summary

In this paper, I have tried to develop a case for examining taxation theory in the context of an appropriate model of political process. I have attempted to indicate why I believe that appropriate model to be one of "Leviathan" government. My reasons are both analytic and methodological.

On analytic grounds, the case for a model in which government is totally constrained by majoritarian electoral processes seems to me to be extremely weak, based both on our understandings of majority rule as a voting procedure and on the simple observation that it would be possible to rely on majoritarian processes much more than is currently done. Moreover, no such model can be used to explain the presence of nonelectoral constraints, including fiscal rules of various types, simply because there is no scope for them. This model can hardly, then, inform any satisfactory treatment of tax theory: taxes would simply emerge from electoral processes (as in early voluntary exchange models).

If such a model is rejected, then we must revert to some form of model in which politicians and bureaucrats do exercise genuine discretionary power. This is in fact a familiar model in conventional policy analysis; but the assumption invariably made is that government will exercise its power in a "desirable" way. Whatever the virtues of this "heroic" model of government as a depiction of what we observe—and I think that is certainly debatable—it does not and cannot be an appropriate model for the derivation of the fiscal constitution. If tax rules are to be devised to apply over a long sequence of periods and to set the framework within which government processes are to operate, we need to have an eye to the worst possible outcomes against which it is the role of those fiscal rules to guard.

It is, of course, true that these fiscal constraints may prevent us at times from doing things we might like to do. This is so because policies have implications not only for us but also for others, and not only now but over the long postconstitutional sequence. This is, I believe, very much the case with tax policy; the choice of tax instruments will, in plausibly constructed models of political process, influence the level of revenues that will be obtained from them. In the absence of explicit and enforced limits on the level of revenues, otherwise attractive tax policies may have consequences that, from the taxpayer's viewpoint, are quite disastrous. The narrowness of focus and the tenuousness of the implicit political assumptions, which characterize orthodox tax advocacy within the economics profession, may be leading us wildly astray.

REFERENCES

Brennan, H.G., and Buchanan, J.M. December 1977. Towards a tax constitution for leviathan. *Journal of Public Economics*.

———. 1980. *The power to tax: analytic foundations of a fiscal constitution*. New York, N.Y.: Cambridge University Press.

Buchanan, J.M. 1975. *The limits of liberty*. Chicago, Ill.: University of Chicago Press.

Downs, A. 1957. *An economic theory of democracy*. New York, N.Y.: Harper and Row.

Friedman, D. 1979. A competitive model of exploitative taxation. Mimeo.

McKenzie, R., and Staaf, R. September 1978. Revenue sharing and monopoly government. *Public Choice* (the journal).

Miller, J.C., III. Fall 1969. A program for direct and proxy voting in the legislative process. *Public Choice* (the journal).

Mueller, Dennis. 1979. *Public choice* (a book). New York, N.Y.: Cambridge University Press.

Phelps, E.S. 1975. *Altruism, morality and economic theory*. Russell Sage Foundation.

Discussion of Richard A. Musgrave, "Leviathan Cometh—or Does He"; and Geoffrey Brennan, "Tax Limits and the Logic of Constitutional Restrictions"

Wallace E. Oates, Discussant

The Brennan paper raises an important set of issues: the effects of the revenue system itself on the size and growth of the public sector. Neoclassical analysis has little to say about all of this; modern incidence studies and most of the optimal-tax literature rely, for the most part, on an exogenously determined level of revenues from which vantage point they examine the distributive and allocative effects of various forms of taxation in a differential-tax framework. Thus, the mainstream of the tax literature is, virtually by definition, silent on the major issues surrounding the tax-limitation debate.

How then do we approach these issues? We obviously need a conceptual framework—a "model" of government—to generate testable predictions about the impact of the fiscal structure on the size (and growth) of the public sector. Brennan's contention is that "the appropriate model for such purposes is a 'monopoly government' or 'Leviathan' model." In short, Brennan postulates that:

(1) The public sector is a revenue maximizer, and that

(2) Electoral processes and moral restraint provide an inadequate constraint on the expansionary propensities of government.

From this, he surmises that the public sector can be expected to exhibit systematic tendencies toward excessive budgetary size, which establishes a prima facie case for tax limitations.

[The author is a member of the Bureau of Business and Economic Research and the Department of Economics, University of Maryland.]

In this regard, I wish to stress that the Brennan paper advances two conceptually distinct theses: the tendency toward excessive size of the public sector and the desirability of constitutional tax limits to constrain this size. I will consider these two propositions sequentially.

Systematic evidence supporting the excessive-size thesis, a premise of the proposal for constitutional limitations on the power to tax, is pretty thin. The Brennan model simply *assumes* that the government seeks to maximize its revenue collections. But it's hard to take this assumption seriously. The public sector is not a monolithic organization with a unified and well-defined set of objectives; we live in a highly fragmented, federal system with a myriad of levels and agencies pursuing a very diverse set of purposes. There are some bits and pieces of evidence to suggest that, under certain circumstances, some forces may operate in the direction of encouraging excessive budgets; particular public agencies may press for inappropriately large budgets and find sympathetic ears in legislative review committees. (See Shepsle[1] for some evidence supporting this contention.) On the other hand, Downs[2] has argued, and Musgrave in his excellent paper notes, that a number of other forces are working in the opposite direction; for example, taxpayer ignorance of the benefits from various public activities may tend to hold certain services at less-than-efficient levels.

It is hard to know how all this comes out in the aggregate. I feel sure that certain public services have been extended excessively; on the other hand, I am also convinced that for plenty of public activities, existing levels are well below that for which marginal benefits become equal to marginal cost. But I feel quite uncertain as to how these plusses and minuses net out. At any rate, simply to characterize the public sector as a revenue maximizer and to move on to a conclusion of an excessively large public budget is not persuasive.

Much, incidentally, was made of this point in discussion at the conference. Both Margolis and Musgrave emphasized caution in transferring the "as-if" market model of man the profit maximizer to the government sector. In particular, Margolis noted that the mechanism for survival in the political sphere is quite different in certain fundamental respects from the mechanics of survival in the market.

1. Kenneth A. Shepsle, *The Giant Jigsaw Puzzle: Committee Assignment in the Democratic House* (Chicago, Ill.: University of Chicago Press, 1978).

2. A. Downs, "Why the Government Budget Is Too Small in a Democracy," *World Politics* (July 1960).

Moreover, Musgrave notes that the businessman's explicit function is to make profits, while the bureaucrat's *supposed* function is to serve the public interest. While the latter is surely suspect as a complete description of bureaucratic objectives, it should at least alert us to the potential differences between market and political behavior. As a political scientist remarked to me some time ago, "The trouble is that political scientists don't understand how markets work, and economists don't understand the nature and use of power."

I doubt if Brennan would take serious issue with much of what I have said here. In fact, he is at pains to point out the importance of explicitly moral considerations in political behavior. He acknowledges the extreme simplicity of the Leviathan model and its failure to capture the complexity of political activity. This, however, is largely beside the point for his purposes. Brennan argues for the Leviathan model not on the grounds that politicians necessarily behave this way, but rather that we should *assume* that power will be abused and should respond by building into the constitution a set of protective measures. This, as I understand it, is his basic argument for tax limits.

This too involves problems, for as Brennan observes, "It is, of course, true that these fiscal constraints may prevent us at times from doing things we might like to do." Tax limits are a constraint on fiscal choice and, as such, may themselves impose costs on the community. This, it seems to me, is not a trivial matter; tax limits are a very inflexible, clumsy instrument for dealing with imperfections in the public sector. A careful "cost-benefit" analysis is surely needed before throwing one's support to the tax-limitation cause. Such a study goes beyond the scope of this note, but I would call attention to one careful evaluation of the pros and cons of fiscal limitations by Helen Ladd in an article where she concludes that "the economic benefits from controls motivated by the desire to limit local public expenditures are likely to be slight, while the costs, in terms of service level distortions, are potentially significant."[3] Even if there exist tendencies toward excessive public budgets, it is far from clear that tax limits are the answer.

In spite of my skepticism regarding the usefulness of the Leviathan model, I enthusiastically support Brennan's efforts to focus attention on some extremely important fiscal matters. Perhaps I can best in-

---

3. Helen F. Ladd, "An Economic Evaluation of State Limitations on Local Taxing and Spending Powers," *National Tax Journal* (March 1978), p. 14.

dicate my support in terms of a current tax issue. Many of us are following with interest the proposal for introduction at federal level of a value-added tax (VAT). The proposal at this stage is clothed in differential-tax garb; that is, Congressman Ullman has suggested that revenues from a value-added tax be used to reduce levels of federal income and payroll taxation. In this form, the proposal has much to commend it. For one, it would serve to reduce the distortions in the existing tax structure working against capital formation and thereby encourage economic growth. More generally, one can muster a number of allocative and distributive arguments on its behalf, most of which we can examine in terms of the traditional tools of tax analysis.

Nevertheless, there remains in the background the troublesome suspicion that the introduction of VAT is not devoid of implications for the size of the federal budget; the adoption of a new broad-based tax may well bring with it an expansion in federal spending relative to what it would have been otherwise. This, if true, would constitute an important additional consideration in the evaluation of the proposal. Unfortunately, it is very difficult to go much beyond a hunch on this. We simply do not have a compelling model of public-sector behavior supported by a systematic body of evidence which will generate predictions on matters like this. While the Leviathan model may be too simplistic for serious predictive purposes, it does at least point our attention to some matters that we must try to understand. As Brennan points out, "it is a profound methodological weakness of standard tax analysis that crucial political assumptions remain entirely implicit."

ALTERNATIVE THEORIES OF THE GROWTH OF GOVERNMENT AND THEIR IMPLICATIONS FOR CONSTITUTIONAL TAX AND SPENDING LIMITS

Peter H. Aranson
Peter C. Ordeshook

Public Sector Size: Scholarship and Politics

There is now a widespread belief that the public sector in the United States is insufficiently constrained and that it has grown too large. A substantial and stable majority of the population (about 78 percent by one poll) favors a constitutional amendment to require a balanced federal budget.[1] Almost enough state legislatures have endorsed a balanced budget amendment to meet the two-thirds requirement specified in Article Five of the U.S. Constitution for calling a constitutional convention to *propose* such an amendment. Nor has the

---

[Peter Aranson is Special Research Administrator, Law and Economics Center, and Professor of Economics, School of Business Administration, Emory University. Peter Ordeshook is Professor of Political Economy, Graduate School of Industrial Administration and School of Urban and Public Affairs, Carnegie-Mellon University.]

1. Gallup (1979). Responding to the question: "Would you favor or oppose a constitutional amendment that would require Congress to balance the federal budget each year—that is, keep taxes and expenditures in balance?" Seventy-eight percent of the respondents answered "yes," 12 percent "no," and 10 percent "no opinion." These percentages have been stable since 1976. Positive responses are open to the interpretation that those who prefer balanced federal budgets *merely* prefer tax revenues to equal expenditures, with no regard for tax or expenditure levels. This interpretation seems to us to be terribly naïve.

143

federal budget received exclusive attention. In 1978 alone, voters in 13 states cast ballots on 15 various tax and spending limits. All but five passed. During that same year, 72 major tax reductions were adopted in 35 states and the District of Columbia. By contrast, major tax increases were adopted in only eight states.[2] The growth of government regulation, too, has attracted severe criticism from members of Congress and even from those whose livelihoods sometimes depend on regulation, the members of the American Bar Association.[3]

Whether or not these actions are ultimately deemed sensible, they do rest on an objectively perceived rapid rate of public-sector growth. Borcherding (1977b, p. 19) points out that "Over the last ten decades public spending has been rising at an annual rate almost two or three percent faster than has Gross National Product." Meltzer (1975, pp. 16–17) reports a 6.4 percent compound annual growth rate in federal tax collections since 1792: "real taxes rose 1.7 times as fast as real output," and public-sector employment, "has grown . . . more than twice as fast as the labor force in the current century." Nutter (1978) confirms the presence of these trends in the 13 major Western democracies, as well as Australia and Japan. The growth of regulation, which is part of the growth of government generally, seems more difficult to measure, and evidence about its expansion remains indirect. Nevertheless, the number of federal regulatory agencies grew from five at the turn of the century to 33 in 1970; another 22 were added in the 1970s (Wallace and Penoyer, 1978, p. iii). The *Federal Register*, which expanded from about 6,000 pages in 1940 to 18,000 pages in 1970, had exceeded 60,000 pages by 1978.

Academic attention to public-sector size, with few exceptions, has

---

2. Information on state action is reported in Advisory Commission on Intergovernmental Relations (1979), pp. 6–30.

3. In 1979 Senator Muskie proposed a "sunset" law, S.2, which would place the existence of several regulatory agencies in cyclical jeopardy; Senator Ribicoff proposed S.262 for himself and S.755 for the Carter Administration, which would require policy-specific, periodic reexamination of various regulations within different agencies; Senator Kennedy proposed S.1291, a "high noon" procedure without the forcing elements of S.2. Senator Percy has introduced S.445, which combines various provisions of the other bills to form a "middle of the afternoon" or "teatime" act. The American Bar Association (ABA) Commission on Law and the Economy recently issued a report (ABA, 1978) proposing various changes in regulatory practices and adopting a generally approving view of deregulation. For a review, see Aranson (1979). The commission's entire set of recommendations was approved by the ABA House of Delegates during its August, 1979, meeting.

only recently focused on the "grand questions" involved: What accounts for changes in the size of the public sector? Are such changes desirable or undesirable? And, are public-sector size and changes in public-sector size directly or indirectly responsive to citizens' preferences? There were few early studies of public-sector size considered as a separate phenomenon. Buchanan (1967, pp. 126–43) and Goetz (1977, pp. 176–87) separately discuss Puviani's (1903) earlier work on the fiscal illusion. Von Mises (1944), in a seldom acknowledged but prescient monograph, noted that the public sector requires bureaucracy for its management, and that bureaucracy is inherently inefficient: too large for any given output.[4] On the other side, Galbraith (1969, chaps. 17–18), and later Downs (1960), argued that the public sector will be too small because of a lack of advertising or because of other systematic inadequacies that lead to a benefit-side fiscal illusion.[5]

Until recently, academic analysis of public-sector size has proceeded on a course that parallels the manner in which the public sector grew: program by program and regulation by regulation. For example, Lindsay's (1975, 1976) studies of Veterans Administration hospitals, while not making specific public policy proposals, lead one to the conclusion that their facilities should be sold off, with veterans' benefits handled on an insurance payment basis (preferably by private carriers). Both veterans and taxpayers would be better off. Browning (1976) provides evidence that, by the federal government's own definition, the poverty problem in the United States would be solved merely by substituting cash payments for the benefits-in-kind that are now given to welfare recipients. The cost to taxpayers would decline for a constant level of benefits, or the benefits would increase for a constant tax level, and probably both taxpayers and welfare recipients could be made better off. Bruce-Briggs (1975) calls attention to the economic foolishness behind present and contemplated expansions of mass transit systems.

All such programs involve government redistributions and purchases of goods and services. Hence, the effects they have on public-

---

4. Jean-Baptiste Say (1827) and others apparently came to a similar conclusion—but for different reasons—much earlier. An enlightening review of the early literature is provided in Toma and Toma (1979).

5. For a review of the "budget size" literature, see Amacher, Tollison, and Willet (1975). The Galbraith and Downs argument appears to be disconfirmed in Clarkson and Tollison (1979).

sector size become directly measurable. Less countable are the effects of regulations. The direct costs of regulation appear small; running various agencies consumes about $5 billion annually; private-sector compliance costs, by contrast, have been estimated at nearly $100 billion (Weidenbaum, 1978). For several reasons, these regulatory compliance costs become reflected in a shrinking of the private sector and thus a *relative* increase in the size of the public sector. For example, the costs of complying with the Occupational Safety and Health Act of 1970 (OSHA) appear to be substantial (Weidenbaum, 1975). Yet, even using the most generous assumptions, the net effects on worker safety remain minuscule—certainly well below the level of statistical significance (Mendeloff, 1979). The compliance costs imposed by OSHA thus must be considered a dead-weight loss. Such losses, moreover, usually go beyond the sum reflected by simple compliance costs. For example, the substantial costs imposed on industry and consumers by various automobile safety regulations have been shown to have made little difference except to shift injury and death from drivers to pedestrians (Peltzman, 1975a, 1975b, 1976). However, Clarkson, Kadlec, and Laffer (1979a, 1979b) have recently pointed out that the cost of complying with these regulations and others covering emissions and fuel economy have worked to Chrysler's severe competitive disadvantage. Their findings can be generalized to most industries with firms of different size where regulations impose fixed costs on each firm. Hence, competition and its economically beneficial effects suffer as an indirect result of federal regulations.

These examples provide only a brief glimpse of the growing number of studies that identify inefficient programs and excessively costly regulations. It has now become apparent that the public-sector problems revealed are neither rare nor idiosyncratic but grow out of one or more systematic failures of representative democracy. As a consequence, academic attention has shifted away from case studies and toward public-sector growth as a generic phenomenon.

Not surprisingly, those who study public-sector failure as a general problem have developed theories to explain the phenomenon and sometimes have gone beyond theory construction to consider correctives and reforms. This essay examines the implications that certain theories explaining *inefficient* public-sector growth hold for reforms to stem it. We begin by discussing demand-side and supply-side explanations of inefficient growth. Then, the implications of these explanations for tax and spending limitations generally and for a fiscal federalism in particular are considered.

Theories of Public-Sector Growth

We arbitrarily divide explanations for public-sector growth into two categories: demand-side explanations and supply-side explanations. This division simply differentiates between actions taken, respectively, in the private and public sectors. As we shall see, the division breaks down at certain points.

Demand-side Explanations

Demand-side explanations for public-sector growth assume two very general forms. The first form looks to broad demographic, economic, and political changes to explain the (perhaps derived) demand for a public sector of a given size. The second form views political demands as existing in a quasimarket for private goods to be supplied at collective cost. Representative of the first form of demand-side theories is the recent work of Meltzer (1975, 1979) and Meltzer and Richard (1978, 1979), as well as that of Peltzman (1979). The Meltzer-Richard theory rests on a simple model of electoral competition in which voters are distributed along a dimension measuring income or wealth, and in which the median voter's preference for redistribution prevails. The sole constraint prohibiting complete redistribution is the supply elasticity of labor. Public-sector growth in the United States is explained as the result of franchise extensions to lower income residents. In sum, the Meltzer-Richard model contemplates an explicit political market in redistribution, although the redistribution programs adopted can assume many forms.

This approach is far removed from prior substantive interpretations of similar election models. Beginning with Bowen's (1943) paper, the issue dimension on which candidates were presumed to take positions and to be evaluated by voters usually represented alternative levels at which some public good might be produced. By contrast, the Meltzer-Richard explanation views the electoral process as producing a private good for the median voter, as well as goods and bads for other voters, depending on their location on the distribution of wealth or income.

The Meltzer-Richard model is open to certain challenges. First, the redistributive outcome presumably maximizes the median voter's utility. Thomas Moore asks why the median voter would ever consent to an extension of the franchise, since the result displaces him as the median voter.[6] This paradox serves to underline the partial nature of the Meltzer-Richard explanation. Various theories have been advanced for the extension of the franchise. For example, Demsetz (1979) reports that franchise extensions in 19th century England resulted from a coalition of industrialists and workers against large landowners and in support of free trade. One of us argues elsewhere that franchise extensions sometimes result from the political *force majeure* of temporary extraordinary majorities (such as the Democrats enjoyed following the 1964 elections) and at other times from a "prisoners' dilemma" played between the major parties (Aranson, 1980, chap. 8). All three of these explanations plainly go beyond the scope of the Meltzer-Richard explanation. Hence, there must exist other, institutional forces that affect public-sector size. Yet, demand-side preferences for redistribution are certainly also at work.

Second, the robustness of the median voter result has been seriously challenged on both theoretical and empirical grounds (Aldrich and McKelvey, 1977; Hinich, 1977; Page, 1977, 1978; Plott, 1976). In the two decades since the publication of Downs's (1957) seminal work, an extensive and growing literature has developed in public choice and positive political theory. In view of the findings in that literature, most researchers expect the existence of electoral equilibria to be the exception, rather than the rule.

Third, beyond these theoretical and empirical findings, when redistribution becomes the political substance of even the simplest election model, the election game becomes unstable. It has no core.[7] Furthermore, an important empirical generalization about redistribution, Director's Law, predicts redistributions from upper- and lower-income persons toward middle-income voters, a result not contemplated by the Meltzer-Richard explanation (Stigler, 1970; Hansen and Weisbrod, 1969; Hansen, 1970). (They predict redistributions solely from upper-income to lower-income persons.)

Fourth, the Meltzer-Richard explanation has not yet been developed to the point at which it can explain redistributions through regulation.

6. Thomas G. Moore's doubts were offered in discussions at a conference on "The Growth of Government," Carnegie-Mellon University, April 1979.

7. The electoral redistribution problem is partially worked out by assuming coalitions divided by quintiles, in Niskanen (1978, 1979).

The meaning of "the median voter's regulatory bliss point" remains unclear. Moreover, straightforward extensions of simple election models to the regulatory process should not be expected. For, unless preferences for various levels of regulatory purview (for example, quality control and insurance through statutory imposition of liability rules) turn out to be perfectly correlated with income, a multidimensional election game results, in which the existence of an equilibrium outcome is most unlikely.

Elsewhere, we have developed a second demand-side explanation for public-sector growth (Aranson and Ordeshook, 1977, 1978). This explanation shows public-sector growth to result partially from adding programs which grant private, divisible benefits to identifiable formal or informal groups within the population. Several aspects of this explanation have been developed independently, even occasionally by presidential candidates, who sometimes rail against the political clout and "irresponsibility" of "special interests." However, we sought to place certain insights on a firmer theoretical basis. First, we showed that when confronted with a limited political budget, interest-group decision makers will tend to "buy" (lobby for) private, divisible goods, rather than public goods, in the public sector. Second, we showed that the same decision makers, when confronted with the choice to pursue politically their group's own private, divisible benefits or to oppose the public supply of other groups' private benefits, will not offer sufficient opposition to prevent increases in the number of private goods programs that are publicly supplied. Hence, the inherent dynamic of interest-group politics leads to increases in public-sector size.

This demand-side explanation, like that of Meltzer and Richard, exhibits certain problems. First, the model incompletely specifies the parameters of growth. In particular, it provides no explanation of why (and whether) the public sector fails to reach some equilibrium size (perhaps even 100 percent of GNP). That is, public-sector size is explained but not public-sector growth. Of course, we might rely on such ad hoc notions as "political innovation" to explain growth. Alternatively, perhaps no equilibrium exists, and government will eventually (or immediately) account for a much larger share, perhaps all, of GNP.

Demsetz (1979) suggests a reasonable dynamic to explain public-sector growth within the constraints of our explanation. He argues that successive divisions of labor (specialization) have increased over the years. With each new division or form of specialization, yet another interest group comes into being. The result is the potential for more programs to be demanded in the public sector. This dynamic, which was originally discovered by V. O. Key, Jr. (1964, p. 128 and passim.) is extremely attractive to us. But, Demsetz's formulation requires further refinement. Suppose two groups of equal size are constructed out of the members of what was once a single group. Presumably, two publicly supplied programs might replace the one originally granted to the single group. However, unless there are scale economies or other exogenous forces, the combined size of the two subsequent programs need not be larger than the first. Therefore, growth need not occur in the wake of successive divisions, although the initial division of an undifferentiated mass of citizens will create growth.

Another dynamic consistent with our explanation rests on the finding that programs supplied in the public sector share many properties with inferior goods. To see this, consider a consumer or interest group contemplating the purchase of a single commodity. In purchasing that good, the group must choose how much (an amount equal to x) to purchase privately on the "open market" and how much of their resources to allocate towards lobbying for its public provision. If the group allocates y dollars to lobbying or pays some set of public officials a rent y, the expected level of public provision is $\bar{x}(y)$. Assuming risk neutrality, the group's decision problem can then be defined as

$$\max \ u(x + \bar{x}(y)) \qquad\qquad (1)$$
$$\text{subject to } px + y - sB \leq B,$$

where B is the group's budget, s is its tax share, and p is the market unit price of the good.

The conclusions drawn from this information depend on the function $\bar{x}(y)$. The simplest assumption is that $\bar{x}(y)$ exhibits diminishing marginal returns, as in the curves of figure 1a. Notice that for curve $\bar{x}_1(y)$, the consumer or group initially anticipates receiving the good at below market cost, whereas for good $\bar{x}_2(y)$, the cost always exceeds market value. Figure 1b graphs some indifference contours as well as an illustrative budget constraint that corresponds roughly with $\bar{x}_1(y)$. Notice that indifference contours are now simply straight 45° lines, while the budget constraint looks much like a production possibilities curve.

Invoking standard assumptions about preferences, we ask: How is

Figure 1a.

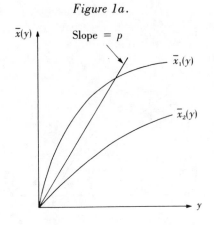

Figure 1b.

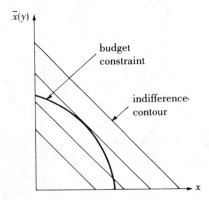

the solution to (1) affected by *s*, the tax rate, which is presumed here to be an independent variable? The answer is straightforward: As *s* varies the budget constraint curve shifts horizontally as shown in figure 2a—to the left as *s* increases and to the right as *s* decreases—so that demand as a function of the budget, $(1-s)B$, looks like the heavy line in figure 2b.

Figure 2b, then, shows that except at a corner solution, the resources spent on lobbying remain a constant as income rises or falls. Thus, ceteris paribus, as the tax rate increases, a greater *proportion* of disposable income is allocated to lobbying and a smaller proportion is allocated to private-sector purchases.

Figure 2a.

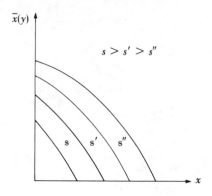

Figure 2b.

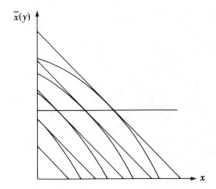

An essentially equivalent result follows from a change in the market price, p. Specifically, for a given s, variations in p affect the budget constraint, as shown in figure 3a, with a corresponding change in demand, as shown in figure 3b. That is, $\bar{x}(y)$ and x are necessarily substitutes.

The relevance of figures 3a and 3b is as follows. If an interest group is successful in securing a private, divisible benefit, then for at least the members of the group the good is public and hence demand increases. But for the short run, at least, the price of that good to everyone increases. And, as figure 3b shows, this increase yields an additional increase in the demand for public provision of that good

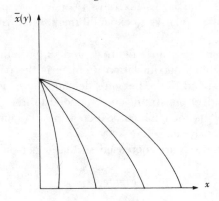

Figure 3a.

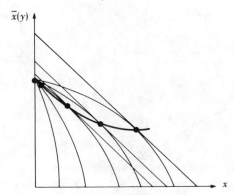

Figure 3b.

by other groups. Taking these two effects together, suppose the members of some group are successful in securing the public supply of their private benefit. Then, for the members of other potential groups, s and p increase, which in turn yields the result that these other groups are willing to shift resources from the private sector to lobbying in the public sector.

Now consider a more general possibility, namely that x and $\bar{x}$ are not the same good. Thus, we write $u(x,\bar{x})$ for a person's utility function, and we assume that indifference contours take the usual convex form rather than the straight line form depicted in figure 1b. What we intend to show is that if x is not an inferior good under the usual budget maximization criterion, it *may* nevertheless be an inferior good in this instance. That is, as tax rates rise, less is spent on private market consumption relative to expenditures for lobbying for the second good.

To see this result, consider figure 4, and suppose that the original solution to a person's maximization problem is the point <u>A</u>. Let the curve <u>OO'</u> correspond to the person's demand curve as a function of income if his budget constraint corresponded to lines parallel to <u>B</u>. Assume that <u>OO'</u> is monotonically increasing (its convexity or concavity is irrelevant here).

Now, suppose taxes are increased so that a person's budget con-

Figure 4

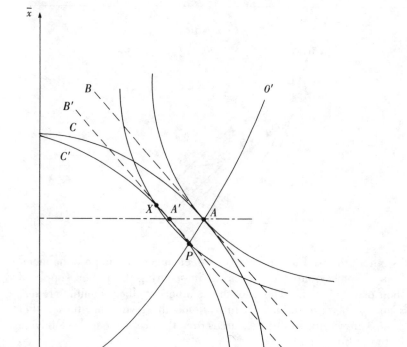

straint shrinks to the curve $\underline{C}'$. From the previous analysis, the line $\underline{B}'$, which is parallel to $\underline{B}$ (that is, there are no price effects from increased taxation), is tangent to this constraint at $\underline{A}'$. Notice that since neither x nor $\bar{x}$ is an inferior good in the traditional sense, the point $\underline{P}$ necessarily lies below $\underline{A}'$. It is straightforward to show that if indifference contours satisfy the usual convexity and continuity assumptions, the new solution to the constrained maximization problem, $\underline{A}'$, is between the points $\underline{X}$ and $\underline{P}$ on $\underline{C}'$. And, since $\underline{X}$ can be above $\underline{A}'$ on $\underline{C}'$, it is possible for $\bar{x}$ to act like an inferior good: As the tax rate increases, ceteris paribus, the relative allocation of income to lobbying increases (provided that a corner solution is not attained).

Of course, the critical assumption of this analysis is that $\bar{x}(y)$ exhibits diminishing marginal returns. This seems a reasonable initial assumption, but it is certainly possible to argue otherwise. There is little if any empirical evidence on this matter. But, the implication that resources allocated to lobbying and related political activities increase as disposable income decreases might seem odd, especially to those familiar with the usual positive correlations found between income and political activity or activism. However, such correlations do not correct for violations of the ceteris paribus conditions of our discussion, such as increased leisure time.

In sum, by the preceding construction, as relative income declines, decision makers turn away from the private sector and toward the public sector for the supply of more and more goods. As noted, relative income might decline because of increased tax shares to support some other group's new publicly supplied program. The first few groups to have their programs publicly supplied create a burden on the members of other groups, who then turn to the public sector in greater numbers. A good example of this phenomenon, but one involving other effects, is government health insurance for those over 65. Medicare and Medicaid have not merely increased the individual tax shares of nonrecipients but have also increased the cost of medical care generally. The result is a growing demand for complete national health insurance.

Finally, it should be noted that public-sector growth through the accumulation of publicly-supplied private benefits fully extends to the regulatory process. Posner (1974) and Stigler (1971, 1974), in their examination of the regulatory process as (implicitly) another aspect of public-sector growth, incorporate the notion that regulation derives from identifiable groups within the population pursuing their private goods in the public sector. Regulation generates private benefits in two distinguishable ways. First, certain regulatory acts help to cartelize particular markets and otherwise generate abnormal rates of return at collective cost. The private-good-public-cost generating aspect of regulation is quite as explicit as when government merely redistributes, say, income. Second, Posner (1971) has pointed out that regulation provides a means for taxing regulated firms, while targeting particular groups to receive the "revenues" thus generated. For example, pre-1978 regulations of the Civil Aeronautics Board (CAB) requiring airline service to very small communities constituted a tax on airlines to subsidize passengers in those communities. Of course, the tax's incidence probably fell largely on passengers on more heavily traveled routes. Recently, the rates of return of many power and telephone companies have been driven to dangerously low levels in response to "consumer advocate" demands for altered rate structures. It now seems clear that the identity and orientation of the regulatory commission's management affects the form of the private benefits distributed but not the fact of their public-sector creation.

Stigler's work is largely empirical and Posner's largely verbal. Neither has constructed a formal, deductive model of the private-goods-producing public-sector phenomena under study. This seems unfortunate because cash and benefits-in-kind transfers on the one hand, and regulatory benefits on the other, represent two distinctly different political methods—technologies—for producing private benefits at collective cost. It would be desirable to understand the process whereby regulation is chosen to produce certain private benefits publicly, while direct grants are chosen to provide others.

Supply-side Explanations.

Supply-side explanations of public-sector growth fall into three general categories. The first category consists of various monopoly models of bureaucratic action (Borcherding, 1977a; Von Mises, 1944; Niskanen, 1971; Orzechowski, 1977; Tullock, 1965). All of these models are informed by the methodological *Weltanschauung* of Buchanan, paraphrasing Adam Smith: "It is not from the benevolence of the bureaucrat that we expect our research grant or our welfare check, but out of his regard to his own, not the public interest" (Tullock, 1965, p. 2). Or, as Niskanen (1971, p. 36) put it, "For a positive theory of bureaucracy . . . the beginning of wisdom is the recognition that bureaucrats are people who are, at least, not entirely motivated by the general welfare or the interest of the state." The monopoly positions of bureaucrats, who then seek to maximize their own welfare, have been analyzed in several places. Niskanen's (1971) work is classic in this regard. More recently, Romer and Rosenthal (1978), as well as Mackay and Weaver (1978a, 1978b) and Denzau, Mackay, and Weaver (1978), have investigated the consequences of bureaucratic agenda control. Tullock (1965) and Lindsay (1975, 1976) demonstrate how the problem of measuring a bureau's *putative* output results in the selection of other outputs to be measured, the quality and quantity of which bureaucrats themselves prefer.

It is hardly true that all monopoly bureau explanations for public sector growth are cut from the same cloth. However, their concentration on the monopoly aspects of public bureaus leads to another question. The conferral of monopoly or monopoly-like positions by government on producers in economic markets can result only in transitional gains, which accrue entirely to those who are producers at the time of conferral (Tullock, 1965; see also Tullock 1978a, 1978b, and 1978c). For example, when the market for taxicab service in a particular city moves from a condition of no regulation to one of prices above competitive rates along with entry control, extant taxicab owners experience a gain. This gain is *only* transitional because subsequent owners would have to buy medallions—permission to operate—from previous owners, the price of which would fully reflect the added returns brought about by the regulatory regime.

Especially in the political process, with increasing numbers of groups seeking private benefits in the public sector, it seems unlikely that the benefits associated with bureaucrats' monopoly positions would not similarly be bid away. For example, Romer and Rosenthal (1978) claim that the rules for voting on school budgets in Oregon communities (with proposed amounts—agendas—fixed by school bureau personnel, and with specified reversion rates if motions fail) give education bureaucrats the ability to secure passage of budgets that are higher than what the median voter would ordinarily approve. They view the resulting addition to budgets, above what median voters would choose, as a measure of the monopoly power of the agenda setters (bureaucrats). Presumably, school system officials, like other bureaucrats, would have some utility for higher budgets (Niskanen, 1971). However, insofar as bureaucrats are elected or appointed by elected officials, the monopoly rents of their positions may be presumed to have been bid away. They may have found it more costly to win their positions (either because of higher campaign costs or more difficult civil service regulations as a consequence of these rents), or they might be using the (additional) discretionary components of their budgets to maintain their positions by paying off specified groups in the population with programs very much akin to private goods. The simplest assumption is that the bureaucrats' market is fully efficient in the sense that gains attributed to their monopoly position remain only transitional. And, if bureaucrats achieve and maintain their positions by catering to the private demands of others, the supply-side and demand-side explanations might merge.[8]

The second category of supply-side explanations for public-sector size grows out of the works of Mayhew (1974) and Fiorina (1977). They view bureau actions as far more passive than do those who offer monopoly bureau explanations. Mayhew implies, and Fiorina believes, that the members of Congress are largely responsible for public-sector growth. Mayhew's analysis points out that electoral incentives lead congressmen to produce private ("particularized") goods for their constituents or for groups within their constituencies. For example, a congressman's constituents probably would not believe him if he claimed credit for being entirely responsible for enacting laws creating real public ("universalistic") goods, such as the achievement of a particular level of national defense. However, the placement of a new defense plant in the congressman's district represents a private, divisible benefit for the residents of that district, and one for which electoral credit might credibly be claimed. Fiorina extends Mayhew's analysis by showing that public-sector growth, accompanied by ever more and larger bureaus, offers congressmen the opportunity to produce private benefits for individual constituents. That is, congressmen act as ombudsmen for their constituents by intervening with

---

8. Some readers of an earlier draft of this essay interpreted our discussion of monopoly bureaus to imply that we do not view bureaucrats as continual rent seekers. This interpretation seems curious, of course, inasmuch as we fully acknowledge the presence of rents themselves as one consequence of bureaucratic decision making. However, the opportunity to find new avenues of bureaucratic (or political) control must itself be reflected in the cost of entry that potential bureaucrats and politicians face. Only if *complete* Knightian uncertainty *completely* prevailed would this not be so, in which case *any* general pronouncements about entry cost and rent seeking would be difficult (though not impossible) to make; at a minimum, positive increments to public-sector size brought about by bureaucratic rent seeking become unpredictable. Nor is it apparent that all increments thus created *perforce* must be positive. The ability to grant individual and corporate income tax exemptions is a case in point.

the bureaucracy on their behalf. The perverse congressional incentive implicit in this formulation is that congressmen should prefer bureaus to be as inefficient as possible, since higher levels of bureaucratic harassment will serve to provide increasing opportunities to carry out ombudsmen services.

Supply-side explanations of public-sector growth that attribute expansion to congressional action implicitly incorporate the notion that legislatures will be responsive to demands for private, divisible benefits supplied at collective cost. Hence, they would not rest uncomfortably beside the theories of political demand developed by us and by Stigler and Posner. Nor would these explanations necessarily conflict with monopoly bureau explanations. But Mayhew and Fiorina fail to address two central problems that might render their explanations incomplete. The first problem is that the role of the president or of strong congressional presidential aspirants (particularly senators) in making public policy appears not to have been considered. One need not postulate the existence of a president-as-welfare-maximizer to understand how the chief executive might be able to put together coalitions to support real public goods legislation and to block private benefits programs. President Carter and Senator Kennedy were largely responsible for the political success of airline deregulation. This counterexample appears to break through the implicit explanatory work Mayhew and Fiorina construct. The airlines certainly did not anticipate the profit-enhancing possibilities of deregulation, nor was deregulation particularly supported by small communities, mainframe manufacturers, and pilots associations. In every sense, airline deregulation went against the grain of private goods legislation. This kind of presidential or senatorial action is not accounted for in most public-sector growth models based on congressional action.

The second problem with this explanation concerns the possible inability of members of Congress to discipline themselves in pursuit of good public policy. The highly touted, recently adopted budget process in the Congress provides little evidence one way or the other. However, Fiorina (forthcoming) argues that the members of Congress enjoy sufficient internal discipline to enforce informal rules of universalism and reciprocity. The result of this enforcement is something for everyone (or more precisely, for everyone's district). But nowhere is there an explanation of why this same internal discipline could not be turned toward the development of Pareto-preferred public policies.

An argument similar to the one we pose concerning the transitional nature of monoply bureau rents surely must apply to members of Congress as well. Whatever benefits grow out of congressional membership must be fully reflected in the cost of winning and maintaining office. Moreover, the frenetic search for yet more ways to divide yet more constituencies to provide private, divisible benefits must not be a terribly satisfying form of congressional service, especially when legislative alternatives appear available. After all, if institutional arrangements in the Congress support reciprocity and universalism, then certainly a higher standard of legislative action, and perhaps even one contemplating a shrinking public sector, might be a less than ephemeral goal.

The third category of supply-side explanations considered here rests on the problem of imperfect information. Elsewhere we have developed a variant of this explanation (Aranson and Ordeshook, 1978, 1980). This variant begins with our earlier findings concerning the political demand for private goods and constructs a plurality-maximizing model of decision making that applies in similar forms to election candidates, legislators in an atomistic framework, and chief executives. It assumes that the voting population can be characterized by citizens' perceptual thresholds for the costs and benefits associated with various privately-consumed, publicly-supplied programs.[9] Supply-side decision makers can proceed incrementally to consider the addition and deletion of various private benefits programs taken one at a time or can proceed globally to fix the total number of programs added and deleted. Table 1 summarizes the findings generated from these assumptions.

As expected, if citizens have high perceptual thresholds concerning program benefits and costs, and if their governors proceed to add and delete programs incrementally, then net results are public-sector growth since more programs are added than deleted. The conjunction of these two assumptions seems to characterize the development of most public policy in the United States today. However, if perceptual thresholds become very low, at least relative to the costs and benefits involved, then incremental procedures lead to net reductions in public-sector size. This pair of assumptions probably characterizes the decisions taken in the White House and in Congress to deregulate

---

9. Perceptual thresholds may derive less from psychophysical properties than from a population's distribution of opportunity costs associated with political action and information gathering and processing.

Table I

SUMMARY OF DECISION PROCEDURE AND THRESHOLD EFFECTS ON
PUBLIC SECTOR GROWTH

		Threshold Distribution	
		Near Zero	*Far from Zero*
Decision Procedure	Global	Net Growth	Qualified Net Reduction
	Incremental	Net Reduction	Net Growth

much of the airline industry because the costs of regulation for the average passenger had grown substantially. With global decision procedures, a somewhat surprising reversal of the previous findings occurs. Global supply-side decision making with extremely low thresholds on the demand side leads to net growth, perhaps of a majoritarian-expropriative variety. But as perceptual thresholds grow larger (depending upon the nature of the threshold distribution), a net reduction in public-sector size results.

When the possibility of legislative coalitions is incorporated into the model, the results become less clear. Nevertheless, under a wide variety of circumstances, the results found to hold with atomistic legislators continue to hold for legislators in coalitions. Coalitions contrived to impose efficiency and block the collective granting of private, divisible benefits programs usually are ineffective. In sum, this model predicts continued public-sector growth by the accretion of private benefit programs, but it can also explain occasional successes in reducing public-sector size.

General Implications for Tax and Spending Limitations

Optimal Public-Sector Size

All of these explanations for public-sector size and growth share one important characteristic. No single explanation or set of explanations provides a measure of how large the public sector ought to be. Most of these explanations arise out of the belief that the public sector has grown too large. Indeed, in many instances that conclusion plainly motivated the original search for explanations for growth. But an explicit statement of how large the public sector ought to be is usually absent from these explanations.

This omission seems unfortunate, for it not only leaves unanswered certain questions concerning the relationship between observed and optimal public-sector size, but also leaves unidentified strategies likely to be successful for making public-sector size optimal. More immediately for our purposes, normative economic theory (for example, welfare economics) and economic explanations for public-sector growth can be vividly juxtaposed. For instance, consider Meltzer's (1975) earlier work on public-sector size. The usual economic paradigm holds that the public sector should correct identifiable market failures: define property rights; produce public goods; suppress public bads; control (private sector) monopolies; and perform certain variants of these tasks. Meltzer states this proposition with the uncommon and admirable pristine clarity of economics:

> The set of data that measures what economists mean by the problem of government does not require a count of the number of units or the tax revenues. It requires measures of efficiency. Ideally, three measures are required. One is an estimation of appropriately defined real wealth in a distortion free world, a world in which the market system works as efficiently as it can. The second is a measure of the distortions removed by government. Governments perform some services that remove distortions and improve the efficiency with which society uses resources. Elimination of private monopolies and reduction of pollution are examples. We would like to count such gains as positive contributions of government. Third, we want to measure the costs of government actions that move society away from the optimum by wasting resources, by prohibiting individuals from choosing freely, by restricting access to opportunity, by encouraging excessive use of some resources and too little of others. (1975, pp. 11–12)

By contrast, the Meltzer-Richard explanation for public-sector growth views the voting decision as the pursuit (through redistribution) of private goods at collective cost. Hence, their explanation provides no easy way, by Meltzer's standards, to calculate whether or not the public sector has reached optimal size. Meltzer is satisfied to say that whether or not optimality has been achieved is irrelevant, for he views the tendency toward growth as inexorable, so the public sector eventually must become too large.

But this view is not helpful if government is not doing what it should be doing, and merely creating (at best) sterile wealth transfers is not one of the appropriate tasks Meltzer had in mind. Under different circumstances, optimal public-sector size might be somewhat easier to identify. For example, the production of some level of a particular public good might replace measurements of redistribution used in the Meltzer-Richard model. In that case, as Bowen (1943) has shown, the median voter's bliss point *sometimes* falls at the correct production rate for that good. Hence, if government were in the business solely of producing that public good, then the median voter's preference would indicate under Bowen's assumptions the appropriate rate of public spending.

However, there appears to be no relationship between this normative view of what government should do and the Meltzer-Richard view (among others) of what it actually does. Or is there? Elsewhere, we argue that optimal public-sector size itself is a public good (Aranson and Ordeshook, 1978). Its production is merely accidental. No one enjoys a measurable incentive to produce the correct level of public spending or the appropriate degree of regulatory intrusiveness. Stated differently, the level of production of public goods, such as national defense, probably reflects the political pursuit of private, divisible benefits through such means as defense contracts, plant and base locations, and higher pay and pension levels for military personnel. Therefore, the level of national defense produced seems largely an external benefit of these political activities. But one might argue that national defense could hardly be produced at anything near optimal levels unless this private political competition for private, divisible gain took place. For example, the weather bureau, which was in the business of creating the public good associated with sophisticated meteorological forecasts, seemed chronically underfunded until its metamorphosis into the National Oceanic and Atmospheric Administration and its simultaneous adoption of constituency-based benefit schemes.

We have now discovered a far more difficult theoretical question. Presumably, perhaps because of the restraints on government functions produced by constitutional mandate, the pursuit of private, divisible benefits in the public sector produces the kind of collective goods that the normative view of welfare economics would intend. Now, however, we find it necessary to specify the relationship between the levels of *private* goods (perhaps as Meltzer-Richard redistributions) *demanded* in the public sector and the levels of *public* goods *produced* by the public sector. We remain only moderately embarrassed that we cannot do so. But, even though particular aggregate taxing and spending levels cannot be adjudged as appropriate or optimal, the advisability of constitutional or other controls on taxing and spending is not eliminated. For, without further information, and with a plethora of case studies demonstrating inefficient growth but far fewer documenting government efficiency, it should be plain that advocates of tax and spending limits are really trying to change lawmakers' incentives.

The Constitutional Question

Some legal commentators, such as Professor Lawrence Tribe, have argued that a constitutional tax or spending limitation amendment would be an inappropriate use of the amendment process in general and of the Constitution in particular. At least in this regard, Tribe and others would *intend* to enshrine forever Mr. Justice Holmes's dissent in *Lochner vs. New York*, 49 L. Ed. 937 (1905): "The Fourteenth Amendment does not enact Mr. Herbert Spencer's Social Statics. . . . [A] constitution is not intended to embody a particular economic theory, whether of paternalism and the organic relation of the citizen to the State or of *laissez-faire*. It is made for people of fundamentally differing views, and the accident of our finding certain opinions natural and familiar or novel and even shocking ought not to conclude our judgment upon the question whether statutes embodying them conflict with the Constitution of the United States." The Constitution, Holmes and (perhaps) Tribe claim, should be neutral as to various economic philosophies and paradigms. In this view, constitutionally imposed tax and spending limits, by formally incorporating the limits into organic law, would circumvent what is properly a legislative decision.

The simple answer is that the Constitution already incorporates various economic limitations on acts of Congress and the states. For example, Article VI provides that, "All Debts contracted and Engagements entered into, before the adoption of this Constitution, shall be as valid against the United States under this Constitution, as under the Confederation." And, the Fifth and Fourteenth Amendments impose due process requirements on the federal government and the states respectively for deprivation of property, while the Fifth Amendment also requires that private property cannot "be taken for public use without just compensation."

The more difficult answer, but one that we believe to be more profound, relies on our conclusion to the discussion about optimal public-sector size, namely, that constitutional tax and spending limitations are really more about the business of changing the incentives of governmental personnel, and less about the substance of public policy. The problem here is to find the least intrusive and disruptive—and putatively the least costly—method to change officeholders' incentives. In particular, these limitations try to break through the private, divisible benefits motivation of public action.

To our knowledge, such a breakthrough has never been systematically and permanently accomplished by any government in history. For a time, public-sector growth in the United States was limited by the checks and balances inherent in the federal Constitution. Since the War Between the States, important and extensive nationalizing forces have been at work in communications, transportation, and commerce. But the relative size of the public sector initially declined. Increased specialization (Demsetz, 1979; Aranson and Ordeshook, 1977), perhaps extension of the franchise (Meltzer and Richard, 1979), and particularly the growth of central administration (Niskanen, 1971; and others), have created a condition whereby all branches of the federal government now reflect almost completely compatible incentives to provide private, divisible goods at collective cost. Simple redistribution from one group to another no longer characterizes the aggregate of political action at the federal level. (Perhaps it never did.) Rather, each and every group finds some benefit from federal spending. Even state and local governments have become indistinguishable from interest groups in their search for increased federal grants.

Again, the demonstration that a significant portion of the growth of government derives from the adoption of inefficient programs comes to us through case by case analysis (polling data mentioned earlier probably reflect the overall effects of this trend). Now the question becomes how the incentives of at least some officeholders might be changed in the least costly and least constitutionally invasive manner. It is difficult to contemplate alternatives to a constitutional tax and spending limit. Various internal reforms of the Congress have been proposed (Fraser and Nathanson, 1975), but these in no way avoid the electoral connection that Mayhew (1974) describes. Indeed, many of these reforms would give bureau personnel an enhanced control over information when interacting with congressional committees. Freeing the president from electoral considerations by limiting him to a single six-year term would itself require a constitutional amendment, and considering the rapidity with which coalitions of minorities form (Mueller, 1973), it seems unlikely that the president would enjoy more than a caretaker government during his last three years in office. Complete public financing of election campaigns to the exclusion of all private contributions would merely shift the political advantage toward those whose contributions are now labor intensive, as well as toward those who enjoy a comparative advantage in illegal activities (Kazman, 1976).

Mr. Justice Holmes's dissent in *Lochner* holds that the Constitution does not enact substantive economic policies. But a constitutional tax and spending limitation speaks only to the aggregate effects of the particular public policies adopted by the legislature. The president and members of Congress would have to balance the federal budget except in times of national emergency (as declared by an extraordinary majority). Accordingly, those who would produce private benefits in the public sector at the margin would of necessity have to find other benefits to delete. Therefore, the minimal expectations from such an amendment would be that the private benefits that continue to be publicly funded would tend to be more nearly efficient, at least by a gross cost-benefit judgment based on the political agenda.

Expectations beyond these minimal ones become less certain, though surely some appear quite plausible. First, constitutional tax and spending limits would stop future public-sector growth attributable solely to past public-sector growth. For example, public employee voting strength forms the basis of certain monopoly bureau explanations (Bush and Denzau, 1977). Increments in that voting strength leading to subsequent public-sector growth would be stopped, except in the unlikely event that the goods and services produced in the public sector suddenly became more labor intensive. Also, long range budget commitments—uncontrollable spending—would be adopted only after the most serious consideration. And, considering the inferior-goods explanation offered earlier, the augmented private demands for public-sector satisfaction would also decline.

Second, a phenomenon now observed to be occurring in California in the wake of Proposition 13 might gain momentum. That is, public-sector decision makers might begin to relegate more activities to private-sector supply. These include garbage collection, some aspects of education, libraries, recreation facilities, and even fire protection. The dynamics involved in this process are extremely complicated because under present arrangements private-sector suppliers of factors for public programs make up part of the programs' supporting constituencies. Where factor producers are monopolistically organized, they are likely to offer substantial opposition to making these activities private. But, where factor markets are competitive, there might be little opposition to supplying the service privately. Therefore, more nearly efficiently produced bureau outputs might be the first to be removed from the public sector. Even so, there would be no added social cost. And, tax shares would decline, providing the general advantages implied in the inferior goods argument.

Regulation and Taxing and Spending

Our work and that of Posner and Stigler point out that regulation provides a means for governmental supply of private benefits as well as for taxation. Both demand-side and supply-side explanations show the public-sector supply of private, divisible benefits to be a politically preferred activity. Direct taxing and spending on the one hand, and regulation on the other, thus become substitutable technologies. As noted earlier, the reasons why one method or the other might be preferred at the margin have not been fully explored. However, a constitutional limitation on tax revenues and spending might lead private-sector demanders and public-sector personnel to turn to regulation for maintaining present divisible benefits as well as for developing new ones. The technological mix between taxing and spending on the one hand, and regulation on the other hand, might now be in equilibrium. Hence, significant alterations in that mix in either direction brought about by exogenous legal constraints would result in less preferred outcomes for public-sector personnel. In some as yet undefined sense, slightly fewer "units of regulation" might be substituted for the now available units of public spending if the level of public spending were to decline. Nevertheless, the public sector might maintain its present size and even continue to grow "off the books," paralleling the growth in the private-sector subterranean economy.

Regulatory sunset laws may provide a useful corrective for this tendency, but only if they force the members of Congress to consider program renewal in appropriate ways. Recall from Fiorina's (1977) work that present bureaucratic regimes probably represent fairly closely the preferences of the members of Congress. Sunset legislation, in and of itself, would serve only to strengthen congressional control of the bureaus. However, if sunset laws are carefully constructed, they might have an improved chance of working. In particular, sunset laws that contemplate extensive reviews of many agencies in a short period of time are likely to reproduce the conditions of incremental legislative decision making with fairly large perceptual thresholds (see table 1). By contrast, if sunset legislation required the review of only one or two agencies each year, and if it specified the route through Congress the reauthorization legislation must take, then a condition of very low thresholds might be induced, as the media turned their attention more completely to the single agency under review. Certainly, the infrequent use of sunset provisions would reduce the possibility of logrolling. Therefore, sunset legislation, properly designed, might be a useful auxiliary to tax and spending limitations.

A discussion of sunset provisions should not draw attention away from our larger concern about the effects of tax and spending limitations on the demand for regulation. While theories of government growth remain incomplete, most, if not all, are consistent with the view that growth in spending and growth in regulatory intrusiveness are part of the same general phenomenon. Thus, a constitutional limitation imposed on growth in one dimension of that phenomenon is likely to affect the other part. The nature of that effect is uncertain, if only because our theories remain incomplete. Hence, any analysis of tax and spending limits also remains incomplete without some attempt to assess the impact of such limits on regulatory activity.

Limitations in a Fiscal Federalism

Implications of State and Local Tax and Spending Limitations

Tax and spending limits at the state and local level commonly arise as a result of popular, referendum voting. Do-it-yourself democracy does not enjoy a good reputation in most western nations. Those paid to specialize in legislating—the legislators themselves—do not appreciate attempts by citizens to circumvent and otherwise constrain their putative rights. Of course, the use of referenda has a long history both in the United States and in Western Europe (Butler and Raney, 1978). Even so, general opposition to the use of referenda grows more out of an academic tradition than out of practical experience.

Beyond rejecting academic disdain, tax and spending limitations imposed by referendum voting might carry one or more of three possible interpretations. First, the increased use of referendum voting in itself probably reflects a shift in the cost-effectiveness of two technologies available to *citizens* themselves for making collective decisions: direct and indirect democracy (Aranson, 1980, chap. 13). This generalization follows from all of the explanations for public-sector growth described earlier. The conflict between the proper role of the state as contemplated in modern welfare economics and in positive theories of collective action, as revealed in our earlier discussion of explanations for public-sector growth, has a parallel—perhaps even an equivalence—in the political science literature concerning the proper role of the legislator (Burke, 1860, p. 219 passim; Eulau et al., 1959). Very generally, legislators may differ as to their "roles" and "focus." The role dimension places at one extreme the preferred Burkean legislator, who tries to be a "trustee." At the other extreme is the "instructed delegate," who seeks merely to register the preferences of those he represents. A second dimension, legislative focus, has the representative attempting to speak for the entire nation at one extreme and solely for his district at the other. Normative positions usually identify the trustee who tries to represent the entire nation as superior to the delegate who seeks merely to represent his district.

Plainly, trustees for national interests would be more concerned with legislating the optimal levels of public goods, while delegates for their district would be more concerned with producing divisible, private benefits for identifiable interests within their districts. That is, the theory of representation in political science and the theory of welfare in economics parallel each other as to their normative intent (Aranson, 1980, chap. 8). However, both demand-side and supply-side explanations for private-sector growth emphasize that legislators' competitive environments lead them to become delegates in pursuit of private goods to satisfy narrow district interests.

Of course, the public sector may be neither more nor less efficient than the private sector at producing such private goods. In that case, tax and spending limitations imposed by referendum voting at the very least would reveal citizens' preferences between the otherwise equivalent outcomes of private choice and public choice. But we have reason to believe that the private sector is more efficient at producing private goods. Hence, referendum voting would probably reveal a preference for private-sector outcomes. Of course, where legislatures are more nearly cost effective in the production of *public* goods, such referendum proposals seem less likely to carry.

More generally, the shift away from the nationally-focused trustee to the delegate focused on the district or special-interest groups signals a theoretical reduction in the productivity of legislators. We suspect that is why citizens increasingly seem willing to turn to the use of referendum decision-making processes. The mechanism that actuates such a citizen preference, following the disintegration of the legislators' comparative advantage, is probably the recognition that what is being done more and more in the public sector should not be done or could be done as well or better in the private sector. Again, the underlying cause of the decisions actuating a preference for the use of referenda concerns the generation of bad legislative decisions brought about by a shift in legislators' incentives to play a particular role with a particular focus.

An alternative meaning of the increased use of referenda to impose state and local tax and spending limitations seems theoretically attractive, although certainly not in the minds of legislators and bureaucrats. That is, referendum voting, especially when it imposes limitations, provides a check on public-sector decision makers' aggregate output and forces them to operate under global decision procedures. This is true because referenda go beyond simple two-candidate elections in that they force the consideration of issues apart from those at an "individualized" level. Referenda, therefore, often bring about a shift from incremental to global, aggregative decision making in legislatures. Thresholds concerning *specific* programmatic issues probably remain large, and thus, considering the findings listed earlier in table 1, a relative shrinking of the public sector might be expected.

Finally, the dullest possible interpretation one could place on state and local tax and spending limits imposed by referenda is that they merely reflect the demand for a private good for the individual voter in the form of a tax cut. This has been argued to be the case with California's Proposition 13. However, the fact of a majority vote for such a motion would again indicate that the legislature has failed to do its job. Thus, whether or not the coin of legislative exchange is in private, divisible goods or in public goods, the tax cost would have been demonstrated to be greater than that sustained by an electoral (referendum) equilibrium. Again, therefore, that limitations might be adopted suggests that direct democracy, at least in this instance, might represent a preferred technology for citizens to use to reveal their own preferences.

State and Local Governments as Interest Groups

The extensive federal support now given to state and local governments has turned these jurisdictions into interest groups with respect to the federal government. This relationship was never more apparent than in then-Senator Muskie's reaction to the growing number of state legislatures that have called for a federal constitutional convention on the balanced budget issue. Muskie responded that Revenue Sharing would be the first program to be cut. He thus aligned himself with public-sector personnel everywhere who, when threatened by tax and spending limits, focus upon a divisible program that might greatly hurt the proponents of limits without affecting others. (Significantly, Muskie said nothing about federally-funded, state-supervised welfare programs.)

Considering state and local dependency on federal funding, the demand-side explanations for public-sector growth, and especially those resting on the public-sector pursuit of private, divisible benefits, suggest a problem with tax and spending limits at the state and local level. In particular, when budgetary limits are reached, state and local governments might turn even more than they do presently to the federal government for relief. The centralizing tendency of this development surely would be costly. But this prediction must rest on the belief that state and local governments do not now fully exploit their possible net returns from lobbying the federal government. Tax and spending limitations imposed on state and local legislatures certainly will not simultaneously increase the level of any fungible political resources state and local officeholders might now enjoy. Therefore, state and local governments will have no apparent way to increase their access to federal funds.

Nevertheless, a different shift might occur. Interest groups that now extract benefits from the public sector at state and local levels, or who simply use these governments as a conduit for federal funds, might find themselves cut off from an expansion of those benefits. Of course, as we argued earlier, overall demands on the public sector may decline as the result of tax and spending limitations, and additional fungible political resources will not suddenly fall into the hands of such groups. But some increase in demands on the federal government may be experienced as a result of state and local tax and spending limitations. Finally, state and local governments *without* tax and spending limitations may also experience increased demands for the supply of divisible benefits.

This last problem resembles the one associated with shifts of crime rates accompanying increased law enforcement or severity of sentences in a particular municipality. Chicago's decision to "get tough" with cat burglers increases the rate of second story work in Milwaukee. Of course, a net reduction in the *aggregate* crime rate of the two areas taken together will be noticed, since the expected cost of burglary for burglars will increase. Also, Milwaukee might itself increase its protection of private residences and stiffen penalties. The parallel should be obvious: Tax and spending limitations enacted in one state or municipality can lead to their adoption elsewhere. We would also expect that any demand shift away from state and local governments and toward the federal government by private interest groups will probably help to stimulate the movement toward a national tax and spending limitation amendment.

REFERENCES

Advisory Commission on Intergovernmental Relations. Winter 1979. *Intergovernmental Perspective*, vol. 5.

Aldrich, J. H., and McKelvey, R.D. 1977. A method of scaling with applications to the 1968 and 1972 presidential elections. *American Political Science Review*, vol. 71.

Amacher, R.C., Tollison, R.D., and Willet, T.D. 1975. A budget size in a democracy: a review of the arguments. *Public Finance Quarterly*, vol. 3.

American Bar Association Commission on Law and the Economy. 1978. *Federal regulation: roads to reform*. Washington, D.C.

Aranson, P.H. 1979. The uncertain search for regulatory reform: a critique of the ABA commission on law and the economy's exposure draft: *Federal regulation: roads to reform*. Coral Gables, Fla.: Law and Economics Center Working Paper 79–3.

————. 1980. *American government: strategy and choice*. Cambridge, Mass.: Winthrop.

Aranson, P.H., and Ordeshook, P.C. 1977. A prolegomenon to a theory of the failure of representative democracy. In *American re-evolution: papers and proceedings*, ed. R. D. Auster and B. Sears. Tucson, Ariz.: University of Arizona Department of Economics.

————. 1978. The political bases of public sector growth in a representative democracy. Prepared for delivery at the Annual Meeting of the American Political Science Association.

———. 1980. Incrementalism, the fiscal illusion, and the growth of government in representative democracies. In *Economics of public and private organization: selected papers from the Interlaken conference on analysis and ideology*, ed. K. Brunner and R. Hayden. Rochester, N.Y.: Center for Study in Government and Business.

Borcherding, T.E., ed. 1977a. *Budgets and bureaucrats: the sources of government growth*. Durham, N.C.: Duke University Press.

———. 1977b. One hundred years of public sector growth. In *Budgets and bureaucrats: the sources of government growth*, ed. T. E. Borcherding. Durham, N.C.: Duke University Press.

Bowen, H.R. 1943. The interpretation of voting in the allocation of economic resources. *Quarterly Journal of Economics*, vol. 58.

Browning, E.K. 1976. How much more equality can we afford? *The Public Interest*, vol. 43.

Bruce-Briggs, B. 1975. Mass transportation and minority transportation. *The Public Interest*, vol. 40.

Buchanan, J.M. 1967. *Public finance in democratic process: fiscal institutions and individual choice*. Chapel Hill, N.C.: University of North Carolina Press.

Burke, E. 1860. *The Works of Edmund Burke, with a Memoir*. New York: Harper and Brothers.

Bush, W., and Denzau, A.T. 1977. The Voting Behavior of Bureaucrats. In *Budgets and bureaucrats: the sources of government growth*, ed. T.E. Borcherding. Durham, N.C.: Duke University Press.

Butler, D., and Raney, A., eds. 1978. *Referendums: a comparative study of practice and theory*. Washington, D.C.: American Enterprise Institute.

Clarkson, K.W., Kadlec, C.W., and Laffer, A.B. 1979a. Regulating Chrysler out of business. *Regulation*, vol. 3.

———. 1979b. *The impact of government regulations on competition in the U.S. automobile industry*. Boston, Mass.: H.C. Wainwright.

Clarkson, K.W., and Tollison, R.D. 1979. Toward a theory of government advertising. In *Research in law and economics*, ed. R.O. Zerbe, Jr. Greenwich, Conn.: Jai.

Demsetz, H. 1979. The growth of government. Prepared for delivery at a conference on the Growth of Regulation, Hoover Institution, Palo Alto, Calif.

Denzau, A.T., Mackay, R.J., and Weaver, C.L. 1979. Spending limitations, agenda control, and voters' expectations. *National Tax Journal*.

Downs, A. 1957. *An economic theory of democracy*. New York, N.Y.: Harper and Row.

———. 1960. Why the government budget is too small in a democracy. *World Politics*.

Eulau, H., et al. 1959. The role of the representative: some empirical observations on the theory of Edmund Burke. *American Political Science Review*, vol. 53.

Fiorina, M.P. 1977. *Congress: keystone of the Washington establishment*. New Haven, Conn.: Yale University Press.

———. Forthcoming. Legislative facilitation of government growth: universalism and reciprocity practices in majority rule institutions. In *The causes and consequences of public sector growth*, ed. P.H. Aranson and P.C. Ordeshook.

Fraser, D.M., and Nathanson, I. 1975. Re-building the House of Representatives. In *Congress in change: evolution and reform*, ed. N.J. Ornstein. New York, N.Y.: Praeger.

Galbraith, J.K. 1969. *The affluent society*. New York, N.Y.: New American Library.

Gallup, G. March 1979. *The Gallup index*, vol. 164.

Goetz, C.J. 1977. Fiscal illusion in state and local finance. In *Budgets and bureaucrats: the sources of government growth*, ed. T.E. Borcherding. Durham, N.C.: Duke University Press.

Hansen, W.L. 1970. Income distribution effects of higher education. *American Economic Review*, vol. 60.

Hansen, W.L., and Weisbrod, B.A. 1969. *Benefits, costs, and finance of public higher education*. Chicago, Ill.: Markham.

Hinich, M.D. 1977. The median voter is an artifact. *Journal of Economic Theory*, vol. 16.

Kazman, S. 1976. The economics of the 1974 Federal Election Campaign Act amendments. *Buffalo Law Review*, vol. 25.

Key, V.O., Jr. 1964. *Politics, parties, and pressure groups*. New York, N.Y.: T.Y. Crowell.

Lindsay, C.M. 1975. *Veterans Administration hospitals: an economic analysis of government enterprise*. Washington, D.C.: American Enterprise Institute.

———. 1976. A theory of government enterprise. *Journal of Political Economy*, vol. 84.

Mackay, R.J., and Weaver, C.L. 1978a. Commodity bundling and agenda control in the public sector. Virginia Polytechnic Institute and State University Center for Study of Public Choice Working Paper CE 78–8–16.

———. 1978b. Monopoly bureaus and fiscal outcomes: deductive models and implications for reform. In *Policy analysis and deductive reasoning*, ed. G. Tullock and R.E. Wagner. Lexington, Mass.: D.C. Heath.

Mayhew, D.R. 1974. *Congress: the electoral connection*. New Haven, Conn.: Yale University Press.

Meltzer, A.H. 1975. Too much government? Prepared for delivery at a conference on "The economy in disarray," University of Chicago Law School.

———. 1979. The size of government in non-slave states. Prepared for delivery at the Annual Meeting of the American Political Science Association.

Meltzer, A.H., and Richard, S.F. 1978. Why government grows (and grows) in a democracy. *The Public Interest*, vol. 52.

———. 1979. A rational theory of the size of government. Pittsburgh, Pa.: Carnegie-Mellon University, Xerox.

Mendeloff, J. 1979. *Regulating safety: an economic and political analysis of occupational safety and health policy*. Cambridge, Mass.: MIT Press.

Mueller, J.E. 1973. *War, presidents, and public opinion*. New York, N.Y.: Wiley.

Niskanen, W.A., Jr. 1971. *Bureaucracy and representative government*. Chicago, Ill.: Aldine Atherton.

———. 1978. The prospects for a liberal democracy. In *Fiscal responsibility in constitutional democracy*, ed. J.M. Buchanan and R.E. Wagner. Boston, Mass.: Martinus Niehoff.

————. 1979. The democratic leviathan. Prepared for delivery at the Annual Meeting of the American Political Science Association.

Nutter, G.W. 1978. *The growth of government in the west*. Washington, D.C.: American Enterprise Institute.

Orzechowski, W. 1977. Economic models of bureaucracy: survey, extensions, and evidence. In *Budgets and bureaucrats: the sources of government growth*, ed. T.E. Borcherding. Durham, N.C.: Duke University Press.

Page, B.I. 1977. Elections and social choice: the state of the evidence. *American Journal of Political Science*, vol. 21.

————. 1978. *Choices and echoes in presidential elections*. Chicago, Ill.: University of Chicago Press.

Peltzman, S. 1975a. *Regulation of automobile safety*. Washington, D.C.: American Enterprise Institute.

————. 1975b. The effects of automobile safety regulation. *Journal of Political Economy*, vol. 83.

————. 1976. The regulation of automobile safety. In *Auto safety regulation: the cure or the problem?* ed. H.C. Manne and R.L. Miller. Glenn Ridge, N.J.: Thomas Horton and Daughters.

————. 1979. The growth of government. Prepared for delivery at a conference on The Growth of Government, Carnegie-Mellon University.

Plott, C.R. 1976. Axiomatic social choice theory: an overview and interpretation. *American Journal of Political Science*, vol. 20.

Posner, R.A. 1971. Taxation by regulation. *Bell Journal of Economics and Management Science*, vol. 2.

————. 1974. Theories of economic regulation. *Bell Journal of Economics and Management Science*, vol. 5.

Puviani, A. 1903. *Teoria della Illusione Finanziaria*. Palermo, Italy: Sandron.

Romer, T., and Rosenthal, H. 1978. Political resource allocation, controlled agendas, and the status quo. *Public Choice*, vol. 33.

Say, J.B. 1827. *A treatise on political economy*. Philadelphia, Pa.: Grigg.

Stigler, G.J. 1970. Director's law of public income redistribution. *Journal of Law and Economics*, vol. 13.

————. 1971. The theory of economic regulation. *Bell Journal of Economics and Management Science*, vol. 2.

————. 1974. Free riders and collective action: an appendix to theories of economic regulation. *Bell Journal of Economics and Management Science*, vol. 5.

Toma, E.F., and Toma, M. 1979. Constitutional spending limits from a history of thought perspective. Prepared for delivery at the Annual Meeting of the Western Economic Association.

Tullock, G. 1965. *The politics of bureaucracy*. Washington, D.C.: Public Affairs Press.

————. 1969. The transitional gains trap. *Bell Journal of Economics*, vol. 6.

————. 1978a. Efficient rent seeking. Virginia Polytechnic Institute and State University Center for Study of Public Choice Working Paper CE 78–2–6.

————. 1978b. Rent seeking. Virginia Polytechnic Institute and State University Center for Study of Public Choice Working Paper CE 78–2–8.

————. 1978c. The backward society: static inefficiency, rent seeking, and the rule of law. Virginia Polytechnic Institute and State University Center for Study of Public Choice Working Paper CE 78–7–1.

Von Mises, L. 1944. *Bureaucracy*. New Haven, Conn.: Yale University Press.

Wallace, M.B., and Penoyer, R.J. 1978. Directory of federal regulatory agencies. St. Louis: Center for the Study of American Business Working Paper 36.

Weidenbaum, M.L. 1975. *Government-mandated price increases: a neglected aspect of inflation*. Washington, D.C.: American Enterprise Institute.

———. 1978. The impacts of government regulation. St. Louis, Mo.: Center for the Study of American Business Working Paper 32.

Discussion of Peter H. Aranson and Peter C. Ordeshook, "Alternative Theories of the Growth of Government and Their Implications for Constitutional Tax and Spending Limits"

Julius Margolis, Discussant

Myths about government abound. Though it would be foolish to say that myths outnumber truths, or that foolishness about government outweighs wisdom, it would be wise to confront most statements about government with a demand for evidence. While the above remarks are made to introduce comments on the Aranson-Ordeshook paper (referred to as A. & O. hereafter), they have been indirectly, rather than directly, provoked by the paper. Thinking about the A & O arguments and other recent theses about government growth heightened my awareness of our ignorance about government and how often the analysis of the public sector is the handmaiden of political bias rather than a searching for truth. Certainly, prior to thinking about the A & O paper, it would never have entered my mind to challenge their statements that in the last century the government has been growing far more rapidly than the GNP, with the result that it now accounts for one-fourth to one-half of the economic activity of the non-Socialist industrial nations. If this "fact" is less clear than I had thought, my new skepticism (or is it confusion) about our knowledge of government is even more increased by the inappropriate way we have of evaluating public-sector growth. What follows is a somewhat disjointed set of observations on government growth and limitations provoked by the Aranson and Ordeshook paper.

The comments will be divided into three sections. The first section challenges their basic argument that a tax or expenditure limitation will lead to a more efficient government. I then question whether this is of great consequence since efficiency in government is not of great

importance. The next section argues that the way we have measured
economic activity has contributed to a misreading of the growth of
government and of the private sector. The argument is that the household economy has increased more than the government. The final
note is methodological plea for less attention to comparative static
models and more use of history and data.

I. Challenge to Their Basic Thesis and Their Favorite Solution

My objections to their basic thesis center around the arguments
about the importance of efficiency; while my objections to their favorite
solution, an expenditure or tax limitation, are that it is very likely
to lead to greater social inefficiency, I also assert that efficiency
consequences are not very important. Since I reject the primacy of
an efficiency objective, my objection to their argument is directed not
only against their logic and evidence, but also against their basic
framework. There are many reasons why a person could oppose the
expansion of government, and if a contraction of the government led
to an increase in inefficiency I suspect that the opponents of government would be prepared to pay the price. I will first discuss the A
& O solution, assuming that efficiency is of major significance, and
then criticize its importance.

1.   *Their Favorite Solution: Will limiting the number of persons
producing bads make things better or worse?* I believe that the correct
answer would be: It most likely will make things worse, but it is an
empirical question and we do not know how to go about answering
it. It is an empirical question because the average level of efficiency
of the government may well decline under a budget limit, but whether
the total will decline is based upon the amount of decline in average
efficiency versus the decline in amount of growth. Furthermore any
change in efficiency due to changes in scale of expenditures may be
swamped by the nature of the alternative mechanisms the government
will adopt to replace its frustrated budgeted activities.

A & O say "even though particular aggregate taxing and spending
levels cannot be adjudged as appropriate or optimal, the advisability
of constitutional or other controls on taxing and spending is not eliminated. For, without further information, and with a plethora of case
studies demonstrating inefficient growth, but far fewer documenting
government efficiency, it should be plain that advocates of tax and

spending limits are really trying to change lawmakers' incentives."
(p. 164) On the contrary, the constitutional tax limitation advocates
make no efforts to change the incentives; they simply attach a limit
on the amount of taxing or spending by government. The limitations
do not restrict the amount of inefficiency that could be created by
government; they do not restrict the amount of intrusiveness by government; they only limit the budget. The argument made by A & O
is that with a limitation there would be competition to procure the
private benefits of government activities and that somehow the "more
efficient" outcome would survive. Implicitly they have a LALE theory
of the budget: i.e., Last Adopted Least Efficient. I will argue that a
LALE model will lead to increasing inefficiency, and then question
their evidence about the inefficiency of government.

LALE is a poor rule for government. To some persons LALE may
be viewed as an efficient form of decision making by a government.
The supporters of LALE may assert that the government ranks all of
its budgetary opportunities according to beneficial output and adopts
spending programs sequentially down the list until it reaches the
budgetary limit. Expand the budget and it takes on less productive
activities; restrict the budget and it drops the activities with least
payoff. Of course, A & O do not overtly credit government with this
order of rationality, but they imply it when they say that the "minimal
expectations from such an amendment [a constitutional tax and spending limitation] would be that the private benefits that continue to be
publicly funded would tend to be more nearly efficient, at least by
a gross cost-benefit judgment based on the political agenda" (p. 166).
I.e., limit the total budget and any additional activity must be "more
efficient" than the activity it displaces; with the consequence that in
time the government would become efficient. Of course, the argument
can become totally circular if efficiency is claimed simply because
one alternative is chosen over another. I do not believe that there is
any merit to the argument that a limitation would encourage efficiency,
and I will discuss this below. Once persuaded that limitations do not
offset efficiency I believe that most persons will still retain their
attitudes towards limitations since I do not believe that one's policy
attitudes towards the size of government are molded by attitudes
towards efficiency.

The LALE theory of the budget, instead of being an efficiency
model, is the favorite of the vested bureaucracy, who assert that the
officials and programs protected by seniority are the more productive

and beneficial. It is not surprising that officials of funded agencies oppose new entrants that compete for the budget. The consequence of this opposition is that growth, if it is to take place, will not be by the transformation and expansion of existing agencies, where growth may be disruptive of the distribution of bureaucratic power, but by the addition of new agencies; sometimes to foster new activities, but often just to accomplish the same objectives in a different way. Old bureaus are dominated by personnel trained in one set of skills, familiar with one type of technology, responsive to one set of clients, and so on. If the bureaucrats can survive by performing familiar tasks they will prefer to do so. It has often been noted that survival is the dominant objective of bureaucrats.[1] As a consequence the bureaucracy becomes a formidable ally of the beneficiaries of existing government programs in defending those programs.

The beneficiaries of government programs are not only those who gain by the outputs of the programs, but also all those who profit from the sale of inputs to mount the program. Therefore an existing program can claim as support the bureaucracy, the suppliers of inputs, the users of outputs, and the many indirect beneficiaries. Against this alliance of supporters of old programs there are the potential gainers of a possibly new program and a set of potential contractors who have not yet invested in supplying the government. There are interesting differences in the gains and costs of new and old programs which give decided advantages to the old, and which make it likely that a stationary government will become increasingly inefficient.

The asymmetry between the incidence of benefits of new and old public programs is very similar to the well-known differences between the short-run and long-run elasticities. The short-run is less elastic than the long-run, so for the near future, which dominates in the political world, the losses of the losers are magnified while the gains of the gainers are diminished. The same phenomenon is captured in the sentence: Losses are certain, while gains are uncertain. The relevant factors are that the beneficiaries of the old services had adapted many other activities to the level of consumption of the public services. A decline in a public service means that beneficiaries would have to change many other activities. (E.g., a cut-back in bus service may lead to a decision to buy a car, or to move, or to get a different

---

1. See James Wilson, *Political organization* (New York, N.Y.: Basic Books, 1973).

job.) Initial losses will be decidedly greater than future steady state losses, after adjustments have been made. In the case of benefits the same is true except the gains are small until there is an adjustment of other activities. Consequently, the public bias to preserve the old. If political costs are related to magnitude of benefits and costs, and it is reasonable to assume so, the contributions of the supporters of the old will exceed those of the new.

The public's bias in favor of the old is reinforced by the bureaucracy and the contractors. Hence the strange situation that though the government responds to changes by adopting new technologies, adjusting to new markets, adding new products, and so on, typically these take place by adding new bureaus, without disturbing the old bureaus. If one prevented the growth of the budget it is true that pressure would be increased to transform the old bureaus, but inefficiency of the old bureaus may have to assume huge proportions before changes are acceptable. Average inefficiency (whatever that means) of the government may increase over time with a fixed budget. Changes in taste and technology may make a constant flow of public outputs increasingly obsolescent. A new agency, even if inefficient, may so greatly dominate the old that the average inefficiency would fall with the addition of the new. In any case, the results are an empirical question.

2. *Their Basic Thesis: The Inefficient Government and the Virtues of Efficiency.* A & O say, "This essay examines the implications that certain theories explaining inefficient public-sector growth hold for reforms to stem it." (p. 146) In fact the theories are not restricted to inefficient public sector growth, but they deal with the growth of government which is assumed always to be inefficient. A & O believe that if they knew the causes of inefficient growth, or really just growth, then they would know how to alter incentives to limit the growth. Implicit in the argument is a statement that if public sector growth was "efficient" then there would be no cause to limit it. The criticism that I will stress is the role assigned to efficiency, the proposition that even if the government were efficient most critics of government would support limitations, and the proposition that supporters of government would defend it, even if inefficient. In fact I think it reasonable to argue that many critics would be more opposed to an efficient government and that many supporters are heartened by its inefficiency.

Is government overwhelmingly inefficient? A & O assert that there is overwhelming documentation about government inefficiency and far fewer studies asserting government efficiency. Since there is no incentive for a government agency to be efficient it would be strange if they were. The government has a monopoly position on certain functions, such as income and wealth redistribution, the cultural integration of society, the establishment and enforcement of laws, the reduction of instability, protection against disasters, and so on. It is not the efficiency of government programs that determines how officials would be judged but the performance of government programs to achieve the above and similar objectives. Is there a box-score on government programs? While I was writing this comment, the newspapers reported a Council of Environmental Quality study by Myrick Freeman which claimed that in 1978 14,000 lives were saved due to reduced air pollution and that the benefits of air pollution control were $21.4 billion, $4.8 billion more than the costs of complying with the act (*Los Angeles Times:* April 22, 1980). I have no brief for the CEQ report. However there are myriads of studies which report similar success, though the benefits-costs calculation is rare. What is the frequency of the Freeman-type studies as against those cited by A & O? Would a critical assessment of *all* of the studies be highly critical of the government? I am sure that an assessment would show the government is inefficient, since no weights will be given to the objectives peculiarly suited to government. If the study were thorough, and therefore beyond the current capacity of economic analysis, so that the socially accepted objectives would be given appropriate weights, it is possible that the sum of benefits would exceed the costs. Despite the general view that the government is wasteful and that taxes should be lowered, the public supports (according to many surveys) the reduction of very few, usually no, programs other than welfare. The largest government redistribution program, and the one dominating the increase in taxes, is the social security program which has the resounding support of the public.

The above argument claims that it is expected and proper for government to be inefficient. Similar inefficiency would be expected of a church, a marriage, and any number of other institutions which produce nonmarketed or nonmarketable products (of which more will be said later). Of course, there is no virtue in inefficiency and it is reasonable for men of good will to try to reduce it. Economists who oppose inefficiency should be applauded and helped, but not when they make efficiency the single objective—and especially not when they propose radical programs to achieve this objective. And it goes without saying that they should be severely faulted if their proposal has not been adequately researched. Social reformers are rightfully faulted because the government programs they espouse often are dominated by unforseen consequences which too often have very perverse effects. It would be ironic if the counterrevolutionaries who seek to dismantle the government should fall victim to the same disease of unintended consequences.

At a superficial level an efficient outcome should always be preferred. The only thing implied by this preference is that one would choose the alternative which has the same number of inputs and more outputs. Unfortunately, for those who are concerned with efficient behavior in churches, families, fraternal organizations, or governments, there are no mechanisms which can force efficient behavior and certainly leaders of religious, social, or governmental organizations are not chosen because of their capacities to be efficient. The goals sought in these institutions are elusive, difficult to identify and measure, but this does not make them any less significant than objects which can be bought in supermarkets. In fact, men die for honor, love, pride, nation, even greed, but rarely to preserve or enhance efficiency.

The issue about efficiency and government is not just the existence of objectives such as redistribution for which there will be trade-offs with efficiency, but that often an efficient solution will be considered immoral. For instance the sale of votes, which might be Pareto-optimal, would be considered illegal and morally reprehensible. The sale of a spot on a waiting list on a court calendar would be considered a gross violation of justice. There are many, many circumstances where quasimarket institutions would make outcomes more efficient but the discussions about these possibilities are "unthinkable." (Witness the great difficulties in organizing a dialogue on educational vouchers.)

A more important disregard for efficiency is the widespread government intervention to prevent the citizenry from suffering too many disappointments. Every president and presidential candidate must exude compassion, no matter how much he should appear as independent as a pioneer or as a fiscally responsible skinflint. He must be prepared to help all those who are disappointed by the results of the competitive race. And yet the spirit of the competitive mobile markets is that most will be disappointed. Workers who invest in one skill will be disappointed since there will have been technological changes, relative wages will have changed, and their incomes would be less than anticipated and certainly less than their aspirations. There are demands for entrepreneurial protection by regulations; and by consumers who invest heavily in material capital and who demand that government assure quality control. Often these demands for individual or group protections from change are rightly viewed as burdens placed upon the productive potential—they create inefficiency. These public acts are the provision of private benefits through government. But identifying the private benefit does not reduce by one iota the social goal of shielding the citizenry from the rigors of uncertainty and disappointment.

The assertion that the government is inefficient as it provides private goods is too often a reflection of our own inadequacies as analysts rather than a judgement about government. Our assumptions about the evaluation mechanism of individuals is highly simplistic. The most unsophisticated man in the street knows that an index of satisfactions must include a set of relative terms, e.g., where you stand relative to your peer group, or relative to your expectations, or relative to where you were last year, or. . . . Our measures of "poverty" are relative and so should be our measures of "happiness."[2] The proof that a government intervention leads to a lowered level of output evaluated by a utility argument devoid of relative terms has little merit. An intervention which reduces variances is very likely to lead to an increase in the utility of the aggregate.

The distressing, at least to the free marketeer, aspect of the more realistic set of utility arguments is that capitalism is fraught with disappointment. The market adjustment process is constantly doling out unhappiness. If the aggregate is growing, one is tempted to believe that there are more happy persons than unhappy. At least two issues should be considered before we rest content with this argument. First, even if there are more happy than unhappy persons associated with market growth, a slim majority of contented may provide a highly unstable society. Second, folklore and psychology tell us of the greater disutility of pain than the utility of pleasure. In economics we refer to it in terms of declining marginal utility of income or risk aversion,

---

2. See Richard Easterlin, "Does Economic Growth Improve the Human Lot?" in Paul David and M. Reder, eds., *Nations and Households in Economic Growth* (New York, N.Y.: Academic Press, 1974).

but, whatever the mechanism, it is clear that unhappiness is more persistent and troublesome than happiness. It is no wonder that many seek the golden mean of comfort. We do not want to burden the reader with too many homilies, but it is this folk wisdom which helps explain public interventions that seem to provide only private benefits but may also be responding to social judgements about policies which cannot be satisfied by the competitive market as it functions in Western society. (In Japan the market is less severe and there seems to be less direct public action.)

II. Has Government Really Grown? How Should It Be Compared?

The usual measure to demonstrate the runaway growth of government is the ratio of government expenditures or revenues to G.N.P. This ratio has shown a dramatic growth over the past century in almost all nations and has grown even more rapidly since WW II. However there remains a need to interpret both parts of the ratio, the data for government as well as gross national product. The real phenomena underlying these numbers have changed greatly over the same period, casting doubt on the most simple and straightforward interpretation of the changing ratios. After thinking about the problem and casually reading in economic history I am convinced that the inferences commonly drawn about the scale of government are quite wrong. The critics of government see tyranny, while its defendants see a growth of community. Neither has taken place. Possibly, this is because neither group has had a very clear idea about what has been taking place in regard to government. In the past two centuries, many things have been happening other than the change of G/G.N.P. and these may have swamped the effects of changes in G/G.N.P.

The G.N.P. measure and structural changes: One of the great faults of the G.N.P. measure is the absence of evaluation of nonmarketed and nonmarketable items. (The difference between a nonmarketed and nonmarketable transaction is that a nonmarketed transaction could be and sometimes is part of a market exchange, while a nonmarketable activity could not be so performed. E.g., the preparation and serving of a meal is usually a nonmarketed activity while the eating of the food is nonmarketable. I.e., there is no transaction which results in someone eating the meal for you.) Many government services are nonmarketed output, rather than nonmarketable, so quasimarket evaluation is possible, but I am not as interested in this much debated point as in the changes in magnitude of nonmarketed output in the household sector.

Two major seemingly countervailing trends have dominated the past century. Organizations have grown in size and prominence. Collectivities have become more numerous and powerful. But at the same time individuals have become less controlled by the collectivities in the sense that over generations less of their time is put into activities controlled by collectivities. I.e., individuals have more leisure time than ever. By leisure time we mean time not used to produce marketed output. These are hours that individuals spend with themselves, families, or friends. These hours are not subject to direct control of any collective.

"Leisure time" activities are highly productive. Many of the nonwork hours are used for sleep and eating necessary to maintain the physical stock of persons but far more are used in exchanges of friendship and love, recreation, human investment, and so on. Some of these activities require no capital, but many of them require large amounts of capital—household durable goods such as automobiles, houses, vacuum cleaners, tools, and so on. The growth of individual, nonmarketed production casts a new light on the growth of that colossus called the government. The power of individuals to act without the collectivity has grown. At another level it casts doubt on the measures we assign to government growth.

The changes in the work versus nonwork time are dramatic. The preindustrial guild worker labored from sunup to sundown, but he had a great many feast days. On the average he worked a 54 hour week. The early 19th century industrial worker averaged around a 69 hour week. He worked a 12 hour stint in winter as well as summer and the feast days had been abandoned.[3] By the beginning of the 20th century the average work week had fallen only to 65 hours, but by 1970 it had fallen to 40.[4] Vacations, week-ends and the eight-hour day are only part of the reduced time at the work place. We start working at least ten years later in life and end it at least ten years earlier. It would not be too unreasonable to guesstimate that the current generation works at a marketable product for less than half

---

3. See E. M. Phelps-Brown, "Labor Force," *International Encyclopedia of Social Sciences* (New York, N.Y.: Macmillan, 1968).

4. See Stanley Lebergott, *The American Economy* (Princeton, N.J.: Princeton University Press, 1975), p. 92.

the time of those of 100 years ago. Not only is the individual freer in that he has more leisure time, but the physical and human capital that he now has is enormous compared to preceding generations. The individual has the productive instruments to provide him with services which would have been unthinkable in preceding decades. But the Gross National Product estimate does not consider these dramatic changes in marketed vs. nonmarketed activities. In fact, the household is equipped with a stock of capital and time to use capital which is unprecedented in the history of mankind. The working classes are owners and users of massive amounts of productive human and physical capital. It is not strange that in surveys those whom Marxian thinking would identify as "wage-slaves" identify themselves as middle-class.

A more correct index of valued activity might result in a measure of GNP which is twice as high and therefore an increase in the ratio of government to GNP which is half of what is reported.

Another aspect of the neglected value of time is of great relevance to the understanding of the models of government. I believe that a correct valuation of time and physical and human capital would result in a great change in the figures of the distribution of income and wealth. The wealthy of the past always had leisure time and household capital. It is no wonder that the working class, equipped as it is with the attributes associated with the affluent, call themselves the middle class. They have the resources which permit them to achieve high levels of real utility.

The wealthy groups, in early periods, retired, sent their children to school, took holidays, and so on. The gains in reduced work have accrued to the working classes. Even though the absolute value of time gains may be more for the wealthy because their wages are higher, the relative gains to the poor are much greater.

I will mention only two examples of historical change which go counter to the accepted wisdom on government growth and instead illustrate the area of privatization. First we have the removal of the state from some institutions, religion in particular. States have become ideological, and therefore civil and international wars about beliefs persist, but theology has become private. The churches must compete for the consumer's dollar and though the state generally provides some general subsidy to religious institutions it does not intervene among them.

A second example, following from my previous discussion of household capital, is transportation. The private automobile has been successful in destroying the public bus, the public railroad, and the public trolley. The owner-occupied car is the prime source of transportation. It clogs the highways, it pollutes the air, it makes the city unpleasant. There is no absence of consensus that mass transportation would reduce these burdens. From almost any "objective" test the private auto is highly inefficient, but its use grows, since "America has a love affair with the car." Of course there is huge public investment in the road system and in the policing of the roads, but all of this is ancillary to the use of capital owned by the households. (Incidentally, there is no imputed income from all of this joint use of automobiles and drivers to provide transportation services.) The private sector has grown relative to the public, but GNP data would grossly misrepresent these events.

III. A Methodological Footnote

Comparative static models are a very weak tool by which to explain the massive shift in social and economic activity which has taken place over a century. A model which uses a few variables and which assumes that over this period everything of interest is exogenous and constant is not likely to have much power. Whatever structure could be assigned to a model to capture the essence of 1860 would seem to have little bearing to the world of 1970. In any case, as one views these two worlds one asks whether the theories outlined by A & O are likely to explain the changes that have taken place. Of course, to explain total social and cultural change over a century was not their task—they were only looking at government. However, a major change such as the scale of government is one of the massive changes in society and is to be understood only as associated with other trends. At this point we require, beyond more painstaking gathering and processing of data, more insights, synthesis, creative leaps, and so on. This is not to deplore analytical models of the government sector. On the contrary, they are absolutely essential to treat certain problems such as the consequences of adopting or abandoning revenue-sharing; the characteristics of good benefits-costs studies; the probable characteristic of a regulatory procedure; and so on. The value of these studies should not blind us to their limitations in dealing with the grand questions of history.

As a final note I would like to enter a plea for more descriptive empirical studies. We have too few time series about government, reliable comparative studies, and data about the borderlines of government as public corporations, regulatory agencies, and so on. We do not have any institutes or research centers which systematically gather and characterize the results of studies about government. All of this has been left to political science, much to our loss. With more attention to historical data, we are less likely to have models (such as the Meltzer-Richard model discussed by A & O) which depend upon the preferences of the median voter to explain massive changes in the scale of government, while the suffrage laws have not changed the relative position of the median voter over the period of the study!

ON THE INITIATIVE-REFERENDUM OPTION AND THE CONTROL OF MONOPOLY GOVERNMENT

Arthur T. Denzau
Robert J. Mackay
Carolyn L. Weaver

The recent proliferation of tax and expenditure limitations and the much noted success of Proposition 13 in California suggest that the conventional view of the collective choice process is seriously misleading. According to this view, citizens, operating within a framework of democratic institutions, effectively control the political process either directly or indirectly through the vigorous rivalry of competing politicians.[1] That widespread dissatisfaction with the size of government and the mix of its activities is observed alongside the support of substantial majorities for cuts in the status quo level of spending

[Arthur Denzau, Robert Mackay, and Carolyn Weaver are Associate Professor, Professor, and Assistant Professor, respectively, in the Department of Economics and Center for Study of Public Choice, Virginia Polytechnic Institute and State University, Blacksburg, Virginia.]

ACKNOWLEDGMENTS: The authors wish to thank Geoffrey Brennan, Roger Faith, Joseph Reid, and participants in the COUPE Conference on Tax and Expenditure Limitations for helpful comments on the first draft of this paper. The research for this paper was supported by the National Science Foundation under Grant SOC 79–08561.

1. See Bowen, Black, Downs, Becker, Stigler, and Tiebout for examples of these types of models. See Reid for an interesting critique of this view of government.

191

and taxing suggests that it is time for economists and political scientists to take seriously the imperfections and monopoly elements inherent in political markets.[2] Once this change in perspective is accomplished, a new set of problems comes clearly into view. For example, what devices do citizens have for controlling the monopoly power of government and how effective are they in accomplishing this task? In addition, how can the effectiveness of these devices be improved or new ones designed?[3]

It is the purpose of the present paper, therefore, to examine some aspects of the politics and economics of initiative-referendum options, in general, and tax and expenditure limitations, in particular. The analytical framework that we use envisions a political world in which participation in the political process is costly and, hence, limited. As voters find it too costly to monitor or control the government on a day-to-day basis, the operations of the government are assumed to be controlled by a dominant coalition composed of "high demanders" and the bureaucracy, subject only to a limited referendum check by the voters.[4] Within such a setting, certain voter groups may well find it advantageous to carry the struggle for control to a higher plane and attempt, through one-shot efforts at constitutional amendments, to limit the monopoly power of the government.[5]

In this political-institutional environment, constitutionally arming citizen-voters with the direct initiative option would seem, on the one hand, to provide a promising and potentially effective means of constraining the inherent monopoly powers of government. This optimism,

---

2. See Niskanen (1968, 1971, 1975), Bartlett, Borcherding, Buchanan, Brennan and Buchanan, Fiorina and Noll, Mackay and Weaver (1978a,b, 1979, 1981), Denzau and Mackay, Romer and Rosenthal (1978, 1979) and Wagner and Weber for examples of models that recognize monopoly power in public supply and attempt to determine its impact on fiscal outcomes. See Tullock (1965, 1971a), Mackay and Weaver (1978a) and Shepsle (1979) for a discussion of the imperfections resulting from political failures of various types.

3. See Barro for an examination of various institutional arrangements, such as the length of a politician's term in office, as devices for controlling the behavior of politicians. See Wagner for a general discussion of the control of politicians and bureaucrats within the framework of the agent-principal relationship.

4. See Shepsle (1978a) for empirical evidence supporting the view that legislative review committees, for example, tend to be dominated by "high demanders" of the respective bureau's output.

5. For a more detailed discussion of why it may pay voters to carry the struggle to the constitutional level instead of facing it at the day-to-day operational level see Denzau, Mackay, and Weaver (1979a).

on the other hand, must be tempered by the recognition that the exercise of the initiative option is costly and, thus, plagued by potentially serious organizational problems. The free-rider problem is especially likely to be serious in view of the "public goods" characteristics of initiatives—one can vote for and benefit from the passage of a proposal, once it has been placed on the ballot, regardless of whether or not one contributed to the cost of the initiative.[6] These considerations raise several important questions. To what extent is the initiative-referendum option, in its various forms, actually an effective control device? What are the key determinants of the effectiveness of this device? Moreover, is it possible that the mere presence and potential use of the initiative option significantly constrains the actions of the government even without it actually being used? If so, what are the likely implications for fiscal outcomes such as the total budget, its composition and the distribution of net gains from collective action? Alternatively, is it possible that the existence of the initiative option, given the costs and problems of utilizing it, fails to impose any binding constraints on the government's action? If so, then what are the causes of this failure?

This paper attempts to provide some preliminary theoretical answers to these questions by addressing them within a consistent framework where the interaction between the government and voters is modeled as a monopoly game.[7] In addition, the analysis focuses explicitly on the costs of using the initiative option as a control device and incorporates these costs into the decision calculus of both the government and the voters. The implications of this analysis for the workings of a political market characterized by significant monopoly power on the supply side are examined in some detail.

Section 1 develops the demand side of the political market by deriving, from an underlying direct utility function and budget constraint, the voter's induced public-sector preference function. This function is defined over the levels of expenditure on the governmental unit's various activities and the cost of initiating a proposed change in the state of the public sector. Section 2 presents, as a reference

---

6. The organizational problems may involve much more than simply the free-rider problem since the government may be able to use threats of retaliation to lower the gains from organizing and to diminish the range of successful proposals. See Denzau, Mackay, and Weaver (1979a) for a discussion of these issues. See also note 4.

7. See Kats for a general definition of a monopoly game and examples of both market and nonmarket monopoly games.

point, the political equilibrium that results from the operation of a monopoly government in the absence of any constitutional provision for direct citizen initiative. The government is run by a dominant coalition of "high demanders" who operate subject only to a limited referendum or rejection check by the voters.[8]

The next two sections examine the impacts on the government's monopoly power of introducing various initiative-referendum options. The focus of each section is on deriving the comparative static implications of alternative political-institutional arrangements in a monopoly game setting. In particular, section 3 examines the case of an unrestricted initiative-referendum option in which voters are able, through the initiative process, to put forth detailed proposals involving specified levels of spending for each of the governmental unit's activities which are then implicitly paired against the status quo in majority rule elections. Each voter, however, must bear some cost of initiating a proposal. Section 4 examines the case in which the initiative option is restricted to total budget levels, with the government determining the budgetary mix that would be applied to any expenditure limit in the post-limitation period.

In both section 3 and section 4 the nonmonopolistic voters are assumed to act as independent Nash agents. Section 5, on the other hand, examines the case of collusive or collective action by the various voter groups in supporting the initiative and putting forward alternative proposals. The organizational problems that plague such collusive efforts, especially the free-rider problem, are addressed. Finally, section 6 contains some concluding remarks. The appendix provides a derivation of the specific public-sector preference functions used in the graphical illustrations.

I. The Demand Side: Voters' Public-Sector Preference Functions

Consider a single governmental unit that undertakes m different activities, the levels at which each of these activities are undertaken being denoted $x_1, \ldots, x_m$, respectively. Each citizen-voter served by this government possesses a direct utility function:

$$U_i = U_i(z_i, \mathbf{x}), \tag{1}$$

---

8. For examples of models of this type see Romer and Rosenthal (1978, 1979), Mackay and Weaver (1978a,b, 1979, 1981) and Denzau and Mackay.

where z_i is his consumption of a privately provided good and **x** equals $(x_1, \ldots, x_m)$. In the absence of an initiative-referendum option, or in its presence when the voter chooses not to bear the cost of initiating a change in the public sector, the voter's budget constraint is given by:

$$y_i \geqq z_i + T_i, \tag{2}$$

where y_i is his income, T_i is his tax bill. (The privately provided good is taken as numeraire.) In the presence of an initiative-referendum option, if the voter chooses to bear the costs of financing the initiative, then his budget constraint is given by:

$$y_i \geqq z_i + T_i + c_i, \tag{3}$$

where c_i is the lump sum cost to the ith voter of financing the initiative. The ith voter's tax bill is given by:

$$T_i = \tau_i B, \tag{4}$$

where B is the government's total budget and τ_i is the voter's share of the cost. The government's total budget is given by:

$$B = \sum_{j=1}^{m} B_j, \tag{5}$$

where B_j is the budget allocated to the jth activity. Finally, each voter has a perceived inverse cost function for the jth activity, ϕ_{ji}, that relates the level at which an activity is undertaken to the budget allocated to that activity:

$$x_j = \phi_{ji}(B_j) \text{ for } j = 1, \ldots, m \tag{6}$$

and where

$$\phi'_{ji} > 0, \ \phi''_{ji} \leqq 0.$$

In this model, a voter's public-sector preference function provides an ordering of possible allocations of the government budget to the various activities, given the voter's income, his tax share, and the cost to him of initiating a proposed change in the public-sector state.[9] This induced preference function can be derived directly from equations (1) to (6). That is:

$$U_i = U_i \left[y_i - \tau_i \left(\sum_{j=1}^{m} B_j \right) - c_i, \; \phi_{1i}(B_1), \; \ldots, \; \phi_{mi}(B_m) \right] \tag{7}$$
$$\equiv V_i(\mathbf{B}, c_i),$$

where $\mathbf{B}$ equals $(B_1, \ldots, B_m)$. With this formulation, $V_i(\mathbf{B}, 0)$ is the voter's utility if he makes no proposal or has a zero proposal cost. The partial derivatives of this induced preference function that are of interest are given by:

$$\frac{\partial V_i}{\partial B_j} \equiv \frac{\partial U_i}{\partial z_i} \; \phi'_{ji} \; [MRS^i_{x_j z_i} - \frac{\tau_i}{\phi'_{ji}}], \; \text{for } j = 1, \ldots, m, \text{ and} \tag{8}$$

$$\frac{\partial V_i}{\partial c_i} \equiv - \frac{\partial U_i}{\partial z_i}, \tag{9}$$

where τ_i / ϕ'_{ji} is the perceived marginal tax cost to the ith voter of another unit of x_j. The voter's ideal point, denoted $\hat{\mathbf{B}}_i$, is given by the solution to the maximization problem:

$$\underset{\mathbf{B}}{\text{Max}} \; V_i(\mathbf{B}, c_i). \tag{I}$$

The solution, found by setting the partial derivatives in equation (8) equal to zero, can be written as:

$$\hat{B}_{ji} = \hat{B}_{ji}(c_i) \; \text{for } j = 1, \ldots, m. \tag{10}$$

Whereas the analysis throughout the paper is presented in fairly general terms, the actual solutions to the government's and voter's maximization problems discussed and presented graphically are based on the special case of a quadratic direct utility function in which the marginal utility of the private good is constant and scaled so as to equal unity. For further simplicity, additional assumptions are made for the graphical analysis so that the induced public-sector preference, for the two activity case, is given by:

---

9. See Denzau and Parks and Mackay and Whitney for analyses of the properties of induced public sector preference functions.

$$U_i = y_i - c_i + \theta_i \sum_{j=1}^{2} (2\hat{B}_{ji} - B_j)B_j \equiv V_i (\mathbf{B}, c_i).^{10} \qquad (11)$$

This particular induced public-sector preference possesses two properties that greatly facilitate the graphical analysis. First, the voter's ideal point is independent of c_i since the income elasticity of demand for the x's are zero. Second, the indifference contours of $V_i (\mathbf{B}, c_i)$ are circular. Figure 1 illustrates such a public-sector preference function, showing for voter a, for example, an indifference contour passing through the point denoted $\mathbf{B}_R$, as well as his ideal point given by $(\hat{B}_{1a}, \hat{B}_{2a})$.

The demand side of the model, in short, is represented by the preference functions illustrated in figure 1 for three voters or groups of voters, denoted a, b and c, respectively. If one thinks in terms of groups of voters, then the voters within any group are assumed to have identical preferences and, moreover, all groups are assumed to be of equal size.[11] Given the configuration of preferences shown in figure 1, voter c (or group c) can usefully be characterized as a "high demander" of the governmental unit's activities. This characterization plays a significant role in the following sections.

II. Monopoly Government in the Absence of an Initiative-Referendum Option: A Reference Point[12]

Consider a political environment in which participation in the political process by voters is costly and hence limited, with the governmental unit of interest being effectively controlled on a day-to-day basis by a dominant coalition composed of "high demanders" of the

---

10. See the Mathematical Appendix for a discussion of the assumptions sufficient to yield (11) as the voter's induced public-sector preference function. This type of preference function has been widely used in the spatial voting literature. See Davis, Hinich, and Ordeshook.

11. Moreover, it is assumed that each of these groups is effectively organized so that c_A, for example, is then to be thought of as the share of the cost of an initiative for a member of group A. Equal sharing in the cost would also be assumed under this interpretation. These assumptions imply that intragroup free-rider problems have been overcome. Section 5 addresses this problem in more detail.

12. The analysis of this section is based on the model of commodity bundling in public-sector supply developed by Mackay and Weaver (1978b, 1979). Other monopoly models of government might have been chosen as the reference point but little of substance would be changed—the moral of the story would be unaffected.

Figure 1

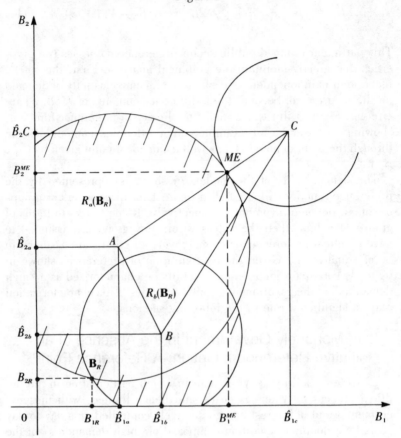

governmental unit's activities and its associated bureaucracy. This
nonrepresentative subset of the population, taken to be voter c in
figure 1, controls the day-to-day operation subject only to a limited
referendum check by the electorate. More specifically, this dominant
coalition confronts voters with a "take-it-or-leave-it" offer in a vote
in which the proposed operation of the government is implicitly paired
against some reversion point involving prespecified levels of spending
for the various activities. If a majority of the electorate rejects the
way the government is currently being operated, the state of the public
sector reverts to the prespecified reversion point, whether it be historically, legislatively, or constitutionally determined. This limited

referendum or rejection check is the only control the voters have over
the operation of the government—the citizen initiative-referendum
option is absent.[13]

The political outcome or voting equilibrium that results from this
institutional arrangement can be found by treating the analytical problem as a monopoly game. Voter c, hereafter referred to as simply
"the government," acts as the monopolist, and knows how voters a
and b will react to the public-sector state he picks. More formally,
voters a and b are assumed to act as independent Nash agents while
the government knows and acts on the basis of their reaction functions.
A later section examines the possibility of collusive action between
voters a and b.

To envision the constraint set facing the government in pursuing
its own objectives in this institutional environment, note that each
voter has an indifference contour passing through the reversion point,
denoted as $\mathbf{B}_R$, where $\mathbf{B}_R$ equals $(B_{1R}, \ldots, B_{mR})$. For any point, $\mathbf{B}$,
the voter has a preference set relative to that point defined as:

$$R_i(\mathbf{B}) = R_i(\mathbf{B}, 0) \equiv \{\mathbf{B'} \mid V_i(\mathbf{B'}, 0) - V_i(\mathbf{B}, 0) \geqq 0\}. \quad (12)$$

The preference set relative to the reversion point is then given by:

$$R_i(\mathbf{B}_R) = \{\mathbf{B'} \mid V_i(\mathbf{B'}, 0) - V_i(\mathbf{B}_R, 0) \geqq 0\}. \quad (13)$$

This set is illustrated for voters a and b in figure 1. If the government
picks a point lying in the interior of a voter's preference set relative
to $\mathbf{B}_R$, then it is assumed that the voter will turn out for a referendum
check and support the government. Alternatively, if the government
picks a point outside of $R_i(\mathbf{B}_R)$, the voter will again turn out but will
now reject the government's action, implicitly supporting the reversion
point. Finally, if the government picks a point on the boundary of
$R_i(\mathbf{B}_R)$ so that the voter is indifferent between that point and the
reversion point, he is assumed to abstain from voting. Since the
referendum check is taken to be a rejection vote, it is assumed that
if the vote is split, then opponents fail to overturn the government's
operation.

The political outcome can now be expressed as the solution to the
following maximization problem:

---

13. For an example of an existing institutional arrangement similar to this, see
the discussion in Romer and Rosenthal (1978).

$$\underset{\mathbf{B}}{\text{Max}}\ V_c\ (\mathbf{B},\ 0)$$

$$\text{s.t. } \mathbf{B}\ \varepsilon\ \underset{i=a,b}{U}\ R_i(\mathbf{B}_R).$$

(II)

In words, the government's maximization problem involves choosing the budget vector, **B**, such that it maximizes its own utility subject to the budget vector being an element of the union of voter a's and voter b's preference sets. Any point within this union, if supported by c, is a sustainable political outcome, incapable of being overturned in the referendum or rejection check.

The solution to this problem is illustrated in figure 1 for a particular configuration of voter preferences. Figure 1, which includes the ideal points for all three voters, shows the preference sets for voters a and b as determined by the reversion point, $\mathbf{B}_R$. The shaded region is the union of these preference sets and, thus, is the constraint set facing the government. Given this constraint set, the best the government can do is to operate at the point labeled ME with an expenditure of B_1^{ME} on activity 1, and B_2^{ME} on activity 2. As illustrated, the political equilibrium lies on the contract curve between voters a and c and on the frontier of voter a's preference set, leaving voter a just indifferent between the reversion point and the government's actual operation at ME. When the rejection check is called, the vote will be split, with voter c voting in favor of the status quo and voter b voting it down. Since the vote is split, opponents fail to obtain the needed majority to overturn the government's operation.

In this equilibrium, the governmental unit's total budget far exceeds the most desired budget level of either voter a or voter b, and the gains from collective action are clearly biased in the direction of the dominant coalition, voter c. This equilibrium is taken as a reference point for the analysis of initiative-referendum options presented in the following sections. The introduction of various initiative-referendum options is shown to provide additional constraints on the government's behavior that may or may not be binding, with resulting implications for the size of the government budget, its composition, and the distribution of gains from collective action. In essence, the focus of the remainder of the paper is on the comparative statics of alternative political-institutional arrangements.[14]

---

14. See Shepsle (1978b) for a similar attempt to derive comparative static results for alternative amendment control procedures.

III. Monopoly Government with an Unrestricted Initiative-Referendum Option

Suppose now that citizen-voters possess a degree of control over the operations of the government through their ability to directly initiate changes in the public sector. The initiative-referendum option examined in this section permits voters to put forth detailed proposals involving specified levels of spending for each of the activities of the governmental unit. The most comprehensive form of referendum check would be an unrestricted initiative consisting of a proposed budget vector, $(B'_1, \ldots, B'_m)$, which would be paired against the current operation of the government in a majority rule election. This form of control over the government need not be complete, of course, for the initiative option may be costly to exercise. Recognizing this, and assuming further that the cost to voter a or b of initiating a proposal, denoted c_a and c_b, respectively, must be borne directly by the voter, it should be clear that this control device is likely to be only partially successful in offsetting the monopoly power of the government.

In modeling the effectiveness of this control device, the government is still treated as a monopolist that knows how the voters will react to its own actions. Moreover, the other voters are assumed to know each other's preferences and to take them into account in deciding whether or not to bear the cost of an initiative, since each voter requires the other's support for his initiative to be successful. As before, the voters are assumed to behave independently and noncollusively. While, in general, this form of initiative check is shown to dilute the monopoly power of the government in controlling political outcomes and generally leads to a reduction in government budgets, the monopoly power is by no means eliminated altogether.

In order to examine the individual voter's decision calculus in this political environment, let the gain that either voter a or b attains by initiating and successfully bringing about a change in the public sector from $\mathbf{B}$ to $\mathbf{B}'$ be given by:

$$G_i\,(\mathbf{B},\,\mathbf{B}';\,c_i) \equiv V_i\,(\mathbf{B}',\,c_i) - V_i\,(\mathbf{B},\,0).^{15} \tag{14}$$

Using this gain function, several other analytical concepts are useful. Consider, first, the *zero gain set* relative to $\mathbf{B}$:

---

15. Since c_i is assumed throughout to be fixed, and since the voter must always incur this cost when initiating a proposal, it is suppressed in the notation as: $G_i\,(\mathbf{B}, \mathbf{B}') = G_i\,(\mathbf{B}, \mathbf{B}'; c_i)$.

$$I_i \, (\mathbf{B}; \, c_i) \, = \, \{\mathbf{B}' \mid G_i \, (\mathbf{B}, \, \mathbf{B}') \, = \, 0\}. \tag{15}$$

This set contains for voter i each budget allocation proposal which, taking into account his cost of initiating that proposal, provides the same level of utility as some status quo budget allocation $\mathbf{B}$. It differs from the standard preference relation of indifference between $\mathbf{B}$ and alternative budget allocations which is defined in the absence of initiative costs:

$$I_i \, (\mathbf{B}) \, = \, \{\mathbf{B}' \mid \mathbf{B}' \, I_i \, \mathbf{B}\}.^{16}$$

The *positive gain set* relative to $\mathbf{B}$ can be defined in a similar way as:

$$P_i \, (\mathbf{B}; \, c_i) \, = \, \{\mathbf{B}' \mid G_i \, (\mathbf{B}, \, \mathbf{B}') \, > \, 0\}. \tag{16}$$

This set contains for voter i each proposal which though costly to initiate, is preferred to $\mathbf{B}$ if attained. Combining the concepts underlying equations (15) and (16), the *nonnegative gain set* relative to $\mathbf{B}$ is defined as:

$$R_i \, (\mathbf{B}; \, c_i) \, = \, \{\mathbf{B}' \mid G_i \, (\mathbf{B}, \, \mathbf{B}') \, \geqq \, 0\}; \tag{17}$$

and the *nonpositive gain set* relative to $\mathbf{B}$ as:

$$R_i^{-1} \, (\mathbf{B}; \, c_i) \, = \, \{\mathbf{B}' \mid G_i \, (\mathbf{B}, \, \mathbf{B}') \, \leqq \, 0\}. \tag{18}$$

The latter equation simply defines the complement of the positive gain set.

Finally, the *individual inertia set*, representing points from which no change initiated by voter i is worth the cost to him, is given by:

$$R_i^{-1} \, (\hat{\mathbf{B}}_i; \, c_i); \tag{19}$$

with its boundary

$$I_i \, (\hat{\mathbf{B}}_i; \, c_i). \tag{20}$$

---

16. Ignoring the initiative costs, economists often use the preference relation, R_i, and its decomposition into indifference (I_i) and strict preference (P_i) to characterize individual choice. One reads $\mathbf{B}^1 R_i \, \mathbf{B}^2$ as "i considers $\mathbf{B}^1$ to be *at least as good as* $\mathbf{B}^2$." Similarly, $\mathbf{B}^1 \, I_i \, \mathbf{B}^2$ is read as "i is *indifferent between* $\mathbf{B}^1$ and $\mathbf{B}^2$" and $\mathbf{B}^1 P_i \mathbf{B}^2$ as "i considers $\mathbf{B}^1$ *to be strictly better than* $\mathbf{B}^2$."

This set differs fundamentally from those defined in equations (16), (17) and (18) in that it is unaffected by the state of the public sector chosen by the government.

Using these analytical concepts, the voter's decision concerning whether or not to initiate a proposal to change the public-sector state, and what change to propose can be formulated as follows. Before incurring the cost of putting forth such a proposal, of course, the voter must be assured that $\mathbf{B}'$ is superior to $\mathbf{B}$ for the other nonmonopolist, as voter c will always vote against the initiative. Voter a, for example, will pay the cost of the initiative only if his gain is strictly positive and voter b also prefers the change. His maximization problem is:

$$\hat{G}_a\,(\mathbf{B}) \equiv \underset{\mathbf{B}}{\text{Max}}\; G_a\,(\mathbf{B},\,\mathbf{B}')$$
$$\text{s.t.}\;\; \mathbf{B}'\;\varepsilon\;P_b\,(\mathbf{B};\,0). \tag{III}$$

The maximization problem can be formulated for voter b in an analogous manner.

The ability of voter a or voter b to influence public-sector outcomes can now be formulated as well. In particular, if for either voter, $\hat{G}_i$ ($\mathbf{B}$) is positive, point $\mathbf{B}$ will be overturned by one of the two initiating a change.[17] The sets of points for which $\hat{G}_i$ ($\mathbf{B}$) are nonpositive thus act as constraint sets on the actions of the government. These sets are referred to as *conditional inertia sets*, denoted $\hat{\,}G_i^{-1}$, and are defined as:

$$\hat{G}_i^{-1} \equiv \{\mathbf{B}\} \mid \hat{G}_i\,(\mathbf{B}) \leqslant 0\}. \tag{21}$$

The graphical derivation of such a set can be illustrated for voter a with the use of several points in figure 2. First, consider the budget allocation given by point $\mathbf{B}^1$. Relative to this point, voter a has a large positive gain set the boundary of which is marked as $I_a\,(\mathbf{B}^1;\,c_a)$. The boundary of the positive gain set (i.e., the zero gain set) relative to point $\mathbf{B}^1$ can be found by setting

$$V_a\,(\mathbf{B}';\,c_a)\;=\;V_a\,(\mathbf{B}^1,\,0) \tag{22}$$

---

17. This statement must be qualified somewhat to recognize that when both voters have $\hat{G}_i$ ($\mathbf{B}$) positive there may be a potential intergroup free-rider problem. Again, see section 5 for a further discussion of this point.

Figure 2

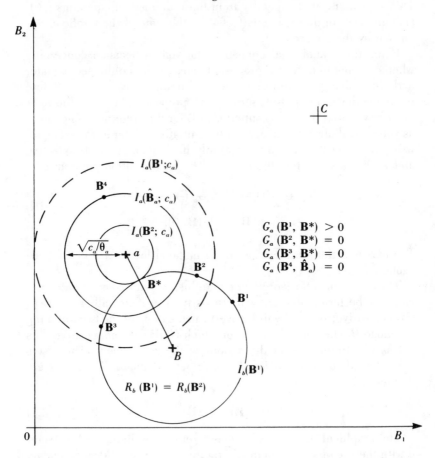

$G_a(\mathbf{B}^1, \mathbf{B}^*) > 0$
$G_a(\mathbf{B}^2, \mathbf{B}^*) = 0$
$G_a(\mathbf{B}^3, \mathbf{B}^*) = 0$
$G_a(\mathbf{B}^4, \hat{\mathbf{B}}_a) = 0$

and solving for the set of all points, $\mathbf{B}'$, that satisfy this equation. For the induced public sector preference function given by equation (11), it is shown in the Mathematical Appendix that the zero gain set defined by a point such as $\mathbf{B}^1$ is a circle given by:

$$(B_1 - \hat{B}_{1a})^2 + (B_2 - \hat{B}_{2a})^2 = r^2 \tag{23}$$

where the radius of the circle, r, equals $\sqrt{(d_a^1)^2 - c_a/\theta_a}$ and d_a^1 equals $\sqrt{(B_1^1 - \hat{B}_{1a})^2 + (B_2^1 - \hat{B}_{2a})^2}$. In words, the zero gain set defined by the point $\mathbf{B}'$ is a circle centered around the voter's ideal point with a radius that equals the square root of the square of the distance between $\mathbf{B}^1$ and the voter's ideal point minus the ratio of the voter's agenda cost to his utility parameter. With the zero gain set, I_a ($\mathbf{B}^1$; c_a) as shown in figure 2, it is clear that voter a can initiate a change that would make both himself *and* voter b better off. The best proposal from voter a's perspective would be to initiate a proposed change from $\mathbf{B}^1$ to a point on the contract curve slightly below the point $\mathbf{B}^*$. In this case, then, $\hat{G}_a$ ($\mathbf{B}^1$) is positive and $\mathbf{B}$ is not an element of voter a's conditional inertia set, $\hat{G}_a^{-1}$.

How can a point which is on the boundary of $\hat{G}_a^{-1}$ be found? If $\mathbf{B}^*$ was an element of voter a's zero gain set relative to some point, then that point would be on the boundary of the conditional inertia set. More precisely, consider the circle centered on voter a's ideal point and passing through $\mathbf{B}^*$. Let the radius of this circle be denoted by W^*. If a point on I_b ($\mathbf{B}^1$) can be found such that this circle is the zero gain set defined by that point, then that point is an element of $\hat{G}_a^{-1}$. The distance between such a point, denoted by $\mathbf{B}^2$ in figure 2, and voter a's ideal point can be found by noting that W^* must equal $\sqrt{(d_a^2)^2 - c_a/\theta_a}$ and then solving for d_a^2. That is,

$$d_a^2 = \sqrt{(W^*)^2 + c_a/\theta_a}. \qquad (24)$$

$\mathbf{B}^2$, then, is that point lying on $I_b(\mathbf{B}^1)$ at a distance of $\sqrt{(W^*) + c_a/\theta_a}$ from voter a's ideal point. In other words, if the status quo is $\mathbf{B}^2$, then the best voter a can do, without making voter b worse off, is to propose a change to $\mathbf{B}^*$; but his resulting gain is zero, since the zero gain set defined by $\mathbf{B}^2$, denoted $I_a(\mathbf{B}^2; c_a)$ in figure 2, passes through $\mathbf{B}^*$. If the status quo point were further from voter a's ideal point, the gain would be positive; if closer the gain would be negative. Thus $\mathbf{B}^2$ is on the boundary of $\hat{G}_a^{-1}$. Since voter a's utility function is symmetric around the contract curve between the ideal points of voters a and b, point $\mathbf{B}^3$ is similarly on this boundary.

A different collection of points is also on this boundary. In the Mathematical Appendix it is shown that the boundary of an individual inertia set, I_i ($\hat{\mathbf{B}}_i$; c_i), for the induced public-sector preference function given by equation (11) is a circle with a radius of $\sqrt{c_i'/\theta_i'}$. Voter a's individual inertia set is shown in figure 2. Consider now the point $\mathbf{B}^4$ which is on the boundary of voter a's individual inertia set. From

$\mathbf{B^4}$, voter a could propose a move to his ideal point, that would receive voter b's support. By definition, however, voter a's gain is zero, and again $\mathbf{B^4}$ is on the boundary of $\hat{G}_a^{-1}$. For some initial points, the constraint in maximization (III) is, thus, not binding and the boundary of the conditional inertia set is merely the boundary of voter a's individual inertia set. Figure 3 illustrates $\hat{G}_a^{-1}$ in its entirety.

In view of this characterization of the responses of voters a and b to alternative budget allocations, the government's maximization problem can be characterized as follows. The government simply chooses that budget allocation which maximizes its own utility subject to not having this choice overturned by an initiative and referendum. Stated formally:

$$\text{Max } V_c\,(\mathbf{B};\, 0)$$
$$\text{s.t. } \mathbf{B} \; \varepsilon \bigcap_{i=a,b} \hat{G}_i^{-1} \qquad\qquad \text{(IV)}$$

The relevant constraint set is given by the intersection of the voters' conditional inertia sets and merely guarantees that no initiative will be successful so long as there is no collusion between the voters in putting forth proposals.

A graphical depiction of this equilibrium is contained in figure 3. To simplify, it is assumed that voter b's initiative cost, c_b, is large enough that his conditional inertia set contains voter a's set. $\hat{G}_a^{-1}$ is then the only binding constraint. Given this set, voter c optimizes by picking point ME_1, the equilibrium for this monopoly game. While the new equilibrium, in this example, lies on the contract curve between the ideal points of voter c and voter a since the boundary of $\hat{G}_a^{-1}$ is the boundary of voter a's individual inertia set here, such a placement of the equilibrium will not always occur. If, instead, voter c's ideal point had been lower than where it is now located, the new equilibrium might have occurred at a point such as $\mathbf{B^2}$. Importantly, however, in either case, the new equilibrium involves a much smaller budget than at ME, and this would be the case even if the reversion point had been on the boundary of $\hat{G}_a^{-1}$ (e.g., at $\mathbf{B^3}$). In general, the move from a simple referendum or rejection check to an initiative system, even if the initiative process is costly, lowers the equilibrium budget level.

The effectiveness of the initiative-referendum process in controlling the monopoly power of the government depends critically, of course,

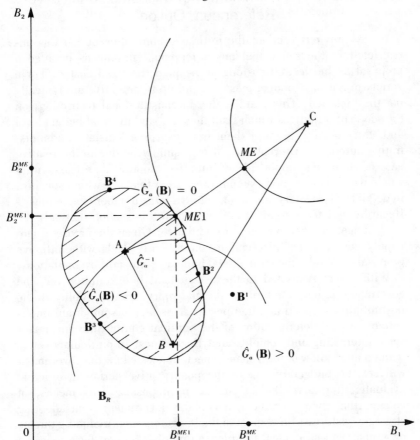

Figure 3

on the value of the c_i's—the cost of initiating a proposal and having it placed on the ballot for a referendum. Notice that in figure 3, for example, the new equilibrium, *ME*1 is a distance equal to $\sqrt{c_a/\theta_a}$ from voter a's ideal point. If c_a and c_b had been large enough, the equilibrium at *ME* may have been in the interior of the intersection of $\hat{G}_a^{-1}$ and $\hat{G}_b^{-1}$. In this case, the cost of initiating a proposal is so great that the presence of the initiative-referendum option, even in its unrestricted form, provides no additional constraint on the exercise of the government's monopoly power. Its usefulness as a control device is then nil.

IV. Monopoly Government with a Restricted Initiative-Referendum Option

In the previous section, the initiative-referendum option was un-restricted in the sense that any voter could initiate as detailed a proposal as he desired so long as he paid the fixed cost c_i. For a variety of reasons, budget measures put up by initiative are typically not this detailed. This may be due to constitutional restrictions on the scope of initiatives which limit them to, say, the total budget level and, thus, legally prohibit them from usurping legislative-adminis-trative authority. Alternatively, it may simply be due to the relative ease of obtaining support for an initiative proposal that deals with a single issue such as total expenditures rather than one which specifies in detail the budgetary allocation across a large number of activities.[18] Regardless of the reason, it is assumed in this section that only the total budget can be controlled by initiative. Given the nature of mo-nopoly government, this section consequently deals with initiative proposals that take the form of total budget or expenditure limitations.

With voters restricted to the use of total budget initiatives, the government is left to determine the budgetary mix that applies in the postinitiative or postlimitation period. This fact has important impli-cations for the determination of the political equilibrium and raises some interesting and complex analytical issues. In particular, voters a and b must know or form some expectation as to how the government will set the budgetary mix in the postinitiative period in order to evaluate alternative budget limitation proposals. This means, of course, that there may be gains to the government from adopting strategic postures with respect to the budgetary mix, including threats or punishment strategies, in order to diminish support for a proposal or reduce the chances that an initiative effort will be successful in gaining the required signatures.[19] This type of strategic behavior cer-tainly took place in California before the passage of Proposition 13.[20]

Without passing judgement on the actual importance of these stra-tegic considerations, this section makes the analytically more tractable assumption that voters expect the government or dominant coalition

---

18. See Shepsle (1972) for an analysis of the potential gains to political candidates from adopting vague platforms.

19. See Denzau, Mackay, and Weaver (1979a) for an analysis of these issues.

20. There is some preliminary evidence from California that these threats were not carried out to a significant extent. See Balbien.

simply to accept a successful budget initiative and, conditional on
its level, choose the budgetary mix in the postlimitation period so as
to maximize its own utility. For any given budget limit, then, the
government is expected to choose the mix by solving the maximization
problem:

$$\text{Max}_{\mathbf{B}} \; V_C \, (\mathbf{B}, \, 0)$$

$$\text{s.t. } B = \sum_{j=1}^{m} B_j. \tag{V}$$

Each voter takes this expectation into account in deciding both
whether or not to propose an initiative and how to vote on one if it
is proposed. Each voter, thus, expects the set of solutions to (*V*) to
be a constraint on his decisions. This constraint set can be expressed
as follows:

$$C \equiv \{\mathbf{B} \mid \mathbf{B} \text{ is a solution to } (V), \text{ for } 0 \leqslant B\}. \tag{25}$$

   In evaluating the gain from initiating a budget limitation proposal,
each voter must take into account not only that the government will
determine the actual budgetary mix that applies but also that the other
voter's support is necessary in gaining approval at the referendum
stage. Any budget limitation proposal by voter *a*, that is, is expected
to lead to a particular budgetary mix, as given by equation (*25*), and
this combined budgetary outcome must make voter *b* better off than
he is at the status quo point. For voter *a*, therefore, the maximum
gain from proposing a feasible change in the state of the public sector
(i.e., one that will receive majority approval) is given by the solution
to the maximization problem:

$$\hat{G}_a \, (\mathbf{B}) \equiv \text{Max}_{\mathbf{B}'} G_a \, (\mathbf{B}, \, \mathbf{B}')$$

$$\text{s.t. } \mathbf{B}' \; \varepsilon \; P_b \, (\mathbf{B}, \, 0) \cap C. \tag{VI}$$

If the resulting gain to voter *a* is positive, he will pay the cost of
initiating the limitation proposal.
   As in section 2, there will be some set of points for voter *a*, denoted
$\hat{G}_a^{-1}$, such that he initiates no proposals. This is the *conditional inertia
set*, defined by:

$$\hat{G}_a^{-1} = \{\mathbf{B}| \ \hat{G}_a \ (\mathbf{B}) \leqslant 0 \text{ or } P_b \ (\mathbf{B}; 0) \cap C = \phi\}. \qquad (26)$$

Notice that there are two reasons for not initiating a proposal. As before, the gain may be nonpositive and, thus, it is not worth the cost. Alternatively, there may be no feasible change that will gain the other voter's approval. This problem is best seen in figure 4.

Figure 4 illustrates how to locate the boundary of the conditional inertia set. Notice first that voter a's "most preferred" outcome is $\mathbf{B}^{**}$, where his indifference curve is tangent to the straight line

Figure 4

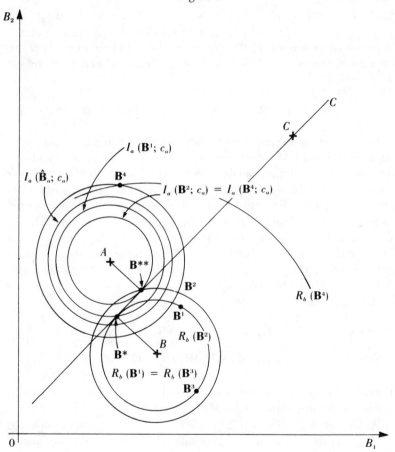

representing C, which is the government's reaction function to total budget limitations.[21] Voter b, similarly, would prefer to be at $\mathbf{B}^*$. From an initial point, $\mathbf{B}^1$, voter a seems to gain by proposing $\mathbf{B}^*$, but since this is not strictly better for voter b, it is not a feasible proposal. In fact, all points that voter b considers indifferent to $\mathbf{B}^*$ will be on the boundary of the conditional inertia set since a small movement in the direction away from voter b's ideal point makes $\mathbf{B}^*$ feasible and yields a positive gain for voter a. Consequently, $\mathbf{B}^1$ and $\mathbf{B}^3$ are on the boundary of $\hat{G}_a^{-1}$. Consider point $\mathbf{B}^2$ which just yields a zero gain set that passes through $\mathbf{B}^{**}$. Point $\mathbf{B}^2$ is again on the boundary of the feasible set, but it is also a zero gain point for voter a. A small movement to lower utility levels for voters a and b will put one in the positive gain set for voter a, implying that $\mathbf{B}^2$ is on the boundary of $\hat{G}_a^{-1}$. Finally, point $\mathbf{B}^4$, which is indifferent to $\mathbf{B}^2$ for voter a, is on that boundary as well since $\mathbf{B}^{**}$ is strictly preferred by voter b, but a's gain is zero. Note that in the region voter b evaluates as better than $\mathbf{B}^1$ but worse than $\mathbf{B}^2$, voter a's best initiative choice varies smoothly on the line segment joint $\mathbf{B}^*$ and $\mathbf{B}^{**}$. The resulting $\hat{G}_a^{-1}$ set is shown in figure 5.

The government's maximization problem is formally the same as (IV) in section 3 except for the new definition of the inertia sets.[22] As before, it is assumed that:

$$\hat{G}_a^{-1} \subset \hat{G}_b^{-1}; \tag{27}$$

implying that voter a's conditional inertia set is the relevant constraint. The new equilibrium is given by $ME2$ in figure 5, and has several properties of interest. First, both $ME1$ and $ME2$ are on the contract curve between voters a and c. For this case, the restricted initiative option moves the new equilibrium to a point that is a distance $\sqrt{(W^{**})^2 + c_a/\theta_a}$ away from voter a's ideal point, where W^{**} is the distance that his ideal point is from his most preferred point along the line C. This compares to the situation at $ME1$ where the equilibrium is a distance of only $\sqrt{c_a/\theta_a}$ from his ideal point. Second, the

---

21. For the case of circular indifference curves the C set is a straight line with a slope of plus one passing that through voter c's ideal point. By "most preferred" outcome, it is meant subject to the constraint imposed by c.

22. For complete mathematical correctness, the government's problem should be stated as finding a supremum rather than maximum since the feasible set is not closed.

Figure 5

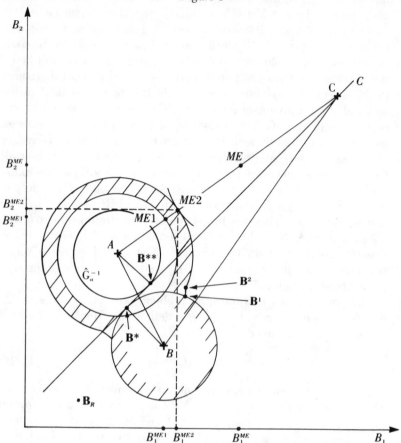

final equilibrium illustrated in figure 5 does not lie along the C set as it would if an actual initiative were passed. Instead, the government is willing to move along its new choice set choosing a new status quo point that involves altering the budgetary mix in exchange for a larger budget. Finally, the change from an unrestricted initiative option to one restricted to total budget levels alone leads, under most circumstances, to a larger government budget or, at a minimum, to one at least as large as before.

In this and the previous section the mere existence of the initiative-referendum option, assuming that the cost of exercising the initiative (i.e., c_a or c_b) is not too large, induces the monopoly government to alter its behavior and, at least to some extent, to be more responsive to voters. As long as the government recognizes the change in its choice set and responds appropriately, there will be no initiative exercised or referendum called. The response by the government to the change in its institutional environment leaves each voter without incentive to try to alter the state of the public sector. In these cases, only if the government makes a "mistake," in the sense of choosing a point in the positive gain set of one of the voters, will an initiative be called and a referendum take place. Importantly, then, the initiative-referendum option can play a key role in controlling the monopoly power of the government even if it is not actually exercised. Its mere presence and potential use constrain the actions of the government and alters fiscal outcomes, redistributing the gains from collective action back towards the voters in general. This result, of course, is similar to the effect of potential entry in constraining monopolistic pricing practices in private markets.

V. The Logic of Participation in the Initiative-Referendum Process

The analysis in sections 3 and 4 is based on a highly simplified model of the initiative-referendum process. The analysis, for the most part, is restricted to a three person world; the hope, of course, being that the lessons learned from this simple model will provide at least some insight into the far more complex reality. The analysis of these sections, however, can be extended somewhat and made richer by simply reinterpreting it in terms of three groups of voters instead of three individual voters. When interpreted in this manner, the voters within any particular group, such as group a, are assumed to have identical preferences. One can then simply think of voters being "stacked up" at each of the ideal points and, to simplify the discussion, assume that the mass of voters at each point is identical.

Within this framework it is fruitful to distinguish between two types of collusive action on the part of voters in attempting to counter the monopoly power of government—intragroup and intergroup collusive arrangements. When the previous analysis is viewed from this large-number perspective, then it is quite clear that these sections are implicitly assuming that all intragroup organizational problems have been overcome. All voters of type a, for example, have formed an effective coalition in which they agree to share the costs of initiating a proposal. Under the restrictive assumptions being made here the group should have no problem, once organized, in reaching an agreement on the actual proposal to place on the ballot since they have identical preferences.

But, in a large number setting it is by no means clear that this group will be able to organize effectively in the first place. Aside from the direct organizational costs, individuals' efforts at organizing the group may well be plagued by a serious intragroup free-rider problem. That is, although each member of group a might gain from a well designed initiative proposal, each member has an incentive to shirk or free-ride off the efforts of the other members of the group. If they are successful in getting a proposal on the ballot, the free-rider can vote for the benefit from the passage of the proposal without bearing any of the costs of the initiative.[23] Unless the group can successfully overcome this free-rider problem and other organizational problems, it is unlikely that they would pose any significant counterthreat to the government's monopoly power. In particular, with many members of the group refusing to participate, the remaining members, even if they do get organized, might find that their share of the cost of the initiative outweighs the gain to them from getting their proposal passed. In other words, the $\hat{G}_a^{-1}$ set for these individuals includes the initial monopoly equilibrium as an element since there has not been a sufficient spreading of the cost of the initiative. To the extent that these problems are serious, the conclusions of sections 3 and 4, about the effectiveness of the initiative option as a control device are overly optimistic.

Even if these intragroups organizational problems are overcome, there may be additional intergroup organizational problems due to differences in preferences that limit the effectiveness of the initiative option. Recall that the previous sections explicitly assumed that voters a and b behaved independently of one another with no coalition being formed. In other words, if voters a and b, or voter groups a and b, are able to get together and work out some cooperative action, then they might be able to further constrain the actions of the government and make themselves even better off.

---

23. See Tullock (1971a) for a further discussion of public decisions as "public goods." See also Auster (1974) and Tullock (1971b) for a formal analysis of the logic or calculus of participation in collective action.

This possibility is worth considering. Assume that groups a and b get together to bargain about both the content of the proposal and the cost sharing arrangement for initiating it. The logic for such bargaining is clear—large gains are available if the two groups can form a coalition to overturn the government manipulated equilibrium.

To see this point, consider the case of an unrestricted initiative option and suppose that group a has the lower initiative cost. Groups a and b will try to reach an agreement on a unique proposal, $\mathbf{B}'$, and some scheme of cost sharing. The latter can be represented by λ_a and λ_b which are the shares of c_a paid by groups a and b respectively. The coalition is not restricted to simple cost sharing but can agree to additional side payments. That is, the shares can lie outside the closed unit interval $[0, 1]$, so long as

$$\sum_{i=a,b} \lambda_i = 1. \tag{28}$$

For some status quo, $\mathbf{B}$, the coalition has a set of viable proposals so long as for some cost sharing arrangement the intersection of their preferred sets (defined relative to $\mathbf{B}$ and $\lambda_i c_a$) is non-empty. Stated formally, there is a viable proposal so long as

$$\bigcup_{\lambda} \bigcap_{i=a,b} P_i (\mathbf{B}, \lambda_i c_a) \neq \phi. \tag{29}$$

If there are viable proposals, the exchange equilibrium between the two groups can be characterized by considering the solution set for the following maximization problem for all $\overline{V}_b$:

$$\operatorname*{Max}_{\lambda, \ \mathbf{B}'} V_a (\mathbf{B}', \lambda_a c_a)$$

$$\text{s.t. } \lambda_a + \lambda_b = 1 \tag{VII}$$

$$V_b (\mathbf{B}', \lambda_b c_a) \geqq \overline{V}_b.$$

It is fairly easy to show that any point satisfying (VII) must lie on the contract curve between groups a and b. Call the set of solutions to (VII) for which both groups are better off $\hat{G}^+(\mathbf{B})$:

$$\hat{G}^+(\mathbf{B}) = \{\mathbf{B}' \mid V_i (\mathbf{B}', \lambda_i c_a) > V_i (\mathbf{B}, 0) \text{ for} \tag{30}$$
$$i = a, b \text{ and } (\lambda, \mathbf{B}) \text{ is a solution VII}.$$

Under certain conditions, involving restrictions on the induced utility function given by equation (11) and the locations of the ideal points of voters a and b relative to the status quo point, it is possible to show that the G^+ ($\mathbf{B}^{ME1}$) set includes the entire contract curve between the two voters. In other words, any point on the contract is, then, a viable and winning proposal that can defeat the status quo, $\mathbf{B}^{ME1}$, for some collusive arrangement involving a specified cost sharing scheme between voter a and voter b. In summary, if groups a and b are able to collude successfully and the government fails to react to the new situation, possibly because it did not believe the collusion would be successful, then these groups will reach an agreement in this case in which they propose some point on the contract curve and share the cost of the initiative in some specified fashion. Once on the ballot, of course, the proposal will pass with groups a and b voting in favor of it while group c is opposed. The final total budget level that results from this successful initiative effort will be between group a's and group b's most preferred total budget levels; that is, between $\hat{B}_a$ and $\hat{B}_b$.[24]

There is one final case that has not been mentioned but is worth considering. Assume the two groups of voters are organized internally but are acting independently of one another—they are not colluding. In this case, an intergroup free-rider problem might develop. To see this possibility, suppose that the government has picked some status quo point that lies outside the conditional inertia set for both groups of voters. That is, each group would find it profitable to finance an initiative proposal that would make it better off while leaving the other voter group at least as well off and possibly, it is important to note, even better off. If it turns out that a is made better off by letting group b put forward its proposal and pay the cost of the initiative rather than by putting forward its own proposal and paying the cost itself *and* if a similar statement is true for group b, then both groups may be led to inaction. Each group, in effect, hopes to free-ride off the action of the other. This intergroup free-rider problem may lead to no effective counter to the government's action and, hence, to the failure of the initiative option as a control device.

---

24. This analysis has not allowed for the possibility that the dominant coalition might counter with an initiative proposal of its own. For a discussion of this possibility and its effects on the likely success and ultimate outcome of initiative efforts see Denzau, Mackay, and Weaver (1979a).

VI. Concluding Remarks

This paper has examined the effectiveness of the initiative-referendum option, in its various forms, as an institutional device for controlling the monopoly power of government and, hence, restricting its expansionist tendencies. The paper illustrated that when the costs to citizens of exercising the initiative option are relatively small, possibly because the requirements for placing a proposal on the ballot are minimal or because voter groups have been able to organize successfully to spread the costs over a large number of individuals, then it may act as a significant constraint on the actions of the government. Moreover, the mere existence of the initiative option under these circumstances may lead to less expenditure even without the initiative option actually being utilized. Also, the more restricted the initiative option is, the less, in general, it constrains the government and the more likely it is that the gains from collective action will be biased away from voters in general and towards the dominant coalition controlling the day-to-day operations of government. Finally, if the costs of exercising the initiative option are large, possibly because of demanding requirements or the inability of voter groups to organize because of the free-rider problem or because of threats of retaliation by the government, then the existence of the initiative option may impose no binding constraints on the government. As a control device, it may then be a complete failure—merely another institutional trapping of "democracy" serving no useful function.

The analysis contained in this paper suggests a number of possible avenues for future research.[25] First, there are other control devices, such as the recall option, to mention only one, that also deserve more careful study and evaluation. Second, there may be ways of improving the existing control devices, such as lower initiative requirements or possibly compensating the initiators of successful proposals, to make them more effective, or there may be new devices that might more effectively constrain the government. Third, from an analytical per-

---

25. The analytical concepts developed in this paper can also be applied to more traditional problems in the theory of voting. For example, Denzau, Mackay, and Weaver (1979b) use the concept of the conditional inertia set—renamed the coalition inertia set—to examine the possibility of majority rule equilibria in a world with positive agenda costs for all voters. In this paper the monopoly game construction of the current paper is dropped, with all voters being treated as Nash agents.

spective, the model examined in this paper should be extended to allow for alternative expectational assumptions on the part of voters and more complex strategies by the government in the context of restricted initiatives. Finally, from an institutional perspective, the analytical framework presented here could be used to evaluate the various features of existing initiative options as they are detailed in actual state constitutions. In short, the general problem of the control of politicians and bureaucrats in a representative democracy deserves much more serious attention—at both the theoretical and the empirical level—than it has received to date from economists and political scientists.

Mathematical Appendix

The Induced Public-Sector Preference Function

The induced public-sector preference functions used in the graphical analysis in this paper can be derived from the voter's direct utility function, assumed to be a quadratic, and given by:

$$U_i = z_i + \sum_{j=1}^{2} \left(\alpha_{ji} x_j - \frac{\beta_{ji}}{2} x_j^2 \right), \tag{A1}$$

for $z_i \equiv$ voter i's consumption of a privately provided good,

         $x_j \equiv$ voter i's consumption of the jth publicly provided good,

$\alpha_{ji}, \beta_{ji} \equiv$ utility parameters,

and his budget constraint given by:

$$y_i = z_i + \tau_i B + c_i, \text{ with} \tag{A2}$$

$$B = B_1 + B_2, \text{ and} \tag{A3}$$

$$B_j = \mu_j x_j \tag{A4}$$

for $y_i \equiv$ voter i's total income,

         $B \equiv$ the total budget of the government unit,

         $B_j \equiv$ the budget allocated to the jth activity,

         $\tau_i \equiv$ voter i's tax share,

         $\mu_j \equiv 1/\Phi_j'(B_j) \equiv$ the reported unit cost of the jth activity, assumed to be the same for all voters,

$c_i \equiv$ the lump sum cost to the ith voter of financing the initiative.

Substituting (A4) into (A3) into (A2) and rearranging and substituting into (A1) to eliminate z_i and then rearranging (A1) yields:

$$U_i = y_i - c_i + \sum_{j=1}^{2} \frac{\beta_{ji}}{2} (2\hat{x}_{ji} - x_j) x_j, \text{ where} \tag{A5}$$

$$\hat{x}_{ji} = (\alpha_{ji} - \tau_i \mu_j)/\beta_{ji} \tag{A6}$$

is voter i's most preferred value of x_j. Equation (A6) is voter i's demand curve for x_j and it is linear, independent of the "price" of the other publicly provided good, and independent of income (i.e., a zero income elasticity of demand). Define $\hat{B}_{ji}$ as voter i's most preferred level of expenditure on activity j, that is,

$$\hat{B}_{ji} = \mu_j \hat{x}_i. \tag{A7}$$

The voter's ideal point is given by $\hat{\mathbf{B}}_i$ which equals $(\hat{\mathbf{B}}_{1i}, \hat{\mathbf{B}}_{2i})$. Substituting (A7) and (A4) into (A5) gives:

$$U_i = y_i - c_i + \sum_{j=1}^{2} \theta_{ji} (2\hat{B}_{ji} - B_j) B_j \equiv V_i(\mathbf{B}, c_i), \tag{A8}$$

where $\theta_{ji} \equiv \beta_{ji}/2\mu_j^2$.

The slope of an indifference contour is given by:

$$\frac{dB_2}{dB_1} \bigg|_{U_i^0} = -\frac{\partial V_i}{\partial B_i} \bigg/ \frac{\partial V_i}{\partial B_2} = -\frac{\theta_{1i}}{\theta_{2i}} \frac{\hat{B}_{1i} - B_1}{\hat{B}_{2i} - B_2}. \tag{A9}$$

Moreover, the indifference contours can be shown to be ellipses of the form

$$\frac{(B_1 - \hat{B}_{1i})^2}{a_i^2} + \frac{(B_2 - \hat{B}_{2i})^2}{b_i^2} = 1, \tag{A10}$$

where $a_i^2 \equiv (\hat{B}_{1i})^2 + (\theta_{1i}/\theta_{2i})(\hat{B}_{2i})^2 + (1/\theta_{1i})(y_i - U_i^0).$

$b_i^2 \equiv (\theta_{1i}/\theta_{2i})(\hat{B}_{1i})^2 + (\hat{B}_{2i}) + (1/\theta_{2i})(y_i - U_i^0).$

The indifference contours will be circles as shown in the figures when θ_{1i} equals θ_{2i}.

Consider the zero gain set relative to point **B** as defined by equation (14):

$$I_i(\mathbf{B}; c_i) = \{\mathbf{B}' \mid G_i(\mathbf{B}, \mathbf{B}') = 0\}.$$

For the induced utility function given by equation (A8) with $\theta_{ji} = \theta_i$ for $j = 1,2$, the zero gain set can be found by solving the following equation:

$$V_i(\mathbf{B}'; c_i) - V_i(\mathbf{B}; 0) = 0. \tag{A11}$$

Solving this equation yields:

$$(B_1' - \hat{B}_{1i})^2 + (B_2' - \hat{B}_{2i})^2 = r^2 \tag{A12}$$

where $r^2 = d^2 - c_i/\theta_i$

and $d^2 = (B_1 - \hat{B}_{1i})^2 + (B_2 - \hat{B}_{2i})^2.$

In other words, the zero gain set relative to **B** is a circle centered at the voter's ideal point with a radius of $\sqrt{d^2 - c_i/\theta_i}$.

Consider the special case of the zero gain set known as the boundary individual inertia set, which is the set of points such that a movement from one of these points to the voter's ideal point leaves him with zero utility after paying the agenda cost. This set of points can be found by solving the following equation:

$$V_i(\hat{B}_i; c_i) - V_i(\mathbf{B}; 0) = 0. \tag{A13}$$

Substituting **B'** equal to $\hat{\mathbf{B}}_i$ into (A12) gives:

$$0 = d^2 - c_i/\theta_i. \tag{A14}$$

Rearranging gives:

$$(B_1 - \hat{B}_{1i})^2 + (B_2 - \hat{B}_{2i})^2 = c_i/\theta_i. \tag{A15}$$

The individual inertia set is, thus, a circle centered at the voter's ideal point with a radius of $\sqrt{c_i/\theta_i}$.

For the public sector preference function given by (A8) the solution to the maximization problem given by (V) can be found by setting the slope of voters c's indifference contour to the slope of the total budget line.

That is:

$$\left. \frac{dB_2}{dB_1} \right|_{U_c^0} = -1. \tag{A16}$$

Solving this equation for B_2 as a function of B_1 and assuming that the indifference contours are circular, gives the following definition for the set C:

$$C \equiv \{\mathbf{B} \mid B_2 = (\hat{B}_{2c} - \hat{B}_{1c}) + B_1\}. \qquad (A17)$$

The graph of this set is shown in figures 4 and 5.

REFERENCES

Auster, R. Fall 1974. The GPITPC and institutional entropy. *Public Choice* 19.

Balbien, J. 1979. Jarvis-Gann and the policy of budgetary reduction in the city of Pasadena: a case study. California Institute of Technology. Mimeographed.

Barro, R. Spring 1972. The control of politicians: an economic model. *Public Choice* 14.

Bartlett, R. 1973. *Economic foundations of political power.* New York, N.Y.: The Free Press.

Becker, G. October 1958. Competition and democracy. *Journal of Law and Economics* 1.

Black, D. 1958. *The theory of committees and elections.* Cambridge, England: Cambridge University Press.

Borcherding, T., ed. 1977. *Budgets and bureaucrats: the sources of government growth.* Durham, N.C.: Duke University Press.

Bowen, H. November 1943. The interpretation of voting in the allocation of economic resources. *Quarterly Journal of Economics* 58.

Brennan, G., and Buchanan, J. 1980. *The power to tax: analytic foundations of a fiscal constitution.* Cambridge, England: Cambridge University Press.

Buchanan, J. 1975. *Limits to liberty: between anarchy and leviathan.* Chicago, Ill.: University of Chicago Press.

Davis, O., Hinich, M., and Ordeshook, P. June 1970. An expository development of a mathematical model of the electoral process. *American Political Science Review* 64.

Denzau, A., and Mackay, R. 1980. Benefit and tax share discrimination by a monopoly bureau. *Journal of Public Economics* 13.

Denzau, A., Mackay, R., and Weaver, C. June 1979a. Spending limitations, agenda control and voter's expectations. *National Tax Journal.*

―――. 1979b. On the possibility of majority rule equilibrium with agenda costs. Blacksburg, Va.: Virginia Polytechnic Institute and State University.

Denzau, A., and Parks, R. June 1979. The derivation of public sector preferences. *Journal of Public Economics* 11.

Downs, A. 1957. *An economic theory of democracy.* New York, N.Y.: Harper and Row.

Fiorina, M., and Noll, R. 1979. Voters, bureaucrats, and legislators. *Journal of Public Economics* 9.

Kats, A. 1974. Non-cooperative monopolistic games and monopolistic market games. *International Journal of Game Theory* 3.

Mackay, R., and Weaver, C. 1978a. Monopoly bureaus and fiscal outcomes: deductive models and implications for reform. In *Deductive reasoning in the analysis of public policy*, ed. G. Tullock and R. Wagner. Lexington, Mass.: D.C. Heath and Company.

——. 1978b. Monopoly and commodity bundling in public supply: a diagrammatic exposition. Blacksburg, Va.: Virginia Polytechnic Institute and State University. Mimeo.

——. 1981. Agenda control by budget maximizers in a multi-bureau setting. *Public Choice*. Forthcoming.

——. 1979. Commodity bundling and agenda control in the public sector: a mathematical analysis. Blacksburg, Va.: Virginia Polytechnic Institute and State University. Mimeo.

Mackay, R., and Whitney, G. 1980. The comparative statics of quantity constraints on conditional demands: theory and applications. *Econometrica*.

Niskanen, W. 1971. *Bureaucracy and representative government*. Chicago, Ill.: Aldine-Atherton.

——. May 1968. The peculiar economics of bureaucracy. *American Economic Review* 58.

——. December 1975. Bureaucrats and politicians. *Journal of Law and Economics* 18.

Reid, J., Jr. June 1977. Understanding political events in the new economic history. *Journal of Economic History* 37.

Romer, T., and Rosenthal, H. Winter 1978. Political resource allocation, controlled agenda, and the status quo. *Public Choice*.

Romer, T., and Rosenthal, H. 1979. Bureaucrats vs. voters: on the political economy of resource allocation by direct democracy. *Quarterly Journal of Economies* 93.

Shepsle, K. 1972. The strategy of ambiguity. *American Political Science Review* 66.

——. 1978a. *The giant jigsaw puzzle: democratic committee assignments in the House of Representatives*. Chicago, Ill.: University of Chicago Press.

——. 1978b. Institutional structure and policy choice: some comparative statics of amendment procedures. St. Louis, Mo.: Washington University. Mimeo.

——. 1979. The role of institutional structure in the creation of policy equilibrium. In D. Rae (ed.) *Sage yearbook in politics and public policy*. Beverly Hills, Calif., Sage Publications.

Stigler, G. Fall 1972. Economic competition and political competition. *Public Choice* 13.

Tiebout, C. October 1956. A pure theory of local expenditure. *Journal of Political Economy* 64.

Tullock, G. May 1965. Entry barriers in politics. *American Economic Review* 55.

——. July/Aug. 1971a. Public decisions as public goods. *Journal of Political Economy* 79.

——. Fall 1971b. The paradox of revolution. *Public Choice* 17.

Wagner, R. 1980. The agent principal relationship in the economic order: the public sector context. *Economics of public and private organizations*. Rochester, N.Y.: University of Rochester Policy Center Publications. 1980.

Wagner, R., and Weber, W. December 1975. Competition, monopoly, and the organization of government in metropolitan areas. *Journal of Law and Economics* 18.

Discussion of A.T. Denzau, R.J. Mackay and C.L. Weaver, "On the Initiative-Referendum Option and the Control of Monopoly Government"

Jerome Rothenberg, Discussant

I. Introduction

Denzau, Mackay, and Weaver have written a useful and provocative paper. Employing a model of monopoly government, they explore how direct methods of citizen involvement, like initiative-referendum options, might mitigate some of the consequences of monopolistic elements of government. Their treatment is neatly performed and their results are almost exactly as expected. Since direct citizen involvement is a sort of entry into a monopolized market, it potentially exercises some mitigation of the "monopolistic exploitation of the market," the extent of this mitigation depending on the size of the "costs" of entry. Since the entry is not "perfect" in terms of the "commodity" being entered in competition, because of a basic asymmetry assumed in monopoly models, mitigation is not complete even for modest "entry costs." In any case, entry costs are likely to be nontrivial, among them being the internal costs of united action—for example, the free-rider problem—so while the initiative-referendum may have some salutory effect in improving the representativeness of government, it should not be counted on to dispel the monopoly in monopoly government.

Since so many economists have for so long treated the public sector as essentially a neutral corrective of private market failures, with no biases or "self-interest" in itself, and with its effectiveness limited only by the intrinsic difficulty of devising perfect policy instruments to cure complex private problems, the recent flurry of work on monopoly government models provides a welcome opportunity to scru-

223

tinize exactly what kind of social rectifier this set of institutions is. It is conceivable that we shall find the reality somewhere between the perfect reflector and high exploiter versions of the public sector— somewhere between always knowing the government is not doing enough and always knowing it is doing too much. Indeed, we shall probably learn something more important. By examining exactly how the different political roles intermesh, how the specific incentive and constraint structures of different participants elicit individual behaviors, and how interactions among these behaviors aggregate into "government action," we shall discover what kinds of transmissional bias occur. They are much more likely to be biases of substance, of pattern, and of mix than simply of too much or too little. The growing, largely theoretical work on monopoly models, and the present very good example, aid in such an inquiry by alerting us to some of the variables on which the functioning of the government system may be sensitive.

The analysis in the present paper is a generally effective, although rather simple, working out of the assumptions of the model. Our ability to interpret that analysis, and the results that punctuate it, depend on carefully understanding these assumptions and how they have been taken over into the analysis. In doing so, we find some unanswered questions about and disturbing discrepancies with what seem to be their real world counterparts. We find damaging oversimplifications and arbitrary asymmetries. The discussion of these will be treated in terms of central issues they raise.

II. The Capture and Monopolization of Government: How, Who, What

How is government monopolized? Monopoly government models differ from one another in this regard, but they agree in emphasizing that information about government operations is crucial to control, and that such information is costly. Facing high costs of understanding and/or monitoring government action, most individuals will be content to remain largely uninformed and thus largely uninvolved. Some specially interested individuals, however, will find it worthwhile to invest in this information and thereby dominate the government. Monopolistic exploitation stems from this dominant coalition's ability to direct and control government activities.

A. What Part of Government Is Monopolized?

One critical issue here concerns what part of government is captured and exploited in this manner. Three possibilities are: the legislative process, the chief executive, individual administrative agencies (the bureaucracy). The question is important because different kinds and costs of information, different mechanisms of influence, and different kinds of exploitation, are involved in each. The three present very different opportunities for disproportionate influence and quite different consequences. These differences are quite relevant to the characterization of a "monopolistic status quo" in contrast to a world with initiative-referendum options.

The present paper does not really raise this issue at all. It leaves the nature of monopolistic control defined only in terms of outcomes: a set of dominant preferences and agenda control. This is seriously incomplete and does not properly characterize the dominant group, their self-selection, their retention of unity and control, and their formulation of operating strategies. All of these help determine the extent and nature of monopolistic exploitation and response to potential challenge by outsiders. Moreover, participatory costs and internal coalitional problems are discussed for outside challengers but not for the dominant group. The characterization of actual and potential constraints against monopolistic exploitation is thus left seriously incomplete.

B. Who Dominates?

The dominant group is characterized as a high demander coalition. Is this warranted? Does it stem from the assumptions concerning the source of limited access to participation? Is this consonant with the real world?

The source of limited access to private participation in government—whether legislative or administrative—is alleged to be the costs of information. If adequate information is expensive, only those for whom the difference between participation and nonparticipation is worth the cost will bother to seek access. There are three variables here: (1) what objective difference in policy and/or practice would result from participation? (2) what is the utility difference to the private participant of this objective difference? and (3) what are the costs of effective participation?

   (1) Expected Change—This depends on the pattern of private preferences for public action in the given field and the expected pattern of active private intervention in government among groups bearing those preferences. This differs for legislative and administrative participation: expected intervention in the former is likely to be potentially more competitive than in the latter—legislative influence seeks

advantages for the active *at the expense of* the passive; administrative influence often simply seeks special privileges which, while indirectly disadvantageous to the passive via overall budget pressure, need not directly counter their interests.

(2)   A given objective change in policy and/or operations can have very different utility impacts for different private groups. A government-induced rise of 10 cents a bushel for wheat obviously means more to wheat farmers than to city dwellers or even to cotton farmers. Similarly, minimum wage or tariff levels, the stringency of an antitrust criterion, the specification of required emission control equipment, or the selection of one antitank weapon over another, has much greater impact on directly affected groups than on groups affected only via indirect linkages.

(3)   The cost of relevant information is not equal for all private individuals. At least three kinds of information are required: (a) knowledge of the present public policy and governmental operations, (b) knowledge about the significance or effect of this present situation, (c) knowledge about the probable consequences of alternative modifications of policy/operations. Groups with substantial private activities in the relevant field are likely to generate much of all three types of information simply in the course of these activities. Participatory information costs for them are likely to be considerably lower than for groups with a less active private commitment to the field.

For influencing the legislative function, the upshot of the foregoing is that participation is most likely for those whose stakes between participation and nonparticipation are highest. But these need not be "high spenders" for a number of reasons. First, it is a drastic over-simplification of governmental activity to characterize the intensity of its intervention in terms only of "the size of public goods," and make that essentially proportional to the size of the public budget. Equal budgets can be spent in ways that involve markedly different kinds and degrees of intervention within any part of the private sector.

Second, even where the size of the public budget is a fair approximation of the size of utility impact for interested parties, there are types of public interventions in which the most interested private parties want the *least* intervention—the *smallest* budgets! Regulatory policy is replete with examples.

Third, expected gains from participation depend on the expected marginal impact of participation, and this, in turn depends on the perceived distribution of private preferences on the issues concerned. A group with preferences for a degree of public intervention far in

excess of the overwhelming majority of citizens is most unlikely to
believe that it can dominate government by its participation. Thus,
very small extremist groups are *not* likely to constitute the core con-
trollers of monopoly government.

It is not only the unrepresentativeness of extremism that can deter
participation, it is the *pattern* of preferences overall. If more than one
group decide to participate, their respective preferences can lead
either to a strengthening coalition between them (if their positions are
relatively close to one another) or to a mutual cancelling-out of competition (where their positions are distant). The latter prospect does
not make the participation of either—or both—irrational; rather, pre-
vention of dominances by a highly contrasting position may be the
very reason for a group to participate. Since extremist influence is
most likely to elicit just this sort of opposing participation, dominance
of the legislative process of government by especially "high—or low—
spenders" is not highly probable. The issue of what kinds of groups
are most likely to exert disproportionate influence bears heavily on
what kinds of bias a "monopolized government" is likely to display
in its actual operations. In sum, desire for "big spending" is not a
good predictor of who will dominate the legislative process of a government with imperfect access, even for issues where citizen preferences *are* tolerably approximated by size of government budget.
Rather, it is a complex of both relative sizes of different groups and
the pattern of their preference positions. The analytic presuppositions
of many monopoly government models on this score, including the
present one, are seriously misleading, especially because they use
the "big spender" characterization of monopolization to infer that an
inevitable—and serious—overenlargement of government will be the
result. This simply does not follow from the fundamentals of the
theory. Imperfectly representative legislatures may generate serious
biases, but the sheer size of spending is not necessarily the most
important aspect of them, and a definitive direction of bias in this
dimension is not so casually inferrable in any case.

The case is different for "monopolization" involving administrative
processes. If administrative agencies are characterized as simply rub-
ber stamps for dominant citizen participation, the analysis is the same
as above. But if monopolization is deemed to stem from the ability
of nonelected officials to insulate themselves against scrutiny, control
and oversight by their elected—or even appointed—superiors, then
a different analysis is appropriate. Under a customary assumption,

bureaucrats (private as well as public) are supposed to want to maximize size—both to enhance power and prestige and to increase security (although the latter seems more relevant to private than to
public bureaucrats). Here is a source of the notion that imperfectly
representative government is government controlled by the big spenders.

Administrative monopolization has its analysis of sources, constraints, and modifications of power; but it is a different analysis from
that of the present paper, with it strategic sizing up of opposing *voter*
groups. Voter groups do have a role to play, since strategically placed
voter groups that support the presumed agency exploitation of the
lapse of hierarchic control can sometimes protect it against its superiors. But this scenario is somewhat inconsistent with the supposed
source of agency free-wheeling in its own monopolization of information about what is really going on. Private groups can be supporting
only imperfect external symptoms, not the real action going on. In
any case, a much more subtle type of analysis is required to understand a public-private interface in the agency monopolization case
than in the present kind of monopoly government model.

Monopolization of the chief executive is like that pertaining to the
legislative process, except that it is much less credible, since the role
is much more visible. Citizen access is far less easy to choke off,
especially to choke off radically by a smallish group. The informational
and access imperfections occurring elsewhere in government are likely
to be much less extreme here. At worst, models of "oligopolistic
government," but not "monopoly government," might apply.

C. Single Issue vs. Multiple Issue Dominance

The present model characterizes the dominant coalition as big
spenders *over the whole set of public goods* provided by government,
not simply for a single public good. The graphical analysis in two
dimensions shows the dominant coalition's most preferred position as
far out on dimensions B_1 and B_2. Does this follow from the fundamentals of the theory? It does not. In fact, an attempt to make it
consistent with the theory must grapple with difficult issues that *are*
the focus of the present paper, and are therefore presumably relevant.
The issues are dealt with for "outsider" groups, but treatment is
completely missing for the more important situation of "insider"
groups.

In brief, the theory establishing grounds for differential voter access to government focuses on special interest groups as the most likely active participants. But special interest groups are notoriously single-issue oriented. Their special concern, their special information advantage, lies with one type of public good (i.e., the one-issue area). This means that for any *pair* of issues—like B_1 and B_2 in the paper—there is likely to be a *different* dominant group (or even competing groups) on each issue. Insofar as both *are* high spenders, they will find themselves *competitors* for a limited government budget, *not* natural allies. They will only be allies if they coalesce—i.e. form an explicit or implicit coalition. A coalition of the appropriate type is one that establishes a log-rolling relationship. But a log-rolling relationship need not be formed between only high spender groups, or even dominant single-issue groups. Since each coalition precludes others, a more general theory of coalitions must be delineated before it can at all be accepted that a dominant two-issue coalition will form under the circumstances cited, and that it will have the characteristics alleged in the paper.

III. The Consequences of Monopolization

While some of the consequences of monopolization are carefully worked out, their significance is not clear because other consequences are omitted or inadequately dealt with. Most important of these are the nature of the instrument of exploitation and a more general consideration of coalition strategy.

The chief instrument of monopolistic exploitation is the ability of the dominant coalition to force an all-or-nothing option onto the public. This results from both a control of the agenda in initiating proposed action and in severely curtailing amendment to such initiations. It indeed constitutes a powerful control, and it is not at all surprising that considerable surplus is generated thereby. But such agenda control is not very credible in terms of observable reality, at least in the U.S. It seems true of neither legislative nor administrative control. It is true that proposed legislation and administrative practice are often initiated by special power groups—congressional committees, bureau chiefs. But the latter are subject to review, negotiation, modification by the department head and by the chief executive and/or his representatives (the Office of Management and Budget). Moreover, the Executive often initiates important new programs as part of comprehensive new policies. In the legislature, committee hearings and deliberations, and plenary debate and amendments can modify, veto or even supplant proposals initiated by a power group. Both absolute budget size and specific programs are capable of such offset to attempted all-or-nothing control. Thus, even in the absence of a threat to upset the power base of the dominant coalition, a give-and-take process of some flexibility is likely to determine governmental outcomes. The power to issue and enforce decision on all-or-nothing options is not convincing.

Discussion of strategic interplay between the dominant coalition and outsider groups, between outsider groups, and within the dominant coalition is either skimpy or largely absent. When facing the need to gain additional support, toward which outsider group or groups does the dominant group turn? In the graphical analysis, the answer is superficially simple: toward whichever group involves a compromise that gives the dominant group highest utility. But the simplicity stems from the three-person model being treated. Much richer issues are involved when the three groups have different relative size, and/or when more than three parties are involved. When relative group size varies, a given dominant coalition will generate *different* outcomes as its proportion of the total voter population varies: the smaller it is the more or the larger are the outside groups with which it must compromise in order to retain some control (effective majority)—in other words, the less the probable "bias" in governmental outcome will be. Moreover, general strategic interplay among dominant and outsider groups will depend not only on the preference positions of the groups but on their relative numbers as well. These important issues are avoided. The interactive process is made almost casually determinate by a misleadingly simple model variant.

Another simplification is misleading, centrally so in terms of the question of the probable extent of monopoly bias. When the initiative-referendum option is discussed, the obstacles to coalition formation by outsider groups are stressed, notably the free-rider problem. Our earlier discussion argues that a "dominant coalition" is also a coalition, and that its composition is not "natural" or obvious—perhaps not even determinate. It too must come into being by being created, and its continued actions are constrained by the need to maintain the agreed coordination of behavior by its members. It too has free-rider problems as well as all the other problems of coalitions generally. Yet none of these are even mentioned, let alone examined closely in the overall multigroup strategic interplay being characterized. It is simply assumed that dominant coalitions form, continue, and strategically interact without any of these basic issues being relevant. This is misleading, perhaps seriously so in terms of the central questions about the degree to which government *can* be monopolized and how much the monopolizing group can exploit from its position.

IV. The Initiative-Referendum Option

These comments are already extended. I shall simply raise some issues briefly about the treatment of the initiative-referendum option.

Most important, the significance of the availability of the initiative-referendum option depends on how much monopolistic control is exercised in the imperfect representation government without referendum. My comments above suggest that it may be considerably less, considerably harder to achieve and maintain, considerably more constrained in operation, than is presumed in the paper. The large potential change wrought by the initiative-referendum option should therefore be modified. It offers outsiders not a sole opportunity for access but only a different kind. Given the large number of voters who must be appealed to instead of the much smaller number of contending (but "outsider") influence groups, the referendum must very likely be a much cruder negotiating instrument for strategic interplay than more continuous forms of access suggested above.

A second issue concerning this access option is that the cost of participating in its use is quite inadequate. Each exercise of the option is deemed in the paper to have a fixed total cost, which is simply divided equally within the groups. Discussion of the free-rider problem is a useful exception to this. But the problem is larger. For one thing, the cost of using the initiative-referendum should be treated as a variable. It varies by degree of comprehensiveness with respect to policy issues (e.g., the number of public goods dealt with) and the degree of specificity proposed. It varies by number of voters reached—and converted to participation. Selling a referendum is a form of production and has its own characteristic inputs and technology. Number of "sales" and the distribution of the costs of production are not nearly so straightforward as in the present paper. Their complexity bears on the strategic use of the option, by whom used, and with what probable success. The treatment in the paper is almost definitional compared to this. While the analytic results seem reasonable in terms of general direction, a more precise quantitative evaluation seems desired by the authors and by the reader as well, given the authors' empirical concern over the seriousness of the problem of monopoly government and how it can best be ameliorated. The present paper will not nearly give a close enough evaluation to support policy recommendations about the advisability of resorting to referenda to solve our governmental problems.

To conclude, we must be grateful to Denzau, Mackay, and Weaver for raising important questions concerning the structure and operation of government in so clear and provocative a way that we compliment them, first by taking their questions seriously, second, by being led to examine the issues more deeply than we had previously, and finally by asking them for more. We certainly cannot expect satisfactory treatment of most of the complications requested: that would be nothing more than a counsel of perfection. But considerably more attention to them is needed before one can give serious credence to any policy recommendation that may emerge from this literature.